The Mating GAME

This book is respectfully dedicated to my teachers, particularly Ellen Berscheid, Saul Kassin, Peter Murphy, Stephen Fix, Elizabeth Estill, and Ron Norton. Your wisdom, intellect, humor, and love of learning have illuminated my life. Thank you.

The Mating GAME

A Primer on Love, Sex, and Marriage

PAMELA REGAN
California State University, Los Angeles

SAGE Publications
International Educational and Professional Publisher
Thousand Oaks ▪ London ▪ New Delhi

For information:

 Sage Publications, Inc.
2455 Teller Road
Thousand Oaks, California 91320
E-mail: order@sagepub.com

Sage Publications Ltd.
6 Bonhill Street
London EC2A 4PU
United Kingdom

Sage Publications India Pvt. Ltd.
B-42 Panchsheel Enclave
Post Box 4109
New Delhi 110 017 India

Printed in the United States of America

Library of Congress Cataloging-in-Publication Data

Regan, Pamela C.
The mating game : a primer on love, sex, and marriage / Pamela Regan.
    p. cm.
Includes bibliographical references and index.
ISBN 0-7619-2636-4 (pbk.)
  1. Man-woman relationships. 2. Love. 3. Sex. 4. Mate selection.
5. Marriage. I. Title.
HQ801 .R334 2003
306.7--dc21

                            2002152026

This book is printed on acid-free paper.

              05 10 9 8 7 6 5 4 3 2

Acquisitions Editor:	Jim Brace-Thompson
Editorial Assistant:	Karen Ehrmann
Production Editor:	Sanford Robinson
Copy Editor:	D. J. Peck
Typesetter:	C&M Digitals (P) Ltd
Cover Designer:	Michelle Lee

Contents in Brief

Contents

Preface

"The Art of a Perfect Relationship" *(Mademoiselle)*
"Sex Survey: What Other Couples Do" *(Cosmopolitan)*
"Love vs. Lust: How You'll Know the Difference" *(Woman's Own)*
"What Women Really Want" *(Men's Fitness)*
"How to Stop Loving Someone Who Doesn't Love You Back" *(Woman's Own)*
"Are You Wedding Obsessed?" *(Cosmopolitan)*
"Turn a Friend Into a Lover" *(Men's Health)*

These quotations, taken from the headlines of several contemporary men's and women's magazines, underscore the deep interest (and even fascination) with which many of us approach topics of love, sex, and romance. And our interest is certainly justified. The intimate connections that we establish with other people, whether for a few moments or for a lifetime, affect our emotional and physical well-being and even the survival of our species. Without love and sex—without mating and pairbonding and reproduction—we would feel empty, isolated, and lonely; our societies would wither; and humankind would literally perish.

My goal in writing this book is to bring together in one text past and present theory, supposition, and knowledge about three important aspects of human mating dynamics: love, sex, and mate selection and marriage. The first section of the text considers the topic of love and begins with an exploration of theoretical discourse (and empirical investigation) into the nature of love. Special attention is given to the two love types that have received the most scrutiny from social and behavioral scientists: passionate love and companionate love. The section ends with a consideration of problematic aspects of love relationships, including unrequited love, obsession, mismatched love styles, and loss of passion.

The second section of the text explores relational sexuality. We examine men's and women's beliefs and attitudes about the role of sex in dating and marital relationships, and we consider sexuality—frequency, preferences, and practices—in beginning and established relationships. Problematic aspects of relational sexuality are considered, including sexual aggression, sexual dissatisfaction, and sexual infidelity. The third section of the text focuses on mate selection and marriage. The text presents theoretical frameworks for understanding human mating, summarizes research on mate preferences, and explores attraction and courtship. Theories of relationship development are discussed, as is research on conflict and dissolution and on mate choice and marriage. The final section summarizes what is currently known about individual differences in relationship orientation. We consider how maleness and femaleness, global personality traits, and interpersonal belief systems may influence a person's romantic opportunities, behaviors, and outcomes.

In addition to discussing these important and interesting aspects of human mating relationships, this text is highly "reader friendly." For example, each chapter includes a detailed outline that serves to guide readers through the material, and I provide a list of key concepts (with page references) to assist readers in identifying and comprehending important terms, theories, and findings. Each chapter also presents readers with a set of recommended readings and discussion questions that are designed to spark debate and discussion about the chapter content. Most, if not all, of these essential pedagogical elements are missing from current texts in this area. I hope that their inclusion will promote active learning and enhance readers' educational experiences.

Love, sexuality, and mate selection are fundamental human experiences that only relatively recently have begun to receive scientific attention. I believe that the comprehensive review and up-to-date information contained in this text will not only provide answers to questions about these important life events but also encourage readers' interest in the diverse and multidisciplinary field of interpersonal relationships and human mating.

PART I

LOVE

Most people eagerly seek out love and believe that forming a successful love relationship is essential for their personal happiness. Although all of us are likely to experience various types of love and enter into a number of different kinds of love relationships over the course of our lifetimes, social and behavioral scientists have tended to focus on the type of love that occurs in long-term romantic relationships. This kind of love is linked with a variety of important personal, interpersonal, and societal outcomes, including marriage and other forms of long-term pairbonding, sex and reproduction, and social support. For example, most people living in contemporary societies will marry only individuals they love and will leave individuals they no longer love. Thus, love—and the relationships it produces and fosters—clearly plays a significant role in human lives.

The following three chapters explore the topic of love. Chapter 1 presents some of the more commonly used typologies of love and their associated measurement instruments. Chapter 2 considers the two types of love that have received the most intense scrutiny from relationships researchers: passionate and companionate love. Finally, Chapter 3 examines the dark side of love, including unrequited love, obsession, mismatched love styles, and loss of passion.

1

General Theories of Love

Chapter Outline

Throughout history, scholars from a variety of disciplines have speculated on the nature of love. For example, as early as 1886, the German physician and pioneering sexologist Richard von Krafft-Ebing (1886/1945) identified five types of love: *true love, sentimental love, platonic love, friendship,* and *sensual love.* Several decades later, psychotherapist Albert Ellis (1954) proposed additional love varieties: "Love itself . . . includes many different types and degrees of affection, such as conjugal love, parental love, familial love, religious love, love of humanity, love of animals, love of things, self-love, sexual love, obsessive-compulsive love, etc." (p. 101).

One of Ellis's contemporaries, religious theoretician C. S. Lewis (1960/1988), devoted an entire book to a discussion of types of love. Drawing on earlier distinctions made by Greek philosophers, he proposed four main varieties. *Affection* (or *Storge*, pronounced "Stor-gay") is based on familiarity and repeated contact and resembles the strong attachment seen between parents and children. This type of love is experienced for and by a wide variety of objects, including family members, pets, acquaintances, and lovers. Affectionate love has a "comfortable, quiet nature" (p. 34) and consists of feelings of warmth, interpersonal comfort, and satisfaction in being together. The second variety of love depicted by Lewis is *Friendship* (or *Philias*). Common interests, insights, or tastes, coupled with cooperation, mutual respect, and understanding, form the core of this love type. Lewis argued that Friendship, more than mere companionship, "must be about something, even if it were only an enthusiasm for dominoes or white mice" (p. 66). *Eros*, or "that state which we call 'being in love'" (p. 91), is the third variety of love. Unlike the other love types, Eros contains a mixture of "sweetness" and "terror" as well as a sexual component that Lewis referred to as Venus. Erotic love also is characterized by affection, idealization of and preoccupation with the beloved, and a short life span. The final love type is *Charity*, a selfless and "Divine Gift-love" that has no expectation of reward and desires only what is "simply best for the beloved" (p. 128).

Contemporary social and behavioral scientists also have proposed taxonomies that specify types or varieties of love (for reviews, see Hendrick & Hendrick, 1992; Sternberg & Barnes, 1988). Two of the more common classification schemes were developed by psychologist Robert Sternberg (e.g., 1986, 1998) and sociologist John Lee (e.g., 1973, 1988).

THE TRIANGULAR THEORY OF LOVE

Sternberg (e.g., 1986, 1998) conceptualized love in terms of three basic components that form the vertices of a triangle: intimacy, passion, and decision/commitment (Figure 1.1). The *intimacy* component is primarily emotional or affective in nature and involves feelings of warmth, closeness, connection, and bondedness in the love relationship. The *passion* component is motivational and consists of the drives that are involved in romantic and physical attraction, sexual consummation, and related phenomena. The *decision/commitment* component is largely cognitive and

Figure 1.1   Sternberg's Triangular Model of Love. The three components of love are indicated at the vertices of the triangle. The various types of love produced by different combinations of the components are in brackets.

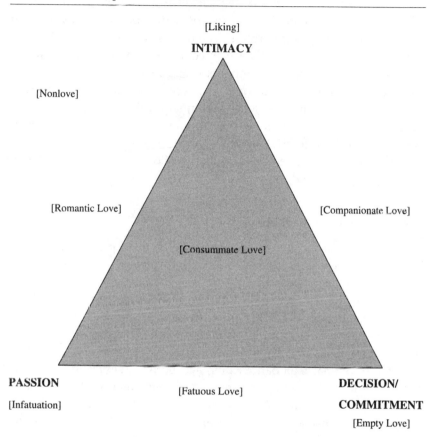

[Liking]

INTIMACY

[Nonlove]

[Romantic Love]   [Companionate Love]

[Consummate Love]

PASSION

[Infatuation]   [Fatuous Love]   **DECISION/**

COMMITMENT

[Empty Love]

SOURCE: From Sternberg, R. J. (1988). Triangulating love. In R. J. Sternberg & M. L. Barnes (Eds.), *The psychology of love* (pp. 119-138). New Haven, CT: Yale University Press. Copyright © 1988 by Yale University Press. Adapted with permission.

represents both the short-term decision that one individual loves another and the longer term commitment to maintain that love.

According to Sternberg, these three love components differ with respect to a number of properties, including *stability, conscious controllability,* and *experiential salience.* For example, the elements of intimacy and decision/commitment are usually quite stable in close relationships (once they occur and become characteristic of a relationship, they tend to endure), whereas passion tends to be less stable and predictable. In addition, whereas people possess a great deal of conscious control over the commitment that they make to relationships and possess at least some degree of control over their feelings of intimacy, they actually have very little conscious control over the amount of passion that they experience for their partners. The three components also differ in terms of their experiential salience. Specifically, an individual is usually quite aware of the passion component, but awareness of the intimacy and decision/commitment components can be extremely variable. That is, a person may experience feelings of intimacy (e.g., closeness, connection, warmth) without explicitly being aware of those feelings or even being able to identify what he or she is feeling. Similarly, a person might not consciously realize the full extent of his or her commitment to the relationship and the partner.

Types of Love Relationship

The three basic components of love combine to produce eight different love types, summarized in Table 1.1. *Nonlove* (no intimacy, passion, or decision/commitment) describes casual interactions that are characterized by the absence of all three love components. Most of our personal relationships (which are essentially casual associations) can be defined as nonlove. *Liking* (intimacy alone) relationships are essentially friendship. They contain warmth, intimacy, closeness, and other positive emotional experiences but lack both passion and decision/commitment. *Infatuation* (passion alone) is an intense, "love at first sight" experience that is characterized by extreme attraction and arousal in the absence of any real emotional intimacy and decision/commitment. In *empty love* (decision/commitment alone) relationships, the partners are committed to each other and the relationship but lack an intimate emotional connection and passionate attraction. This type of love is often seen at the end of long-term relationships (or at the beginning of arranged marriages). *Romantic love* (intimacy + passion) consists of feelings of closeness and connection coupled with strong physical attraction. *Companionate love* (intimacy + decision/commitment) is essentially a long-term, stable, and committed friendship that is characterized by high amounts of emotional intimacy, the decision to love the partner, and the commitment to remain in the relationship. This type of love is often seen in "best friendships" that are nonsexual or in long-term marriages in which sexual attraction has faded.

Table 1.1   Sternberg's Typology of Love Relationships

	Love Component		
Kind of Love Relationship	Intimacy	Passion	Decision/Commitment
Nonlove	Low	Low	Low
Liking	High	Low	Low
Infatuation	Low	High	Low
Empty love	Low	Low	High
Romantic love	High	High	Low
Companionate love	High	Low	High
Fatuous love	Low	High	High
Consummate love	High	High	High

NOTE: According to Sternberg (e.g., 1986), the three basic components of love—intimacy, passion, and decision/commitment—combine to produce eight different types of love relationship. For example, infatuation-based relationships are characterized by relatively high levels of passion but relatively low levels of intimacy and commitment.

Couples who experience *fatuous love* (passion + decision/commitment) base their commitment to each other on passion rather than on deep emotional intimacy. These "whirlwind" relationships are typically unstable and at risk for termination. Finally, *consummate love* (intimacy + passion + decision/commitment) results from the combination of all three components. According to Sternberg, this is the type of "complete" love that many individuals strive to attain, particularly in their romantic relationships.

Because the three basic components of love occur in varying degrees within a relationship, most love relationships will not fit cleanly into one particular category but will reflect some combination of categories.

Measurement

Sternberg (1998) developed a 45-item scale to assess the three basic elements of love. The Intimacy subscale consists of 15 items designed to reflect feelings of warmth, support, self-disclosure, trust, and other aspects of intimate connection. Examples include "I receive considerable emotional support from _____," "I feel close to _____," "I feel that I can really trust _____," and "I share deeply personal information about myself with _____." The 15 items that make up the Passion subscale are designed to capture the more intense, physical, and exciting elements of romantic relationships, including "Just seeing _____ excites me," "I especially like physical contact with _____," "I adore _____," and "I fantasize about _____." The Decision/Commitment subscale contains 15 items that assess feelings of stability, commitment, and permanence. Examples include "I view my commitment to _____ as a solid one," "I have confidence in the stability of my relationship with _____," "I plan to continue in my relationship with _____," and "I will always feel a strong responsibility for _____."

Interestingly, although this scale was designed to measure three distinct aspects of love—intimacy, passion, and decision/commitment—empirical evidence suggests that it may actually measure one general aspect of love. For example, psychologists Clyde and Susan Hendrick (1989) administered the Triangular Love Scale to a large sample of men and women. Their results indicated that the three subscales were highly intercorrelated and also that the items formed a unifactorial scale. In other words, the scale appeared to measure one global love dimension rather than three distinct elements or components of love. Perhaps for this reason, the scale has not received widespread use among social scientists interested in examining people's love experiences.

THE COLORS (STYLES) OF LOVE

Another contemporary theory of love, and one that has produced a widely used measurement instrument, is the typology developed by Lee (e.g., 1977, 1988). In this novel approach, each variety of love is likened to a primary or secondary color (hence the title of Lee's [1973] book, *Colours of Love*).

Primary and Secondary Love Styles

According to Lee, there are three primary colors or styles of loving. The first, *eros*, is an intensely emotional experience that is similar to passionate love. In fact, the most typical symptom of eros is an immediate and powerful attraction to the beloved individual. The erotic lover is "turned on" by a particular physical type, is prone to fall instantly and completely in love with a stranger (i.e., to experience "love at first sight"), rapidly becomes preoccupied with pleasant thoughts about that individual, feels an intense need for daily contact with the beloved, and wishes the relationship to remain exclusive. Erotic love also has a strong sexual component. For example, the erotic lover desires the beloved sexually, usually seeks some form of sexual involvement fairly early in the relationship, and enjoys expressing his or her affection through sexual contact. In sum, the erotic lover is "eager to get to know the beloved quickly, intensely—and undressed" (Lee, 1988, p. 50).

The second primary color of love is *ludus* (or game-playing) love. The ludic lover views love as a game to be played with skill and often with several partners simultaneously. The ludic lover has no intention of including the current partner (or partners) in any future life plans or events and worries about any sign of growing involvement, need, or intense attachment from the partner. As the quintessential commitment-phobe, the ludic lover avoids seeing the partner too often, believes that lies and deception are justified, and expects the partner to remain in control of his or her emotions. In addition, ludic lovers tend to prefer a wide variety of physical types and view sexual activity as an opportunity for pleasure rather than for intense emotional bonding.

Storge is the third primary love color. Described by Lee (1973) as "love without fever or folly" (p. 77), storge resembles Lewis's concept of Affection in that it is stable and based on a solid foundation of trust, respect, and friendship. Indeed, the typical storgic lover views and treats the partner as an "old friend," does not experience the intense emotions or physical attraction to the partner associated with erotic love, prefers to talk about and engage in shared interests with the partner rather than to express direct feelings, is shy about sex, and tends to demonstrate his or her affection in nonsexual ways. To the storgic lover, love is an extension of friendship and an important part of life but is not a valuable goal in and of itself.

Like the primary colors, these primary love styles can be combined to form secondary colors or styles of love. The three secondary styles identified by Lee contain features of the primary love styles but also possess their own unique characteristics. *Pragma*, a combination of storge and ludus, is "the love that goes shopping for a suitable mate" (Lee, 1973, p. 124). The pragmatic lover has a practical outlook on love and seeks a compatible lover. He or she creates a shopping list of features or attributes desired in the partner and selects a mate based on how well that individual fulfills the requirements (similarly, he or she will drop a partner who fails to "measure up" to expectations). Pragmatic love is essentially a faster-acting version of storge that has been quickened by the addition of ludus.

Mania, the combination of eros and ludus, is another secondary love style. Manic lovers lack the self-confidence associated with eros and the emotional self-control associated with ludus. This obsessive, jealous love style is characterized by self-defeating emotions, desperate attempts to force affection from the beloved, and the inability to believe in or trust any affection the loved one actually does display. The manic lover is desperate to fall in love and to be loved, begins immediately to imagine a future with the partner, wants to see the partner daily, tries to force the partner to show love and commitment, distrusts the partner's sincerity, and is extremely possessive. This love type is "irrational, extremely jealous, obsessive, and often unhappy" (Lee, 1973, p. 15).

The last secondary color of love is *agape,* a combination of eros and storge. Agape is similar to Lewis's concept of Charity and represents an all-giving, selfless love style that implies an obligation to love and care for others without any expectation of reciprocity or reward. This love style is universalistic in the sense that the typical agapic lover believes that everyone is worthy of love and that loving others is a duty of the mature person. With respect to personal love relationships, an agapic lover will unselfishly devote himself or herself to the partner, even stepping aside in favor of a rival who seems more likely to meet the partner's needs. Although Lee believed that many lovers respect and strive to attain the agapic ideal, he also believed that the give-and-take that characterizes most romantic relationships precludes the occurrence of purely altruistic love.

Measurement

Lee's classification scheme inspired the development of several measurement instruments. The most well known and commonly used is the 42-item Love Attitudes Scale (LAS) designed by the Hendricks and their colleagues (Hendrick & Hendrick, 1986; Hendrick, Hendrick, Foote, & Slapion-Foote, 1984). The LAS appears to reliably measure the six love styles and has subsequently been redesigned so that each of the items refers to a specific love relationship as opposed to more general attitudes about love (Hendrick & Hendrick, 1990). A shorter, 28-item version of the scale is also available (Hendrick, Hendrick, & Dicke, 1998). The complete scale, along with its shorter version, is reproduced in Exhibit 1.1.

Exhibit 1.1   The Love Attitudes Scale

Instructions
Please answer the following items as honestly and accurately as possible. Whenever possible, answer the questions with your current partner in mind. If you are not currently dating anyone, answer the questions with your most recent partner in mind. Otherwise, answer in terms of what you think your responses would most likely be.

Response scale
1: strongly disagree
2: moderately disagree
3: neutral
4: moderately agree
5: strongly agree

Items

<u>Eros</u>
1. My partner and I were attracted to each other immediately after we first met.
*2. My partner and I have the right physical "chemistry" between us.
3. Our lovemaking is very intense and satisfying.
*4. I feel that my partner and I were meant for each other.
5. My partner and I became emotionally involved rather quickly.
*6. My partner and I really understand each other.
*7. My partner fits my ideal standards of physical beauty/handsomeness.

<u>Ludus</u>
8. I try to keep my partner a little uncertain about my commitment to him/her.
*9. I believe that what my partner doesn't know about me won't hurt him/her.
*10. I have sometimes had to keep my partner from finding out about other lovers.
11. I could get over my love affair with my partner pretty easily and quickly.
*12. My partner would get upset if he/she knew of some of the things I've done with other people.
13. When my partner gets too dependent on me, I want to back off a little.
*14. I enjoy playing the "game of love" with my partner and a number of other partners.

<u>Storge</u>
15. It is hard for me to say exactly when our friendship turned into love.
16. To be genuine, our love first required *caring* for a while.
17. I expect to always be friends with my partner.

(Continued)

Exhibit 1.1 Continued

---

  *18. Our love is the best kind because it grew out of a long friendship.

  *19. Our friendship merged gradually into love over time.

  *20. Our love is really a deep friendship, not a mysterious mystical emotion.

  *21. Our love relationship is the most satisfying because it developed from a good friendship.

Pragma

  22. I considered what my partner was going to become in life before I committed myself to him/her.

  23. I tried to plan my life carefully before choosing a partner.

  24. In choosing my partner, I believed it was best to love someone with a similar background.

  *25. A main consideration in choosing my partner was how he/she would reflect on my family.

  *26. An important factor in choosing my partner was whether or not he/she would be a good parent.

  *27. One consideration in choosing my partner was how he/she would reflect on my career.

  *28. Before getting very involved with my partner, I tried to figure out how compatible his/her hereditary background would be with mine in case we ever had children.

Mania

  29. When things aren't right with my partner and me, my stomach gets upset.

  30. If my partner and I break up, I would get so depressed that I would even think of suicide.

  31. Sometimes I get so excited about being in love with my partner that I can't sleep.

  *32. When my partner doesn't pay attention to me, I feel sick all over.

  *33. Since I've been in love with my partner, I've had trouble concentrating on anything else.

  *34. I cannot relax if I suspect that my partner is with someone else.

  *35. If my partner ignores me for a while, I sometimes do stupid things to try to get his/her attention back.

Agape

  36. I try to always help my partner through difficult times.

  *37. I would rather suffer myself than let my partner suffer.

  *38. I cannot be happy unless I place my partner's happiness before my own.

  *39. I am usually willing to sacrifice my own wishes to let my partner achieve his/hers.

  40. Whatever I own is my partner's to use as he/she chooses.

  41. When my partner gets angry with me, I still love him/her fully and unconditionally.

  *42. I would endure all things for the sake of my partner.

Scoring
Starred items are those included on the short form of the LAS. To find out
your love style, add up your ratings for the items in each subscale. Divide
this total by 7 (or by 4 if using the short form). You will have scores for the
three primary love styles and for the three secondary love styles. Is your
relationship characterized by one particular style of love? Or is it more
complex than that?

SOURCES: Adapted from Hendrick, C., & Hendrick, S. (1990). A relationship-
specific version of the Love Attitudes Scale. *Journal of Social Behavior and
Personality, 5,* 239-254. Copyright © 1990 by Select Press, Inc. Items reprinted
with permission. Starred items are included in the short form of the scale
from Hendrick, C., Hendrick, S. S., & Dicke, A. (1998). The Love Attitudes
Scale: Short Form. *Journal of Social and Personal Relationships,*
15, 147-159.
NOTE: Response options have been reversed from original source.

Individual and Group Differences in Love Style

Unlike the Triangular Love Scale, the LAS has been used in numerous empirical investigations. In general, the results of these studies
reveal that love experiences vary as a function of individual difference
and group variables. For example, many researchers find that women
score higher on the love styles of storge and pragma than do men,
whereas men tend to score higher on ludus (e.g., Dion & Dion, 1993;
Hendrick & Hendrick, 1987, 1988, 1995; Hendrick et al., 1984, 1998;
Rotenberg & Korol, 1995).

There also are multicultural and cross-cultural differences in love
style. Within the United States, Asian American adults often score lower
on eros and higher on pragma and storge than do Caucasian, Latino,
and African American adults (e.g., Dion & Dion, 1993; Hendrick &
Hendrick, 1986). Latino groups, on the other hand, often score higher
on ludus than do Caucasian groups (e.g., Contreras, Hendrick, &
Hendrick, 1996). And cross-cultural comparisons reveal that
Americans tend to be endorse a more storgic and manic approach to
love than do the French, who in turn tend to demonstrate higher levels
of agape (e.g., Murstein, Merighi, & Vyse, 1991).

These differences notwithstanding, it is important to keep in mind
that not all individuals possess one approach or style of loving. A man or
woman may adopt numerous love styles, and a person's love style may
change over his or her lifetime or during the course of a given relationship. For example, the preoccupation and intense need associated with a

manic love style may occur more often during the beginning stages of a romantic relationship, when the partners are uncertain as to their feelings and the future of their association. Over time, however, these feelings may be replaced by more erotic, storgic, or agapic feelings.

THE PROTOTYPE APPROACH: MENTAL MODELS OF LOVE

Some researchers, rather than following the theoretical "top-down" approach adopted by Sternberg and Lee (and others), have taken an empirically driven "bottom-up" approach to delineate the nature of love. One such technique, the prototype approach, involves collecting data directly from men and women about their knowledge, beliefs, and attitudes—their mental representations—of the concept of love. Researchers who use the prototype approach are interested in exploring what people think of when they are asked about love, how they differentiate love from related concepts (e.g., liking), how they form their conceptualizations of love, and how these conceptualizations or mental representations influence their behavior with relational partners.

The Hierarchy of Love

According to Eleanor Rosch (e.g., 1973, 1975, 1978), an early pioneer in the use of prototype analysis, natural language *concepts* (e.g., *love, dog, apple*) can be viewed as having both a vertical and a horizontal dimension. The former concerns the hierarchical organization of concepts or relations among different levels of concepts. Concepts at one level may be included within or subsumed by those at a higher level. For example, the set of concepts *fruit, apple,* and *Red Delicious* illustrate an abstract-to-concrete hierarchy with superordinate, basic, and subordinate levels.

Using the methods originally developed by Rosch, some researchers have investigated the hierarchical structure of the concept of love. Psychologist Phillip Shaver and colleagues (Shaver, Schwartz, Kirson, & O'Connor, 1987), for instance, found evidence that *love* is a basic-level concept contained within the superordinate category of *emotion* and subsuming a variety of subordinate concepts that reflect types or varieties of love (e.g., *passion, infatuation, liking*) (see Figure 1.2). That is, most people consider passion, infatuation, and liking to be types of love, which in turn is viewed as a type of positive emotion.

Figure 1.2   The Hierarchy of Love and Other Emotions. Research
conducted by Phillip Shaver, Beverley Fehr, and their
colleagues (Fehr & Russell, 1991; Fischer, Shaver, &
Carnochan, 1990; Shaver, Schwartz, Kirson, & O'Connor, 1987)
suggests that *love* is a basic level concept contained within the
superordinate category of *emotion*. In addition, *love* appears to
contain a variety of subordinate concepts that reflect types or
varieties of love; of these, *maternal love* is viewed as the most
prototypical variety.

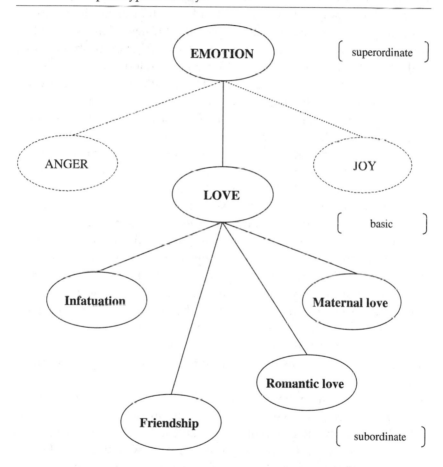

The Prototype of Love

Concepts also may be examined along a horizontal dimension.
This dimension concerns the differentiation of concepts at the same
level of inclusiveness (e.g., the dimension on which subordinate-level

concepts such as *Red Delicious, Fuji,* and *Granny Smith* apples vary). According to Rosch, many natural language concepts or categories have an internal structure whereby individual members of that category are ordered in terms of the degree to which they resemble the prototypic member of the category. A *prototype* is the best and clearest example of the concept (the "appliest" or the most apple-like apple [e.g., *Red Delicious*]). Individuals use prototypes to help them decide whether a new item or experience belongs or "fits" within a particular concept. For example, in trying to decide whether or not he is in love with his partner, a man might compare the *feelings* ("I'm happy when she's here and I'm sad when she's not"), *thoughts* ("I think about her all of the time," "I wonder what our children would look like"), and *behaviors* ("I rearrange my schedule to spend time with her, and we go everywhere together") he has experienced during their relationship with his prototype—his mental model—of "being in love" ("People who are in love miss each other when they're apart, think about each other a lot, imagine a future life together, and spend a lot of time with each other"). If what the man is experiencing "matches" his prototype, he is likely to conclude that he is, in fact, in love with his partner.

The prototype approach has been used to explore the horizontal structure of a variety of relational concepts, including love. Beverley Fehr and James Russell (1991), for example, asked men and women to generate as many types of love as they could in a specified time and then asked another sample of individuals to rate these love varieties in terms of prototypicality or "goodness-of-example." Of the 93 subtypes generated, *maternal love* was rated as the best or most prototypical example of love, followed by *parental love, friendship, sisterly love, romantic love, brotherly love,* and *familial love. Infatuation,* along with *sexual love* and *puppy love,* was considered one of the least prototypical examples of love.

Researchers also have identified the prototypic features (as opposed to types) of love. For example, in an earlier demonstration, Fehr (1988) asked one group of participants to list the characteristics of the concept of *love* and a second group to rate how central each feature was to the concept of love. Features that her participants believed were central or prototypical to love included *trust, caring, honesty, friendship, respect, concern for the other's well-being, loyalty,* and *commitment.* Features that were considered peripheral or unimportant to the concept of love included *see only the other's good qualities, butterflies in stomach, uncertainty, dependency,* and *scary.*

More recently, psychologists Arthur Aron and Lori Westbay (1996) extended Fehr's work by exploring the underlying structure of the prototype of love. These researchers found evidence that the 68 prototypic love features identified by participants in Fehr's (1988) study could be reduced reliably to three latent dimensions that resembled those included in Sternberg's triangular theory of love typology: passion, intimacy, and commitment. Thus, Sternberg's theory appears sound; that is, the love experiences of many men and women do indeed reflect the three basic dimensions he proposed.

SUMMARY

Social and behavioral scientists, recognizing the important role that love plays in human life, have theorized about its nature. In the process, they have proposed a number of typologies or classification schemes that specify types or varieties of love. Other researchers, following a prototype approach, have attempted to delineate the nature of love by examining people's common understandings of love and their love experiences. This body of theoretical and empirical work reveals that there exist a multitude of ways of loving. Love truly is a many splendored—and multifaceted—experience.

KEY CONCEPTS

Storge (p. 4)
Philias (p. 4)
Eros (p. 4)
Charity (p. 4)
Triangular theory of love (pp. 4-5)
Intimacy component (p. 4)
Passion component (p. 4)
Decision/commitment component (pp. 4-5)
Stability property (pp. 5-6)
Conscious controllability property (pp. 5-6)
Experiential salience property (pp. 5-6)
Nonlove (p. 6)
Liking (p. 6)
Infatuation (p. 6)

DISCUSSION QUESTIONS

1. Why have scientists tended to devote so much attention to romantic or passionate love? Do you think that this focus has helped or hindered our understanding of love in general?

2. Although philosophers, poets, and writers have speculated on the nature of love for many hundreds of years, the topic of love has only recently begun to receive scientific attention. What do you think might account for this state of affairs?

3. Describe Sternberg's (1988) triangular theory of love. Select two relationships you have seen portrayed in the media (e.g., books, plays, movies, television). Which type of love does each relationship illustrate? Describe each in terms of the three components of love.

4. Define the three primary and three secondary colors of love. What would be the best pairing of love styles? The worst? Why?

5. Scientists interested in the nature of love have tended to adopt a theory-driven "top-down" approach (e.g., Sternberg, Lee) or a data-driven "bottom-up" approach (e.g., Fehr, the prototype researchers). What does each approach contribute to our understanding of love? Is one better than the other? Why or why not?

RECOMMENDED READINGS

Hendrick, C., & Hendrick, S. S. (1989). Research on love: Does it measure up? *Journal of Personality and Social Psychology, 56,* 784-794.

In this classic article, the authors examine whether the available love instruments actually measure what they purport to measure.

Lee, J. A. (1973). *Colours of love: An exploration of the ways of loving.* Toronto: New Press.

This book serves as a wonderful introduction to the author's theory. Although out of print (check the library or a used book store), it is well worth the effort to locate it.

Kephart, W. M. (1967). Some correlates of romantic love. *Journal of Marriage and the Family, 29,* 470-474.

Simpson, J. A., Campbell, B., & Berscheid, E. (1986). The association between romantic love and marriage: Kephart (1967) twice revisited. *Personality and Social Psychology Bulletin, 12,* 363-372.

In 1967, Kephart asked a group of men and women whether love was essential for marriage. Twenty years later, Simpson and his colleagues did the same. The results revealed that attitudes about the association between love and marriage had changed dramatically over time, particularly among women.

Sternberg, R. J., & Barnes, M. L. (Eds.). (1988). *The psychology of love.* New Haven, CT: Yale University Press.

Although dated, this book remains a valuable reference tool for people interested in understanding social scientific views of love.

2

Passionate and Companionate Love

Chapter Outline

M ost people would probably agree that "being in love" with someone is a very different experience from "loving" that person. However, scientists have been relatively slow to make this same distinction. In fact, it was not until the early 1970s that theorists and researchers began to recognize that passionate love was more than simply an intense or extreme version of liking (e.g., Berscheid & Walster, 1974; Rubin, 1970, 1973). Now, the distinction between these two love experiences—exciting, intense *passionate* love and stable, affectionate *companionate* love—is maintained by most social and behavioral scientists.

PASSIONATE LOVE: A "SEXY" KIND OF LOVE

Of all the varieties of love that have been identified by theorists and researchers, passionate love (also called erotic or romantic love) has received the lion's share of attention. This particular type of love has assumed special importance in relationships research and in theoretical discourse on love for a number of reasons. First, passionate love appears to be a cross-cultural universal, experienced by men and women around the world (Jankowiak & Fischer, 1992; Sprecher, Aron, et al., 1994). Second, passionate love has become an essential part of the marriage contract in many human societies; most people say they will not marry without it (Simpson, Campbell, & Berscheid, 1986). Third, the absence or loss of passionate love seems to be a factor in relationship dissolution; many people leave marriages and other romantic relationships when their feelings of passionate love decline or end (Berscheid, 1985). And fourth, current social psychological theory suggests that passionate love is the type of love most closely associated with sexuality (Regan, 1998c, 2000a).

Defining Passionate Love

I hope to hold you in my arms before long, when I shall lavish upon you a million kisses, burning as the equatorial sun.

—From a letter written by Napoleon Bonaparte to Josephine, Spring 1797 (Hall, 1901)

Marie! Marie! Oh let me repeat that name a hundred times, a thousand times over; for three days now it has lived within me, oppressed me, set me afire. I am not writing to you, no, I am close beside you. I see you, I

hear you. . . . Eternity in your arms. . . . Heaven, hell, all is within you
and even more than all.

—From a letter written by famous Hungarian
composer Franz Liszt to Marie d'Agoult,
December 1834 (Tamplin, 1995)

Although various definitions of passionate love have been proposed, a review of the theoretical and empirical literatures suggests that the state of being in love is characterized by at least three primary features.

Emotional Intensity

Passionate love is an intensely emotional experience. In his classic book, *The American Sexual Tragedy,* psychologist Albert Ellis (1954) noted that "the romantic lover is changeable, and frequently goes from one violent passion to another" (p. 102). Two decades later, social psychologists Ellen Berscheid and Elaine Hatfield [then Walster] (1974) applied a well-known theory of emotion to the experience of passionate love in an effort to delineate its essential features. Specifically, these scientists proposed that men and women experience passionate love when a minimum of two conditions occur. First, they are extremely aroused physiologically (an essential ingredient for any strong emotion). Second, they believe that this arousal is caused by the partner and therefore is appropriately labeled "passionate love."

Some indirect empirical support exists for this hypothesis. Psychologists Donald Dutton and Arthur Aron (1974) conducted a now classic field study in which an attractive woman—a confederate who was working for the researchers—approached men who were walking across two quite different bridges located on the Capilano River in Canada. The Capilano Canyon Suspension Bridge served as the experimental bridge. This narrow, 450-foot-long structure consists of wooden boards attached to wire cables that run across the river. In addition, it possesses several arousal-inducing features, including the following (in the words of the researchers): "(a) a tendency to tilt, sway, and wobble, creating the impression that one is about to fall over the side; (b) very low handrails of wire cable which contribute to this impression; and (c) a 230-foot drop to rocks and shallow rapids below the bridge" (p. 511). The control bridge, located farther up the river, was constructed of heavy cedar, was considerably wider and sturdier than the experimental bridge, did not tilt or sway, and was suspended a mere 10 feet above a small shallow rivulet that ran into the main body of water. As each male participant crossed his respective bridge, the confederate approached him, introduced herself as a research assistant, and asked whether he would fill out a brief questionnaire. She then gave her phone number to those men who completed the questionnaire and invited them to call her if they had any additional questions about the study and wanted to talk further. The results revealed that fully half (50.0%) of the men who had met the young woman while on the scary experimental bridge called her later, compared with only 12.5% of the men who met her while crossing the sturdy control bridge. What explains this result? The men on the suspension bridge had experienced physiological arousal but had attributed their response to the woman rather than to the life-threatening situation, hence their attraction to her and subsequent interest in pursuing additional contact with her. These results certainly suggest that passion, attraction, and similar experiences are fundamentally "emotional" in nature.

In addition, passionate love is assumed to be associated with both positive and negative emotions. Some theorists suggest that passionate lovers alternate between states of joy, fulfillment, and ecstasy when the relationship is going well and between bouts of emptiness, anxiety, and despair when it is not (Hatfield & Rapson, 1993). In their analysis of the elements of romantic love relationships, Keith Davis and Michael Todd (1982) proposed that the exclusivity that characterizes this type of love can result in both the positive "subjective experience of having a special relationship to the loved one . . . [and] the sense of almost unlimited power that lovers feel" and the negative experiences of "possessiveness, jealousy, and excessive dependency" (p. 91).

Interestingly, this particular theoretical assumption has received only partial support. Research generally reveals that passionate love is more strongly associated with positive emotions than with negative emotions. Men and women asked to identify the essential features of passionate love cite many more positive emotional experiences—including happiness, joy or rapture, closeness, warmth, giddiness, and tenderness—than negative ones (Regan, Kocan, & Whitlock, 1998). Similarly, partners who are in love with one another report feeling positive emotions to a greater degree than they do negative emotions (Sprecher & Regan, 1998). However, one negative emotional state—jealousy—does appear to be related to passionate love. Both men and women associate jealousy with the state of being in love (Regan et al.,

1998), and those who love passionately also tend to report feeling or having felt jealous (Sprecher & Regan, 1998).

Fragility

The second feature of passionate love is its fragility. In contrast to more durable types of love, passionate love is viewed by most theorists as an inherently unstable, relatively brief phenomenon. In his discussion of the four general varieties of love, C. S. Lewis (1960/1988) called erotic love "notoriously the most mortal of our loves" and reminded readers that "the world rings with complaints of his fickleness" (p. 113). Existential psychologist Erich Fromm (1956), another of the earlier love theorists, agreed that the "explosive" experience of falling in love with someone is "by its very nature short-lived" (p. 48). This notion has been echoed in more recent discourse. For example, Berscheid (1983) concluded that passionate love, like other intense emotional experiences, has a "swift onset" and is "distressingly fragile." Drawing an analogy to substance addiction, Robert Sternberg (1988) similarly stated that the rapid development of passion is inevitably followed by habituation, so that over time the partner is no longer as "stimulating" or arousing as he or she once was. Once habituation occurs, Sternberg argued, even more time with the loved one is unlikely to provoke the earlier passionate response.

Some cross-sectional and longitudinal research supports the theoretical prediction that passionate love has a brief life span. It is the case that feelings of passionate love initially may increase as a couple progresses from earlier (e.g., casual dating) to later (e.g., steady dating, engaged) courtship stages (e.g., Hatfield & Sprecher, 1986). However, research conducted with married individuals generally finds that passionate love declines over longer periods of time (e.g., Hatfield, Traupmann, & Sprecher, 1984) as well as after major relational transitions (i.e., childlessness to parenthood [Tucker & Aron, 1993]). Researchers who have surveyed dating couples find similar results. For example, with a sample of 197 dating couples, Susan Sprecher and Pamela Regan (1998) examined whether the number of months that each couple had been dating was related to the amount of passionate love the partners reportedly felt for each other. These researchers found evidence that passionate love indeed is related to relationship duration; specifically, the longer a couple had been together, the lower the partners' passionate love scores (although scores were high in all couples).

Sexuality

> *I love everything about him—I want him all the time and I think about him*
> *all the time. I am so in love with him that I get weak even writing down*
> *these words. I can't concentrate, I can't sleep, I don't want to eat. I get so*
> *excited when I know that I'm going to see him, and then when I do see him,*
> *I can't breathe I'm so full of want. When we're together I can't wait for him*
> *to touch me, to kiss me, to hold me. And then I want more! This is how I*
> *know that I'm really in love—these feelings just keep growing stronger and*
> *stronger. This is it!*

—24-year-old woman interviewed by the author

As this quotation illustrates, passionate love and sexuality appear to be intricately connected in the eyes of many individuals. Contemporary theorists and researchers who have speculated on the nature of this love type have linked it with a wide array of sexual phenomena. Some theorists have posited that *desire* is the sexual ingredient that gives passionate love its unique flavor (e.g., Regan & Berscheid, 1999; Tennov, 1979). For example, Berscheid (1988) wrote,

It is all very well to look down one's nose at Sigmund Freud's cursory analysis of romantic love as repressed, suppressed, or frustrated sexual desire, but, for me at least, Freud seems to have gotten smarter as I've gotten older. And, surely, it is no accident that the wisest of the romantic love theorists, Theodore Reik, enti-tled his classic book *Of Love and Lust* (1941) (and not, by the way, "Of Love and Liking"). (p. 372)

Other theorists have targeted *sexual arousal* or *excitement* as an important feature of passionate love (e.g., Hatfield & Sprecher, 1986; Hatfield & Walster, 1978; Shaver, Hazan, & Bradshaw, 1988). Still others believe that passionate love is strongly linked with *sexual depri-vation* (e.g., Hatfield & Walster, 1978), *sexual satisfaction* (e.g., Berscheid & Walster, 1974; Hendrick & Hendrick, 1986), or *sexual activity* (e.g., Shaver & Hazan, 1988). Although these phenomena do not represent the same (or in some instances even similar) concepts, it is clear that passionate love is considered by many social scientists to be a sexually charged experience.

Excitement and Activity. Research strongly supports this theoretical assumption. Numerous studies demonstrate that both behavioral (e.g., intercourse, other sexual activities) and physiological (e.g., sexual excitement, sexual arousal) aspects of sexuality are associated with feelings of passionate love. People who are more passionately in love report experiencing higher levels of sexual excitement when thinking about their partners (Hatfield & Sprecher, 1986; Sprecher & Regan, 1998) and also engaging in more frequent sexual activities with those partners (Aron & Henkemeyer, 1995) than do individuals who are less passionately in love.

In addition, some empirical evidence reveals that sexual activity is one of the primary ways in which couples express and communicate feelings of passionate love. For example, evolutionary psychologist David Buss (1988) asked a sample of 100 men and women to think of people who "have been or are currently in love" and to list acts or behaviors these individuals performed that reflected their feelings. Several behaviors involving sexual intimacy were viewed as integral to the passionate love experience, including "he gave her a prolonged hug," "she nuzzled him," "he made love to her," and "she spent the night with him." Similar results were reported by researchers Peter Marston, Michael Hecht, Melodee Manke, Susan McDaniel, and Heidi Reeder (1998). These researchers interviewed a sample of "in love" couples about the ways in which the partners communicated their feelings of passion to each other. The most common method of expressing passion was through sexual activities, including "making love."

Desire. Motivational aspects of sexuality—sexual desire or sexual attraction—also appear related to passionate love. For example, Robert Ridge and Ellen Berscheid (1989) asked a sample of undergraduate men and women whether they believed that there was a difference between the experience of being in love with another person and that of loving another person. Fully 87% emphatically claimed that there indeed was a difference between the two experiences. In addition, when asked to specify the nature of that difference, participants cited sexual attraction as descriptive of the passionate "in love" experience—and not of the companionate "loving" experience.

Similar results were reported by Regan and her colleagues (1998). These researchers asked a sample of men and women to list in a free response format all of the features that they considered to be characteristic or prototypical of the state of "being in love." Of 119 spontaneously generated features, *sexual desire* received the second highest frequency rating, cited by 66% (*trust* was first, cited by 80%). In other words, when thinking of passionate love, two thirds of the participants automatically thought of sexual desire. In addition, this feature was viewed as more important to the passionate love concept than behavioral sexual events such as *kissing* (cited by only 10%), *touching/holding* (cited by 18%), and *sexual activity or intercourse* (cited by 25%).

Person perception experiments provide additional support for these prototype results. Person perception experiments are commonly used in social psychological research and essentially involve manipulating people's perceptions of a relationship and then measuring the impact of that manipulation on their subsequent evaluations and beliefs. In the first experiment, Regan (1998b) provided a sample of 60 undergraduate men and women with two self-report questionnaires ostensibly completed by "Rob" and "Nancy," a student couple enrolled at the same university. The members of this couple reported experiencing either no sexual desire for each other or a high amount of sexual desire for each other, and they either were currently engaging in sexual activity with each other or were not sexually active. Participants then estimated the likelihood that the partners experience passionate love as well as a variety of other relationship events. As illustrated in Exhibit 2.1, the results indicated that both men and women believed that dating partners who experience sexual desire for each other are more likely to be passionately in love with each other (as well as more likely to experience a variety of other relationship events) than are dating partners who do not desire each other sexually, regardless of their current level of sexual activity.

A second experiment, a conceptual replication of the first, confirmed these results. Here, 48 men and women received information about the members of a heterosexual, dating "student couple" who ostensibly reported either that they were currently passionately in love with each other, that they loved each other, or that they liked each other. Participants then estimated the likelihood that the members of the couple experience sexual desire for each other and the amount of desire that they feel for each other. Analyses revealed that participants perceived partners who are passionately in love as more *likely* to experience sexual desire than partners who love each other or who like each other. Similarly, partners who are passionately in love were believed to experience a greater *amount* of sexual desire for each other than were partners who love each other or who like each other. Interestingly, sexual

Exhibit 2.1 What Do a Couple's Sexual Experiences Tell Us About the Nature of Their Relationship?

	Rob and Nancy Report			
	High Desire + Intercourse	*High Desire + No Intercourse*	*Low Desire + Intercourse*	*Low Desire + No Intercourse*
How likely is it that Rob and Nancy				
1. Are passionately in love with each other?	7.53	6.47	2.00	2.47
2. Like each other?	8.13	8.07	4.73	6.33
3. Are happy?	7.73	7.40	3.60	5.60
4. Are satisfied with their relationship?	7.73	7.13	2.93	5.20
5. Are committed to their relationship?	7.27	7.40	5.60	5.33
6. Trust each other?	7.20	7.27	5.73	6.27
7. Love each other?	6.40	5.47	3.07	3.80

SOURCE: Data adapted from Regan, P. C. (1998b). Of lust and love: Beliefs about the role of sexual desire in romantic relationships. *Personal Relationships, 5,* 139–157.

NOTE: In this study, participants read about a couple ("Rob" and "Nancy") who reported feeling either high or low amounts of sexual attraction for one another and who either were engaging in sexual intercourse or were not. After reading about the couple, participants estimated how likely it was that they experienced a variety of other feelings using a 9-point scale (1: *not at all likely,* 9: *extremely likely*). As you can see from the results, participants thought that Rob and Nancy were much more likely to be in love with each other (and to like each other, etc.) when they sexually desired each other than when they did not sexually desire each other (and it really did not matter whether or not they were having sex). In other words, people associated sexual desire (and not sexual activity) with passionate love; sexual desire seems to be a "sign" that a couple is in love.

desire was believed to be no more likely in a "loving" relationship than in a "liking" relationship, and greater amounts of sexual desire were not believed to occur in loving relationships than in liking relationships. Again, it seems that sexual desire is viewed, at least by young men and women, as an important feature or component of passionate love relationships—and not of relationships characterized by feelings of loving (i.e., companionate love) and/or liking (i.e., friendship).

Not only do people *believe* that passionate love is characterized by sexual desire, but most men and women report *experiencing* sexual desire for the people with whom they are passionately in love. For example, Sarah Meyers and Ellen Berscheid (1996) asked a large sample of undergraduate men and women to list the initials of all the people they currently loved, the initials of all those with whom they were currently in love, and the initials of all those toward whom they currently felt sexual attraction/desire. The researchers' results indicated that 85% of the persons listed in the "in love" category also were listed in the "sexually desire" category, whereas only 2% of those listed in the "love" category (and not cross-listed in the "in love" category) were listed in the "sexually desire" category. Thus, the objects of respondents' feelings of passionate love (but not their feelings of love) also tended to be the objects of their desire.

Research with actual dating couples yields similar results. Regan (2000b) reported that the self-reported amount of sexual desire experienced by men and women for their dating partners (and not their level of sexual activity) was significantly positively correlated with the level of passionate love they felt for those individuals. Their feelings of desire were unrelated, however, to the amount of companionate love and liking they experienced for their partners.

In sum, passionate love is a sexualized experience that is strongly associated with feelings of sexual desire or attraction for the partner, that tends to result in the occurrence of sexual activity, and that appears to be linked with sexual arousal and excitement.

Measuring Passionate Love

There are two basic ways in which to assess passionate love: single-item self-report measures and multi-item scales. Single-item measures typically ask respondents to report on the quantity or intensity of passionate love that they experience for their partners. Examples of such items are provided in Exhibit 2.2.

Exhibit 2.2   Single-Item Measures of Passionate Love

1. How much passionate love do you feel for _____?

     1   2   3   4   5   6   7   8   9
    None   A great deal

2. Rate the intensity of your feelings of passionate love for your current partner.

     1   2   3   4   5   6   7   8   9
    Not at all   Extremely
    intense   intense

3. How deeply are you in love with _____?

     1   2   3   4   5   6   7   8   9
    Not at all   Very deeply
    deeply

4. How strong are your feelings of passionate love for your partner?

     1   2   3   4   5   6   7   8   9
    Very weak   Very strong
     1   2   3   4   5   6   7   8   9
    Not at all   Extremely
    strong   strong

5. How often do you experience feelings of passionate love for your partner?

     1   2   3   4   5   6   7   8   9
    Never   Extremely
                                                            often

    _____ times a day
    _____ times a week
    _____ times a month

6. How often did you experience passionate love in your relationship during the past month?

     1   2   3   4   5   6   7   8   9
    Never   Sometimes   Extremely
                                                            often

Global single-item measures are easy to use and appear to be relatively valid (Sprecher & Regan, 1998). However, many researchers choose to use larger multi-item scales that have been developed specifically to measure the various theoretically important elements of passionate love.

Several different passionate love scales have been constructed over the years. The two most commonly used and empirically sound measures are the Erotic subscale of the Love Attitudes Scale (LAS) (see Chapter 1) and the Passionate Love Scale, developed by Elaine Hatfield and Susan Sprecher (1986).

The Passionate Love Scale represents the most complete measure of passionate love currently available. Drawing on past theoretical conceptualizations, previously developed measures, and in-depth personal interviews, Hatfield and Sprecher (1986) crafted a series of items designed to assess the various components of the passionate love experience. The complete scale is reproduced in Exhibit 2.3. The items clearly reflect what theorists believe are the essential ingredients of passionate love: intense physiological arousal ("Sometimes my body trembles with excitement at the sight of _____"), emotional highs and lows ("Since I've been involved with _____, my emotions have been on a roller-coaster"), and sexuality ("I possess a powerful attraction for _____").

COMPANIONATE LOVE: A "STURDY" KIND OF LOVE

In addition to passionate love, the majority of scientists include a type of love called companionate love in their classification schemes. Variously described as affectionate love, friendship love, true love, attachment, storge, and conjugal love, companionate love reflects "the affection and tenderness we feel for those with whom our lives are deeply entwined" (Hatfield & Rapson, 1993, p. 9).

Defining Companionate Love

> *I hope and pray I shall be able to make you happy and secure during my remaining years, and cherish you my darling one as you deserve, and leave you in comfort when my race is run. What it has been to me to live all these years in [your] heart and companionship no phrases can convey. Time passes swiftly, but is it not joyous to see how great and growing is the treasure we have gathered together?*
>
> —From a letter written by British Prime Minister Winston Churchill to his wife, Clementine, January 23, 1935 (Soames, 1979)

Exhibit 2.3   The Passionate Love Scale

Instructions

We would like to know how you feel when you are *passionately in love.* Some common terms for passionate love are *romantic love, infatuation, love sickness,* and *obsessive love.* Please think of the person whom you love most passionately *right now.* If you are not in love right now, please think of the last person you loved. If you have never been in love, think of the person you came closest to caring for in that way. Try to tell us how you felt at the time when your feelings were the most intense.

Response scale

1	2	3	4	5	6	7	8	9
Not at all true				Moderately true				Definitely true

Items

1. Since I've been involved with _____, my emotions have been on a roller coaster.
2. I would feel deep despair if _____ left me.
3. Sometimes my body trembles with excitement at the sight of _____.
4. I take delight in studying the movements and angles of _____'s body.
5. Sometimes I can't control my thoughts; they are obsessively on _____.
6. I feel happy when I am doing something to make _____ happy.
7. I would rather be with _____ than with anyone else.
8. I'd get jealous if I thought _____ were falling in love with someone else.
9. No one else could love _____ like I do.
10. I yearn to know all about _____.
11. I want _____—physically, emotionally, and mentally.
12. I will love _____ forever.
13. I melt when looking deeply into _____'s eyes.
14. I have an endless appetite for affection from _____.
15. For me, _____ is the perfect romantic partner.
16. _____ is the person who can make me feel the happiest.
17. I sense my body responding when _____ touches me.
18. I feel tender toward _____.
19. _____ always seems to be on my mind.
20. If I were separated from _____ for a long time, I would feel intensely lonely.
21. I sometimes find it difficult to concentrate on work because thoughts of _____ occupy my mind.
22. I want _____ to know me—my thoughts, my fears, and my hopes.
23. Knowing that _____ cares about me makes me feel complete.
24. I eagerly look for signs indicating _____'s desire for me.
25. If _____ were going through a difficult time, I would put away my own concerns to help him/her out.

26. _____ can make me feel effervescent and bubbly.
27. In the presence of _____, I yearn to touch and be touched.
28. An existence without _____ would be dark and dismal.
29. I possess a powerful attraction for _____.
30. I get extremely depressed when things don't go right in my relationship with _____.

Scoring

To find out your passionate love score, add up the ratings you gave to each item. Divide this total by 30.

SOURCE: Adapted from Hatfield, E., & Sprecher, S. (1986). Measuring passionate love in intimate relationships. *Journal of Adolescence, 9*, 383-410. Copyright © 1986 by Academic Press, Inc. Items reprinted with permission.

You have been with me constantly, sweetheart. At Kangerdlooksoah I looked repeatedly at Ptarmigan Island and thought of the time we camped there. At Nuuatoksoah I landed where we were. And on the 11th we passed the mouth of Bowdoin Bay in brilliant weather, and as long as I could I kept my eyes on Anniversary Lodge. We have been great chums dear. In fancy I kiss your dear eyes and lips and cheeks sweetheart; and dream of you and my children, and my home till I come again. Kiss my babies for me.

—From a letter written by Arctic explorer Robert Peary to his wife, Josephine, August 17, 1908 (Tamplin, 1995)

Companionate love, or the state of "loving" someone, consists of several basic features.

Emotional Intimacy

In contrast to passionate love, companionate love is assumed to be associated with primarily positive, and much less intense, emotional experiences. Recall Lewis's (1960/1988) description of affectionate love as "this warm comfortableness, this satisfaction in being together" (p. 32). Relationship scholar Sharon Brehm (1985) described this type of love as built on a solid foundation of respect, admiration, and interpersonal trust and rewards, and Sternberg (1988) similarly depicted companionate love as composed of feelings of emotional intimacy coupled with a firm commitment to the relationship and the partner.

Indeed, research suggests that companionate love is a nearly uniformly positive experience. Recall that Beverley Fehr's (1988) participants identified warm feelings of *trust, caring, respect, loyalty, supportiveness,* and *friendship* as prototypical features of love; more intense experiences, including *euphoria, heart races, butterflies in stomach,* and other signs of emotional arousal, were not considered to be essential features of this type of love. Similar results were reported by Helmut Lamm and Ulrich Wiesmann (1997), who asked university students to write down how they could tell that they "loved" (as opposed to "liked" or were "in love with") another person. The most common indicator of companionate love generated by the participants was *positive mood* (listed by 53%); distinctive indicators (i.e., elements that were listed significantly more frequently for "love" than for "like" or "in love") included such positive affective experiences as *trust* (41%), *tolerance* (21%), and *relaxedness or calmness* (12%).

The participants in a study conducted by psychologist Donna Castañeda (1993) provided nearly identical answers when asked to indicate the qualities and characteristics they believed to be important in a love relationship. Specifically, participants mentioned *trust, mutual respect, communication and sharing, honesty,* and *affection* along with a number of other positive emotions and experiences. Research with dating couples substantiates these survey results. Sprecher and Regan (1998) found that positive emotions (including joy, trust, liking, contentment, satisfaction, liking, and respect) were strongly associated with the amount of companionate love reported by a sample of romantically involved couples.

Durability

Unlike passionate love, companionate love is assumed to be relatively impervious to the passage of time. In fact, some theorists speculate that companionate love may grow stronger over time because it is grounded in intimacy processes (including caring, understanding, and attachment) that require time to develop fully (Hatfield & Rapson, 1993). Other scientists propose that romantic relationships may even progress in a linear fashion from passionate love to companionate love. For example, Sternberg (1988) suggested, "Most romantic love relationships that do, in fact, survive eventually turn into companionate love relationships:

the passion begins to melt, but the intimacy remains. Passion may be replaced over time by long-term and deeply felt commitment" (p. 127).

A similar proposition was made by theorist Bernard Murstein (1988), who noted,

> With unimpeded access to each other and as a result of habituation, bit by bit generalized, overriding passion and longing evaporate and are replaced by liking or trust, although in good marriages, passion may return on specific occasions. . . . Out of the evolving network of shared experiences as a couple—children, family, married life—comes something less ephemeral and more permanent than romantic love. (p. 30)

Certainly, companionate lovers report feeling extremely committed to their partners and desirous of maintaining their relationships; their feelings of companionate love also appear unrelated to the length of their relationships (i.e., time does not appear to have any negative impact on companionate love) (Sprecher & Regan, 1998).

Closeness

Closeness is another feature of companionate love. Love theorists Elaine Hatfield and Richard Rapson (1993) argued that companionate love requires that the partners' lives "must be deeply entwined" (p. 107). Sternberg (1988) similarly suggested that companionate lovers possess mutual understanding, share themselves and their possessions with one another, give and receive emotional support, and demonstrate various other signs of intimate connection and mutuality. A close relationship is defined as one in which the partners' thoughts, emotions, and actions— their lives—are strongly interdependent (Kelley et al., 1983). Companionate love is, in essence, close love; that is, it is characterized by a high degree of interconnection between the two individuals. What one partner says, feels, does, or thinks has a direct impact on the other person.

Measuring Companionate Love

Companionate love can be measured via single items (e.g., "How much caring affectionate love do you feel for your partner?") or multi-item scales. For example, Sternberg (1986) defined companionate love as the combination of intimacy and decision/commitment; thus, the items on his scale that reflect those components provide one measure of companionate love. The Storge subscale on the LAS also may assess this type of love. Perhaps the most commonly used measure of companionate love, however, is the 13-item Love Scale created by Zick Rubin (1970). Sprecher and Regan (1998), in an attempt to create an even "purer" measure of companionate love, added an item that assesses interpersonal trust to Rubin's scale and removed several items that reflected a more passionate love experience. The resulting 7-item, adapted Companionate Love Scale is provided in Exhibit 2.4.

SUMMARY

Although most scientists recognize and maintain the distinction between passionate love and companionate love, both types of love are experienced with some frequency by men and women during their lifetimes. Passionate love is an intensely emotional, fragile, and sexualized experience that has become strongly associated with the marriage contract and the establishment of other types of committed romantic relationship. Companionate love is a more durable, lower keyed experience that is founded on trust, affection, and respect. Although this type of love has received less attention than its more colorful cousin, it is certainly no less essential to human happiness.

KEY CONCEPTS

Passionate love (p. 26)
Sexual excitement or arousal (p. 26)
Sexual behavior or activity (p. 26)
Sexual desire (pp. 26-29)
Single-item measures of love (pp. 29-30)
Passionate Love Scale (p. 31)
Companionate love (p. 31)
Closeness (p. 35)
Companionate Love Scale (p. 36)

DISCUSSION QUESTIONS

1. Compare and contrast the experience of passionate and companionate love. If you had to choose, which would you rather feel for a steady dating partner or spouse? Why?

Exhibit 2.4   The Companionate Love Scale

Instructions

Companionate love is a stable type of love based on feelings of deep affection and caring. Some common terms for companionate love are *affectionate love, friendship love, true love, attachment,* and *conjugal love.* We would like to know how you feel when you love someone this way. Please think of the person whom you love most companionately *right now.* If you do not love someone right now, please think of the last person you loved. If you have never loved someone, think of the person you came closest to caring for in that way.

Response scale

1	2	3	4	5	6	7	8	9
Not at all true				Moderately true				Definitely true

Items

1. I feel that I can confide in _____ about virtually everything.
2. I find it easy to ignore _____'s faults.
3. I would do almost anything for _____.
4. I would forgive _____ for practically anything.
5. I would greatly enjoy being confided in by _____.
6. I care about _____.
7. I feel that I can trust _____ completely.

Scoring

To find out your companionate love score, add up the ratings you gave to each item. Divide this total by 7.

SOURCE: Adapted from Sprecher, S., & Regan, P. C. (1998). Passionate and companionate love in courting and young married couples. *Sociological Inquiry, 68,* 163-185. Copyright © 1998 by Blackwell Publishing, Inc. Items reprinted with permission.

2. Is it possible to feel both types of love—passionate and companionate—for another person?

3. Consider the general theories of love presented previously in Chapter 1. Which types or styles of love reflect the two varieties discussed in this chapter?

4. Select a movie or television scene that, in your opinion, best illustrates the concept of "passionate" love. Do the same for "companionate love." Share your examples with the class and discuss the ways in which the scenes exemplify these two types of love.

5. Consider the many ways in which love has been portrayed throughout history and in literature. Is love a "good" thing? A "bad" thing? Use examples to support your conclusion. (Good sources of information include Bartlett's *Familiar Quotations*, any book of proverbs, and *The Oxford Dictionary of Quotations*.)

RECOMMENDED READINGS

Berscheid, E. (1988). Some comments on love's anatomy: Or, whatever happened to old-fashioned lust? In R. J. Sternberg & M. L. Barnes (Eds.), *The psychology of love* (pp. 359-374). New Haven, CT: Yale University Press.

Long before most other social scientists, the author recognized that lust (sexual attraction or desire) is one of the essential ingredients of passionate love. In this delightful chapter, she calls for social psychologists to reintegrate sexuality, in particular desire, into their discourse on love.

Berscheid, E., & Walster, E. (1974). A little bit about love. In T. L. Huston (Ed.), *Foundations of interpersonal attraction* (pp. 355-381). New York: Academic Press.

This classic article is one of the earliest social psychological commentaries about the nature of love.

3

Love Gone Bad:
Problematic Aspects of
Love Relationships

Chapter Outline

Love and love relationships are associated with a variety of positive events. For example, the experience of loving another person may allow us to feel intimacy, contentment, and satisfaction; to experience passion, joy, and excitement; and to provide and receive emotional and social support. All of these experiences, in turn, can enhance and promote our psychological and even our physical well-being. But there is another side to love as well—a dangerous, destructive, and problematic side that is associated with dysfunction, negative emotion, and other less-than-enjoyable outcomes. This chapter examines the "dark" side of love.

UNREQUITED PASSIONATE LOVE

Folk wisdom (actually, Victorian poet Alfred Tennyson) tells us that "it is better to have loved and lost than never to have loved at all." And perhaps this is sound advice. After all, love is usually associated with a wonderful and rewarding mix of positive outcomes, events, and feelings. However, passionate love—particularly when it is *unrequited* or not reciprocated by the beloved—has the potential to be just as strongly associated with negative outcomes.

In one of the first studies to attempt to explore the dynamics of unrequited love, Roy Baumeister, Sara Wotman, and Arlene Stillwell (1993) asked 71 people who had been in this situation to write autobiographical accounts of their experiences as would-be suitors and rejectors. The results indicated that unrequited lovers experienced a panoply of both positive and negative emotions. Many (44%) would-be suitors reported that their unreciprocated passion caused them pain, suffering, and disappointment; jealousy and anger (which were usually directed at the loved ones' chosen partners); and a sense of frustration. Similarly, 22% experienced worries and fears about rejection. In addition to these unpleasant experiences, however, the lovelorn suitors also reported many pleasant emotional outcomes; in fact, positive feelings far outweighed negative ones in the accounts they gave of their experiences. For example, happiness, excitement, the blissful anticipation of seeing the beloved, sheer elation at the state of being in love, and other positive emotions were reported by the majority (98%) of would-be suitors. More than half (53%) also looked back on their unrequited love experiences with some degree of positive feeling. In explaining this finding, the researchers noted the following:

> Apparently, positive feelings can be remembered in a positive way even if the memory is linked to suffering and disappointment. People remember the warmth of their feelings for another person, and the memory is at least somewhat pleasant. Some of our participants expressed gladness at being able to preserve the friendship that could have been jeopardized if their romantic overtures had become too insistent. Others simply treasured the memory or retained a soft spot in their heart for the one they loved. (Baumeister & Wotman, 1992, p. 60)

When the researchers examined the experiences reported by the rejectors, however, they found little evidence of positive outcomes. Specifically, although roughly one fourth of the rejectors reported feeling flattered by the attention of their potential lovers, the majority also viewed these unwanted advances as annoying (51%), felt uncomfortable about delivering rejection messages (61%), and experienced a host of negative emotions, including anger, frustration, and resentment (70%). In addition, their recollections of the entire experiences were far less suffused with warmth, with only 33% indicating any positive affect in retrospect. The researchers concluded,

> Unlike the would-be lover, it was hard for the rejector to feel that his or her life had been enriched by this experience. For many, apparently, it was a useless and pointless set of aggravations. They were forced to respond to a situation they never wanted, and these responses were difficult for them, bringing uncertainty, guilt, aggravation, all of which went for naught. For some, a valued friendship was destroyed in the bargain. Thus they had plenty to resent and regret. (Baumeister & Wotman, 1992, p. 62)

Unrequited love clearly is an emotionally difficult experience for both the rejector and the would-be suitor. Unfortunately, it also is a common event in the lives of adolescents and young adults, particularly men (Hill, Blakemore, & Drumm, 1997), and there is no easy way in which to recover from romantic rejection. Time is perhaps the only cure.

OBSESSION

At first I thought it was sort of cute and romantic that he wanted to be with me all the time. He would ask me to give him a detailed account of my day, all the places I went, the people I talked with, the things I did.... I felt flattered that I had a boyfriend who loved me so much. But then it got out of hand. I mean, he wouldn't even let me drive to the store by myself! After we broke up, he began calling me at home, usually several times a night. He also started calling me at work, which made things difficult for me with my boss. So I stopped taking his calls at work and I

changed to an unlisted number at home. I think what really made me real-
ize that I needed to take some action and tell people what was going on
was when he started spying on me. One morning, I was standing by the
window looking outside and I noticed his car. He was just sitting there,
watching me. I have no idea how long he had been there, but it really
scared me. I felt trapped and violated.

—32-year-old woman interviewed by the author

I met a woman I thought I liked. She was attractive, bright, seemed to
have a good sense of humor and to be stable and well-grounded. We
went out on a couple of dates, and it turned out that we didn't have that
much in common, so I didn't pursue the relationship. No big breakup or
anything, we just weren't suited to each other. That should have been
the end of it, but it wasn't. She lived about 10 miles from me, and she
would drive over to my neighborhood, park in front of my house, and
then go jogging around the block for what seemed like hours. I would see
her as she passed my house again and again, every single day. She began
to eat in the local restaurants I frequented. She called my house and left
messages about getting together to "work things out." She was every-
where I went and she did her best to invade every single moment of my
day. My friends laughed about it and made jokes about what a lucky guy
I was to have this woman chasing after me, but believe me, it wasn't
funny. Fortunately, I relocated due to my job and I haven't seen her
since.

—46-year-old man interviewed by the author

As we have seen, most people at some time or another become
attracted to or fall in love with individuals who do not reciprocate their
feelings. And although these experiences often are not pleasant, the
majority of men and women manage to deal with them. Sometimes,
however, unreciprocated passion or attachment is associated with
obsessive thinking, psychopathology, and/or inappropriate or even
violent behavior (Meloy, 1989; Mintz, 1980). *Obsessive relational intru-*
sion (ORI) is defined as "repeated and unwanted pursuit and invasion
of one's sense of physical or symbolic privacy by another person, either
stranger or acquaintance, who desires and/or presumes an intimate
relationship" (Cupach & Spitzberg, 1998, pp. 234-235). This phenomenon
also has been called "relational stalking" (Emerson, Ferris, & Gardner,
1998), "domestic stalking" (Dunn, 1999), and "intimate partner stalking"

(Tjaden & Thoennes, 2000) and essentially involves one person (the pursuer) desiring and actively attempting to obtain an intimate relationship with another person (the victim), who either does not want this particular type of relationship or wants no relationship at all.

Surveys of college samples reveal that relational stalking is disturbingly common, with rates ranging from 20% to 30% (e.g., Coleman, 1997; Logan, Leukefeld, & Walker, 2000; Spitzberg & Cupach, 1996). In addition, sizable numbers of men and women report having been the target of behaviors that are implicated in ORI, including receiving unwanted letters, notes, phone calls, visits, or gifts and being followed or watched by a pursuer (Herold, Mantle, & Zemitis, 1979; Jason, Reichler, Easton, Neal, & Wilson, 1984; Leonard et al., 1993; Roscoe, Strouse, & Goodwin, 1994). Research conducted with young adults generally reveals that men and women are equally at risk for this type of victimization (Spitzberg & Cupach, 1996).

To some extent, ORI or relational stalking can be considered a warped version of the normal courtship process. For example, suitors often persist in—and are rewarded for—their efforts to gain attention and affection from potential mates, and even partners who have ended a relationship sometimes "come around" and renew their love and commitment to one another. Given this state of affairs, it is not surprising that a would-be lover would make several attempts to woo a potential or former partner. It is when the individual continues in his or her pursuit despite strong and sustained resistance from the target that these normal aspects of courtship become inappropriate.

Communication scholars Brian Spitzberg and William Cupach (2002) identified several additional ways in which relationships characterized by ORI differ from "normal" intimate relationships. For example, the development of most romantic relationships is marked by reciprocal and progressively deeper levels of self-disclosure, intimacy, closeness, and familiarity (see Chapter 11). In an ORI relationship, however, the self-disclosure that occurs is one-sided, premature, and excessive. In addition, hyperactive possessiveness takes the place of closeness, and familiarity is created through violations of privacy rather than through the mutual exchanges that characterize normal relationships. In sum,

> ORI relationships are characterized by forms of intimacy that are distorted, exaggerated, accelerated, more intense, and more

desperate, compared to the normal prototype for developing intimacy. Although the same dimensions of intimacy that characterize normal relations apply to ORI relations, their manifestations are more forced, fabricated, prematurely escalated, and disinhibited in ORI relations. (p. 206)

Data gathered by Cupach and Spitzberg (1997; see also Spitzberg & Cupach, 1996, 2002) reveal that pursuers use a variety of tactics to promote relationships with their unwilling targets. Some of these strategies are mildly intrusive and invasive, including leaving unwanted gifts and messages, making exaggerated expressions of devotion or affection, and following the target or invading his or her personal space. Moderately invasive and threatening tactics include intentionally sabotaging the target's reputation, spying or otherwise monitoring the target's behavior, and intruding on the target's friends and family. Examples of extremely intrusive and threatening tactics include making verbal or physical threats against the target or his or her loved ones, physically restraining or assaulting the target, sexually coercing the target, damaging the target's property, and invading the target's home or work.

The milder forms of intrusive behavior are the most frequently experienced ones. For example, approximately 60% to 75% of the participants in Spitzberg and Cupach's studies reported that their pursuers engaged in the following activities:

- Repeatedly called the target on the phone and argued with him or her
- Asked the target whether he or she were seeing someone romantically
- Called the target and hung up without speaking
- Begged the target for another chance
- Watched or stared at the target from a distance
- Refused to take hints that he or she was not welcome
- Made exaggerated claims about his or her affection
- Gossiped or bragged to others about the supposed relationship

About 10% to 30% of ORI victims reported that their pursuers had engaged in the following less common, but significantly more invasive and threatening, behaviors:

- Threatened to cause physical harm to the target
- Followed the target from place to place
- Damaged the target's property or possessions
- Exposed himself or herself to the target
- Forced the target to engage in sexual behavior
- Took photos without the target's knowledge or consent
- Sent a multitude of e-mail messages to the target
- Recorded conversations without the target's consent
- Broke into the target's home or apartment

Given the range of invasive and threatening actions in which pursuers commonly engage, it is hardly surprising that victims of ORI and relational stalking often experience a number of negative emotional reactions, including fear, anxiety, paranoia, depression, self-blame, and anger (e.g., Mullen & Pathé, 1994; Spitzberg, Nicastro, & Cousins, 1998; Wallace & Silverman, 1996). In addition, they may curtail their lifestyle or activity patterns, develop a heightened distrust of others, and/or exhibit sleeplessness, illness, and other physical symptoms (see Spitzberg & Cupach, 2001).

There are several ways in which targets may attempt to deal with ORI and stalking (De Becker, 1998; Spitzberg & Cupach, 1998, 2001). One of the most common reactions—and the one that requires the least amount of effort on the part of the target—is *avoidance*. Forms of avoidance include simply ignoring the pursuer, refraining from showing any signs of interest, failing to respond to the pursuer's messages or behavior, not accepting gifts or other tokens of the pursuer's affection, and limiting the pursuer's access to the target. Targets also may employ *direct confrontation*, which includes actions such as admonishing or attempting to reason with the pursuer and requesting that he or she refrain from further contacts. *Retaliation* is another strategy for dealing with unwanted attention. Retaliatory actions range from verbal threats and attempts to belittle or shame the pursuer to physical violence. Finally, *formal protection* may be sought from law enforcement officials or from friends and family.

Each of these coping strategies carries a potential cost. For example, because avoidance is an indirect and somewhat ambiguous strategy, the pursuer may fail to interpret it as rejection. Similarly, because the pursuer's goal is to connect with the target, direct confrontation by the target may prove to the pursuer that persistence pays off—that is, that pursuit will eventually bring contact with the object of obsession.

Retaliation may demonstrate the target's lack of interest; however, it may also anger the pursuer and push him or her to escalating levels of intrusion and threat. A similar outcome may be associated with formal protection efforts; for example, the seriousness of obtaining a restraining order or having police intervene in the situation may trigger anger and heightened aggression from the pursuer (as well as serve to demonstrate that he or she is finally gaining the target's notice).

So, what should a target of obsessive pursuit do? Some professionals believe that statements and actions that directly and unequivocally convey rejection are most effective at managing unwanted attention (e.g., De Becker, 1998). For example, an individual should refuse gifts and other forms of attention offered by the pursuer, should directly state his or her disinterest, and should cease all further contact and communication with that person.

MISMATCHED LOVE STYLES

When a lover whose preferred type of loving is storge becomes involved with a partner whose understanding of true love is some other type, difficulties naturally occur.

—Lee (1973, p. 80)

Another potential problem faced by people who fall in love or who enter love relationships has to do with the match or fit between their general love styles and those of their partners. When two lovers do not share the same beliefs about love and approach to love relationships, some degree of interpersonal and personal distress is likely to result. For example, a person who loves erotically may feel unfulfilled by a low-key storgic partner who expresses his or her feelings through shared activities rather than passionate declarations; the storgic individual, in turn, may feel uncomfortable in the face of the erotic partner's sexual expressiveness and emotional intensity. Similarly, the pairing of a ludic lover who seeks to avoid commitment and a manic lover who desperately requires it will undoubtedly produce negative outcomes for both partners.

Interestingly, only a few researchers have examined the role of love styles in ongoing romantic relationships. In general, there is a tendency for individuals to pair with similar others; erotic lovers join up with other erotic lovers, agapic people pair with other equally selfless individuals, and so on (e.g., Davis & Latty-Mann, 1987; Morrow, Clark, & Brock, 1995). In addition, there is some evidence that love styles are correlated with relationship outcomes. For example, research on dating couples conducted by Susan Hendrick and her colleagues (Hendrick, Hendrick, & Adler, 1988) revealed that men and women who adopted an erotic style of loving tended to feel particularly satisfied with their romantic relationships. In addition, the partners of women who scored high on eros (erotic or passionate love) or agape (selfless love) were highly satisfied, whereas the partners of women who scored high on ludus (game-playing love) were not very satisfied. More recently, Brenda Meeks, Susan Hendrick, and Clyde Hendrick (1998) examined the correlation between relationship satisfaction and various love styles in a sample of dating couples. Their results revealed that men and women who endorsed an erotic or storgic approach to love tended to also be highly satisfied with their relationships; those who loved ludically, however, were less satisfied. Taken as a whole, these results suggest that game playing, lack of friendship, and lack of passion are not conducive to interpersonal happiness.

LOSS OF PASSION

> It's not that I don't desire him anymore, it's simply that I don't desire him as much. In a way, our relationship is stronger now, built more solidly on other, less sexual feelings. But there are times when I have to admit I become a bit nostalgic for the passion that we've lost. It used to be that I would glimpse him making a certain gesture, or hear his voice on the phone, or catch the scent of his cologne, and I would literally be infused with this feeling of desire, of need, of sheer want. And it was almost indescribable, a mingling of the physical and the emotional. But we've been together for a long time, and somehow, somewhere, that feeling just faded. I love him deeply, maybe more than I ever did before, and I know that we'll grow old together, but it's not the same.
>
> —35-year-old homosexual man interviewed by the author

Passionate love frequently fades over time in romantic relationships (Sprecher & Regan, 1998). To some extent, we owe this occurrence to our biological design; our bodies simply are not equipped to sustain for long periods the physiological arousal associated with passionate love, desire, and other intense emotional experiences. It is definitely the case that a sudden loss of passion or an intense "falling out of love" may indicate that some degree of emotional conflict or interpersonal dysfunction exists in a couple's relationship. However, it may also serve as a sign that the couple has moved into a different, and no less positive, relational phase. In Chapter 2, we reviewed evidence suggesting that as passion and excitement fade within a relationship, they are often replaced by trust, acceptance, respect, fondness, and the other elements of companionate love.

In addition, passion, desire, and excitement may fade or fluctuate because of changes in the physical or psychological state of the individual partners that have nothing to do with larger relationship issues. Some people regularly experience fluctuations in their feelings of passion and desire (Kaplan, 1979; Levine, 1984). Others may find their ability and/or motivation to experience passion impaired by poor health, hormonal imbalances, chronic drug use, depression and other mood disorders, and so on (see Regan & Berscheid, 1999). It is hard to feel passionately enthralled by the beloved when one is ill or otherwise feeling poorly. Thus, the sense that one is "falling out of love" with, or even losing some degree of sexual attraction to, the partner is not necessarily a sign that the relationship is in trouble. It is only when one or both partners disagree about or are troubled by some element of their relationship that professional intervention may be helpful.

SUMMARY

Although most men and women find their love relationships to be both positive and life affirming, difficulties may arise. Unrequited passionate love, obsession, mismatched love styles, and loss of passion all are potentially problematic events that may result in extremely negative outcomes. Understanding the types of love that exist, the changes that commonly occur over time in romantic relationships, and the signs and symptoms of interpersonal problems can enable us to effectively alleviate the difficulties that may develop in our love relationships.

KEY CONCEPTS

Unrequited love (p. 40)
Obsessive relational intrusion (p. 42)
Relational stalking (p. 42)
Avoidance (p. 45)
Direct confrontation (p. 45)
Retaliation (p. 45)
Formal protection (p. 45)

DISCUSSION QUESTIONS

1. Is being in love always a positive experience? In what ways can passionate love be problematic?

2. Define obsessive relational intrusion (ORI). How do ORI relationships resemble, and differ from, "normal" relationships? What strategies can victims use to deal with ORI?

3. Which love styles appear associated with interpersonal distress? Can ludic love ever be a "good" experience?

4. Why does passion seem to inevitably fade over time in most romantic relationships? Is the loss of passion a sign of interpersonal dysfunction?

RECOMMENDED READINGS

Baumeister, R. F., & Wotman, S. R. (1992). *Breaking hearts: The two sides of unrequited love.* New York: Guilford.

This book was written for the reading public and presents a nice blend of scientific research and narrative about the experience of unreciprocated love.

De Becker, G. (1998). *The gift of fear: Survival signals that protect us from violence.* New York: Dell.

This is an excellent, if often terrifying, glimpse into stalking. The author discusses his own extensive experiences in working with people (including many celebrities) who have been the recipients of unwanted (and sometimes violent) attention from others. Although many of the stories are graphic and intense, the author gives his readers helpful advice on how to avoid and manage these situations. This is an excellent and informative read.

Spitzberg, B. H., & Cupach, W. R. (Eds.). (1998). *The dark side of close relationships.* Mahwah, NJ: Lawrence Erlbaum.

This edited volume presents a collection of chapters written by theorists and researchers who have explored problematic aspects of close relationships.

PART II

SEX

Sexuality plays an important role in dating and mating relationships. We already have seen, in Chapter 2, that several aspects of sexuality—including excitement, desire, and activity—are associated with feelings of passionate love. This section of the text focuses on *relational* sexuality—sexual responses that occur within the context of romantic relationships. Relational sexuality is very different from the type of sex that involves uncommitted or casual partners. Certainly, relational and casual sex often stem from similar motives such as the need for physical release and the urge to satiate or express sexual desires. In addition, both types of sex often produce similar outcomes ranging from sheer physical pleasure, to sexual satisfaction, to the positive feeling that one is desirable and sexually attractive. These similarities notwithstanding, however, relational sex has additional interpersonal meanings, purposes, and consequences. For example, relational partners may engage in sexual activity to express feelings of love and intimacy, to demonstrate or reaffirm their commitment to each other, or to restore equity in the relationship (see Sprecher & Regan, 2000). Sexual events that occur within a romantic relationship thus have important nonsexual consequences for that relationship.

Chapter 4 explores attitudes about the role of sex in committed relationships. We then discuss sexuality in both beginning (Chapter 5) and established (Chapter 6) relationships. Finally, Chapter 7 explores problematic aspects of relational sexuality, including sexual aggression, sexual incompatibility, and sexual infidelity.

4

Sexual Attitudes

Chapter Outline

In the minds of many individuals, love and sex share an intimate connection. In fact, most men and women view sexual intercourse as most appropriate when it occurs within the context of a committed, long-term, and love-based relationship. As we discuss in this chapter, a large and growing body of research suggests that people are most accepting of sexual activity between married and engaged partners and are least accepting of sex between uncommitted partners or those at very early relationship stages.

BELIEFS ABOUT SEX IN DATING RELATIONSHIPS

Well, I can't speak for anyone else, but for me, the only way I'd have sex with someone was if we were deeply in love. If two people are in love, then sex seems like a natural way to express those feelings.

—19-year-old woman interviewed by the author

The decision to have sex is a personal choice that everyone should be free to make. Some people have sex just because they enjoy it or because they have the chance to do it. That's fine; it's a personal decision. Other people, and I'm one of them, think that sex is best when it's done out of love, with someone you're involved with.

—20-year-old man interviewed by the author

In one of the first empirical investigations of sexual standards, sociologist Ira Reiss (1964) reported that men and women from a national probability sample of the U.S. population as well as students from five high schools and colleges were increasingly more accepting of premarital sexual intercourse between two people as their relationship became characterized by correspondingly greater amounts of affection and commitment; in other words, as the relationship progressed from relatively little affection to strong affection, and then to love and engagement, people believed that intercourse was more acceptable. Similarly, the majority (80%) of the participants in Anne Peplau, Zick Rubin, and Charles Hill's classic (1977) study indicated that it was "completely acceptable" for couples who love each other to engage in sexual intercourse, whereas only 20% found sexual intercourse with a casual acquaintance to be completely acceptable. More recently, sociologists Susan Sprecher, Kathleen McKinney, Robert Walsh, and Carrie Anderson (1988) surveyed a group of men and women and reported that increasing numbers of participants viewed sexual intercourse between two people as acceptable as their relationship stage moved from the first date (28%), to casual dating (41%), to serious dating (72%), to preengagement (77%), and finally to engagement (82%).

Cross-sectional research indicates that American society (as well as many other societies) is becoming more sexually permissive. In particular, although men and women continue to view sex as most appropriate when it occurs between committed relational partners, there is a trend toward greater acceptance of sexual activity in casual dating relationships. Robert Sherwin and Sherry Corbett (1985), for example, examined normative expectations about sexual activity in various types of dating relationships on a college campus. Three groups of students—the first surveyed in 1963, the second in 1971, and the third in 1978—were asked to indicate the extent to which various sexual activities generally were expected to play a part in the relationship between casually dating, steadily dating, and engaged partners. The results provided evidence for increasingly liberal campus sexual norms among both men and women over the 15-year period. For example, none of the men and women in the 1963 sample expected sexual intercourse to occur in a casual dating relationship; by 1978, however, 17% of the men and 9% of the women viewed intercourse as a normal part of casual dating.

The Role of Sex or Gender

One of the most potent correlates of attitudes toward premarital sex is sex or gender. For example, men tend to hold more permissive or positive attitudes toward uncommitted or casual sexual activity than do women (e.g., Oliver & Hyde, 1993). Men also are less likely than women to associate the occurrence of sexual intercourse with love, commitment, and intimacy. When Ira Robinson, James Balkwell, and Dawn Ward (1980) asked a sample of college students to write down their first five responses to the stimulus word *sex*, fewer men (42%) than women (71%) responded with words indicative of love, and fewer men (16%) than women (43%) provided words reflective of marriage or commitment. Similar results were reported by Susan Hendrick, Clyde Hendrick, Michelle Slapion-Foote, and Franklin Foote (1985), who surveyed a group of undergraduates about various sexual attitudes. These researchers found strong sex differences; for example, men were more likely than women to agree that sexual relations with another person did not require commitment to that person, whereas women were more likely than men to agree that sex without love is meaningless.

More recently, sociologists John Roche and Thomas Ramsbey (1993) asked a large sample of college students to indicate how appropriate they thought sexual intercourse would be between partners at five different stages of dating: dating with no particular affection (Stage 1), dating with affection but not love (Stage 2), dating and being in love (Stage 3), dating one person only and being in love (Stage 4), and engaged (Stage 5). Nearly equally high percentages of men (76%) and women (67%) believed that sexual intercourse was appropriate between engaged partners (Stage 5), and nearly equally low percentages (3% of the men, 0% of the women) believed that it was acceptable in the complete absence of commitment and affection (Stage 1). However, men and women clearly diverged in their attitudes about the role of sex in dating relationships in the other relationship stages. For example, 17% of the men, compared with only 1% of the women, believed that intercourse was appropriate when dating partners felt affection but not love (Stage 2). Similarly, many more men (44%) than women (15%) believed that sexual intercourse was acceptable when partners were dating and in love (Stage 3). Thus, both sexes viewed intercourse as increasingly acceptable as a dating relationship became characterized by greater amounts of commitment and affection. However, men believed that sex was appropriate at earlier relationship stages than did women (in fact, more men than women simply believed that sex was appropriate—regardless of relationship stage).

In addition, both sexes seem to know that women are more likely than men to associate sex with love and intimacy. For instance, participants in one study (Regan & Berscheid, 1995) were asked to specify the causes of male and female sexual desire. More than 40% stated that love caused women to experience a desire for sexual activity, whereas fewer than 10% believed that love caused men to want sex. One male respondent mentioned "thoughts of love and romance" as playing an important role in female sexual interest, another noted that "a woman tends to be in love when she feels desire or has sexual intercourse," and one female respondent stated that "often the words 'I love you' will cause sexual desire in a woman."

Based on these results, it might be tempting to conclude that women simply do not experience as much sexual interest for their dating partners as do men or that women just desire less sexual involvement in general in their romantic relationships than do men. This is not the case, however. For example, surveys of adolescents and young adults reveal that both boys *and* girls, and both men *and* women, report thinking about sex often or fairly often (Juhasz, Kaufman, & Meyer, 1986) and experience sexual desire at least once a week (Useche, Villegas, & Alzate, 1990). Similarly, more than 80% of the high school girls who participated in David Muram and his colleagues' (Muram, Rosenthal, Tolley, Peeler, & Dorko, 1991) study reported being sexually excited by their dating partners, regardless of whether or not they actually engaged in intercourse. Thus, it is not that women are less interested than men in becoming sexually involved with their dating partners, but rather that women generally prefer a greater amount of emotional commitment *prior* to sexual involvement.

The results of one study illustrate this phenomenon. Marita McCabe and John Collins (1984) asked men and women to indicate how much sexual activity they desired at three stages of a romantic relationship: on the first date, after several dates had occurred, and when going steady. The researchers found—as we might expect—that men expressed a desire for a higher level of sexual activity at the earlier relationship stages (i.e., on the first date and after several dates) than did women. However, there was no difference in how much sexual activity men and women wanted at the *later* relationship stage of going steady. In other words, both sexes were willing to allow sexual activity to occur in a dating relationship, but men wanted this activity to begin earlier in the development of the relationship than did women, who believed that sex should not occur until there was some evidence of commitment and emotional involvement.

The Role of Culture

Another important correlate of attitudes toward premarital sexual activity is culture. As noted by cross-cultural psychologist Robin Goodwin (1999), human societies vary considerably in the extent to which they permit premarital sex, and this is partly due to whether they are collectivist or individualist in cultural orientation. *Collectivist* cultures are those in which people are integrated into cohesive groups, marriages link families and are sometimes arranged by those families, group boundaries are explicit and firm, and there is a strong emphasis on group loyalty, solidarity, and shared activity. *Individualist* cultures reflect the opposite pattern; people are loosely connected and autonomous, group boundaries are flexible, and emphasis is placed on the fulfillment of personal preferences and goals in romance and other life pursuits. Goodwin's review indicated that young adults in collectivist cultures (e.g., Asia, the Middle East, South America) strongly disapprove of premarital sex, whereas young adults from individualist cultures (e.g., Britain, Belgium, France, Scandinavian countries) tend to hold more permissive attitudes.

Indeed, Susan Sprecher and Elaine Hatfield (1995) asked more than 1,500 college students from the United States, Russia, and Japan to indicate how acceptable they thought sexual intercourse was on a first date, when casually dating, when seriously dating, when preengaged, and when engaged to be married. Although participants from all three cultures disapproved of sex between uncommitted partners (those who were on a first date or those who were casually dating), American students generally were more tolerant of sexual activity between seriously dating, pre-engaged, and engaged partners than were Russian and Japanese students. In America, sex was deemed acceptable as soon as some evidence of the couple's commitment was present. In Russia and Japan, however, the fact that the couple was seriously involved or even engaged was insufficient justification for sexual activity; a marriage vow was required.

BELIEFS ABOUT SEX IN MARITAL RELATIONSHIPS

Although there have been few empirical investigations of marital sexual attitudes, some general conclusions can be gleaned from the available literature. First, sexual intercourse is considered a "normal" part of the marital relationship. Not only do most people view sexual activity as completely acceptable between spouses, but marriage historically has been defined as a socially sanctioned sexual relationship. In Western culture, for example, 17th-century church doctrine specified sexual intercourse as a marital duty for both spouses (Leites, 1982).

Second, marital sex is assumed to be exclusive sex. That is, once an individual is married, the general presumption is that he or she will confine sexual activities to the marital relationship. Data indicate that most men and women possess strong expectations about marital sexual exclusivity (e.g., Wiederman & Allgeier, 1996), disapprove of extramarital sex (e.g., Davis & Smith, 1991; Glenn & Weaver, 1979; Small, 1992), and express negative beliefs about "cheating spouses" (e.g., Sprecher, Regan, & McKinney, 1998). For example, sex researcher Robert Michael and his colleagues (Michael, Gagnon, Laumann, & Kolata, 1994) asked a sample of more than 3,400 adults the following question: "What is your opinion about a married person having sexual relations with someone other than the marriage partner—is it always wrong, almost always wrong, sometimes wrong, or not wrong at all?" (p. 287). Their results revealed that 77% of the sample believed that extramarital sex was "always wrong"—a strong condemnation indeed.

As with many sexual attitudes, men and women differ. Specifically, in comparison with women, men hold more permissive attitudes about extramarital sex (e.g., Oliver & Hyde, 1993; Thompson, 1984) and are more likely to express an interest in having an extramarital sexual relationship (e.g., Buunk & Bakker, 1995; Seal, Agostinelli, & Hannett, 1994; Thompson, 1984). Similarly, although extramarital sexual activity is not considered appropriate for either sex, it seems to be relatively more tolerated or expected for men (for additional discussions, see Reiss, 1973; Reiss & Lee, 1988). Cultural differences exist as well, with adults in Scandinavian countries appearing relatively more tolerant of extramarital sexual liaisons than those in Asian countries and the United States (see Goodwin, 1999; Hatfield & Rapson, 1996).

A third belief about marital sexuality concerns the relative power accorded to each sex in the making of sexual and reproductive decisions. For many years, both men and women believed that choices and decisions about the sexual part of married life—including when and how to initiate sexual activity, the frequency and amount of sex, the timing and number of children, the use of contraception, and so forth—were the responsibility of the male spouse. Witness the following quotation, excerpted from a popular guide to love, courtship, and marriage published in the United States more than a century ago:

> Usually marriage is consummated within a day or two after the ceremony, but this is gross injustice to the bride. In most cases she is nervous, timid, and exhausted by the duties of preparation for the wedding, and in no way in a condition, either in body or mind, for the vital change which the married relation brings upon her. . . . This, then, is the time for all approaches by the husband to be of the most delicate, considerate, and refined description possible. . . . Young husband! Prove your manhood, not by yielding to unbridled lust and cruelty, but by the exhibition of true power in self-control and patience with the helpless being confided to your care! (Jefferis & Nichols, 1896, pp. 202-204)

The authors of this advice manual clearly consider sexual decisions to be a husband's duty and right; he is the one who must demonstrate self-control and guard against yielding to "unbridled lust," who must determine the appropriate time for the wife's initiation into sexual relations, and who must calmly and patiently guide the couple's first and subsequent sexual interactions.

An examination of modern marriage manuals and guides to newlyweds reveals that this particular belief about marital sexuality has undergone significant change during recent years, at least in the United States and Western Europe. Evidence was provided by researchers Martin Weinberg, Rochelle Swensson, and Sue Hammersmith (1983), who analyzed 49 sex manuals published in the United States between 1950 and 1980. During the 1950s and 1960s, for example, writers continued to emphasize differences between male and female sexuality and complementarity in sexual roles (i.e., husband as sexual teacher and wife as sexual learner). By the late 1970s, however, both sexes were depicted as autonomous sexual beings in control of their own sexuality, capable (and desirous) of sexual pleasure, and equally able to enact the parts of sexual teacher and sexual learner. Despite these changes, in many other parts of the world—including Africa, Central America, and India—men continue to be expected to make the major sexual and reproductive decisions (e.g., Bertrand, Makani, Edwards, & Baughman, 1996; Karra, Stark, & Wolf, 1997; Villasmil Prieto, 1997). For example, as discussed by social scientist Elisha Renne (1997), Hausa women living in Nigeria have a range of contraceptive methods available to them but may not use them due to their own (culturally supported) belief that reproductive decisions are more appropriately made by men.

SUMMARY

Researchers have identified a number of beliefs and assumptions about the role of sexuality in dating relationships. For example, although there is a trend toward greater sexual permissiveness or liberalism in many societies, most men and women continue to view sexual activity as most acceptable when it occurs between partners in committed (as opposed to casual or uncommitted) relationships. A number of beliefs also exist about marital sexuality, including the idea that sexual intercourse is a normative part of the marital union and the assumption that spouses should confine their sexual activities to the marital relationship. As we discuss in Chapters 5 and 6, many of these beliefs reflect the sexual realities experienced by men and women in their ongoing romantic relationships.

KEY CONCEPTS

Relational sexuality (p. 51)
Sexual standards (p. 54)
Premarital sexual intercourse (p. 54)
Sexual permissiveness (p. 54)
Collectivist cultures (p. 57)
Individualist cultures (p. 57)
Sexual exclusivity (p. 58)

DISCUSSION QUESTIONS

1. How does relational sex differ from nonrelational sex?

2. Consider the ways in which sexual standards for dating couples have changed over time. Base your answer on empirical evidence gathered from surveys of sexual attitudes.

3. Discuss the ways in which sex or gender and culture are associated with sexual standards.

4. What three general conclusions about marital sexual standards can we draw from the available literature?

RECOMMENDED READINGS

Frayser, S. G. (1989). Sexual and reproductive relationships: Cross-cultural evidence and biosocial implications. *Medical Anthropology, 11,* 385-407.

Hatfield, E., & Rapson, R. L. (1996). *Love and sex: Cross-cultural perspectives.* Needham Heights, MA: Allyn & Bacon.

These two works explore the ways in which different cultures view sexuality and the sanctions they impose on men and women who violate sociocultural sexual norms and taboos.

Oliver, M. B., & Hyde, J. S. (1993). Gender differences in sexuality: A meta-analysis. *Psychological Bulletin, 114,* 29-51.

These authors review research examining sex differences in sexual attitudes and behavior.

5

Sexuality in Beginning Relationships

Chapter Outline

T he beliefs that people hold with respect to the role of sexual activity in dating and marital relationships undoubtedly have implications for their sexual (and nonsexual) interactions with their partners. In this chapter, we examine the role that sexuality plays in the attraction process and in the initial stages of romantic relationships.

SEXUALITY AND THE ATTRACTION PROCESS

As we discuss later, in Chapter 9, there are a number of dispositional attributes or personality characteristics that people find particularly desirable in dates and marriage partners, including intelligence, honesty, a good sense of humor, emotional stability, and interpersonal warmth. Attributes that are related to sexuality—including a potential partner's "sex appeal," sexual history, and amount of sexual experience—also are important determinants of initial attraction.

Sex Appeal

Although many social scientists have explored the characteristics that people find attractive in potential mates, few have investigated the factors that render someone particularly sexually appealing and that thus prompt initial attraction. In an effort to discover the specific features that create "sex appeal," social psychologists Pamela Regan and Ellen Berscheid (1995) asked a group of men and women to list all of the characteristics men and women could possess that would cause them to be sexually appealing to others. According to the participants, sex appeal in women was believed to be primarily a function of appearance (with 90% specifying this attribute) along with dispositional dimensions such as a good overall personality (cited by 23%), self-confidence (17%), and intelligence (15%). Examples of participants' responses include the following:

> *From a male participant:* I think men want women to be willing, attractive, and interesting. It makes the desire stronger when he knows she wants the same thing, although not being able to get sex from her sometimes will do the same thing. Physically, I think a desirable woman would be soft, yet athletic, not fat, but not overly thin, with lots of curves and a nice face. A woman who is experienced and enjoys sex is more desirable than either an inexperienced, shy woman or else an overly experienced, "easy" woman.
>
> *From a male participant:* Her appearance. Nothing else is needed. A man can be with any woman as long as he thinks she looks good. The easiest way to get a man interested in a woman is for his friends to say how good the girl looks. I truly feel that besides the body—no other characteristics are needed.
>
> *From a female participant:* Definitely an attitude that portrays that she wants "it." Flirtation seems to help men become more interested. A confident characteristic that would suggest that she is good at "it." Overall attractiveness (skinny, tall, nice smile).

From a female participant: Could be very thin with long, thin legs, long hair, white teeth. Could be voluptuous—I guess what I'm getting down to is physical attraction.

Male sex appeal was presumed to be caused by a very similar constellation of features. Again, appearance was the most frequently mentioned characteristic (cited by 76%), followed by "sensitivity" or a compassionate and kind disposition (35%), a good overall personality (24%), and a sense of humor (18%):

From a male participant: I think a well-built, strong man would cause desire as opposed to a sloppy, overweight guy or a really skinny guy. I think women desire a guy who is open, honest, and is interested in pleasing them, instead of the opposite. I also think a woman desires men who appreciate her sexual appetites/preferences over ones who force their own wishes on her. Physical qualities would probably include muscles and cleanliness or being well-groomed.

From a male participant: Women like men to be funny and caring. A major thing for women is that they want a man to be sensitive to their needs as women. Physical attractiveness is important to women, although they don't tend to show this as much as men do. I wish I knew more about this question myself—believe me!

From a female participant: A great fit body, and nice clothes. This doesn't mean that's all I'm looking for, but to be sexually attracted—yes.

From a female participant: Based on physical characteristics, I would say the way a person looks such as his face, eyes, lips, and a well-toned body. A man must be caring, kind, and gentle. He must be able to show his feelings and let you know he cares about you.

Thus, although many characteristics can make a person initially attractive and appealing to others, appearance seems to be the most important factor. And the significance people give to appearance is not surprising. In first encounters, before two people have even interacted or started a relationship, the primary piece of information they have about one another is what they can see—each other's appearance.

Sexual History

Sex appeal (and the features that comprise it) is not the only sexual characteristic that influences our attraction to another person. An individual's sexual history also influences how we evaluate him or her.

In general, research reveals that men and women prefer their potential dates and mates to possess lower, rather than higher, levels of previous sexual experience. In a study conducted by Susan Sprecher and her colleagues (Sprecher, Regan, McKinney, Maxwell, & Wazienski, 1997), for example, college students were asked to indicate how desirable they thought three levels of sexual experience were in a marriage partner: no previous sexual experience (i.e., someone who has had no previous partners), moderate sexual experience (i.e., someone who has had few previous partners), and considerable sexual experience (i.e., someone who has had several previous partners). The results indicated that no sexual experience was preferred more than moderate sexual experience, which in turn was preferred more than extensive sexual experience.

Similar results are provided by person perception experiments (in which participants receive information about, and then evaluate, a target individual they believe is a "real" person). In one such study conducted by Laura Bettor, Susan Hendrick, and Clyde Hendrick (1995), a group of college students read a brief vignette about two target persons who were involved in either a casual or a serious romantic relationship. In the casual relationship vignette, "Bob" and "Cathy" had met recently at a grocery store and exchanged phone numbers, and within a week they had gone on their first date, during which they had sex. In the serious relationship condition, the targets were described as meeting a year ago in a grocery store and dating steadily ever since, now feeling that they were in love, and having sex for the first time very recently. After reading the two vignettes, participants were asked to estimate the likelihood that Bob would consider marrying "a girl like Cathy" and that Cathy would consider marrying "a guy like Bob." The results revealed that participants thought that Bob would be much more likely to marry Cathy, and that Cathy would be much more likely to marry Bob, when the relationship was depicted as serious rather than casual. In other words, targets who engaged in sexual intercourse on a first date after they had just met were not considered as "marriageable" as those who waited to have sex until they were in a committed loving relationship. Similar results were reported by Lucia O'Sullivan (1995), who found that people preferred as dates and spouses targets who were presented as engaging in intercourse within a committed relationship rather than those who were described as having uncommitted casual sex.

When considering a potential spouse's sexual history, then, people clearly believe that "less is more" and that any prior sex that has occurred should have been confined to committed rather than casual relationships.

Chastity: No Longer Important?

Although most men and women prefer their dates and mates to possess lower rather than higher levels of lifetime sexual experience, this does not necessarily mean that they desire partners with no sexual knowledge whatsoever. Indeed, data collected over the past several decades suggest that chastity (complete sexual inexperience) has become increasingly *un*important to both men and women. For example, in one of the earliest mate preference studies (Hill, 1945), men and women received a list of 18 attributes that they ranked in terms of importance in a romantic partner. Chastity, defined as "no previous sexual experience," was ranked 10th in importance—about halfway down the list. A replication study conducted some 20 years later (Hudson & Henze, 1969) revealed that chastity had fallen to 15th in importance as a partner attribute. A decade later, another replication study (Hoyt & Hudson, 1981) indicated that chastity had continued its decline into irrelevance; women now ranked this attribute second to last (17th), and men ranked it dead last (18th), in importance. Thus, complete and total sexual inexperience does not appear to be a highly desirable partner attribute. Men and women apparently want someone with "just enough" sexual knowledge.

Some cultures, however, value chastity more than do others. Data collected by psychologist David Buss (1989) indicate that people in several Asian countries (e.g., Taiwan, Japan, China, Indonesia, India) view chastity or "no previous sexual experience" as a relatively important attribute in a potential mate, whereas men and women in a variety of Western European countries (e.g., Belgium, France, Sweden, Italy, Greece, Norway) consider chastity to be irrelevant or even undesirable. Of course, what people say they want and what they themselves do are sometimes quite different. As noted by cross-cultural psychologist Robin Goodwin (1999), premarital sex is quite common among both men and women in contemporary Eastern cultures; therefore, although chastity may be considered a desirable trait, it is not necessarily seen as an indispensable one.

SEXUALITY IN BEGINNING RELATIONSHIPS

Premarital sexual activity is an increasingly common event in the lives of most adolescents and young adults, and the majority of this activity occurs within the context of dating relationships (see Christopher, 2001).

Insofar as many teenagers and college-age adults believe that sex is an appropriate element of committed romantic relationships (Reiss, 1964; Sprecher, McKinney, Walsh, & Anderson, 1988) and believe that sex can bring a couple closer together (Muram, Rosenthal, Tolley, Peeler, & Dorko, 1991), it is perhaps not surprising that most young people have engaged in some form of sexual activity, including intercourse, by 16 years of age (e.g., Brook, Balka, Abernathy, & Hamburg, 1994; Leitenberg & Saltzman, 2000; Zelnik & Kantner, 1980). This section considers research on the first sexual encounter in beginning relationships, including the factors that are important in the decision to have sex for the first time with a particular partner and the different pathways to sexual involvement that a couple may follow. It also considers the ways in which men and women attempt to influence their sexual interactions with dating partners.

The First Sexual Encounter

The first sexual encounter is usually a highly significant event in a developing relationship. Most people remember their first sexual episode in quite vivid detail (Harvey, Flanary, & Morgan, 1986), and romantic partners often have sex to express closeness or love (Jessor, Costa, Jessor, & Donovan, 1983; Leigh, 1989) and report feeling increased commitment to the relationship after becoming sexually intimate (Baxter & Bullis, 1986; Cate, Long, Angera, & Draper, 1993).

The Decision to Have Sex for the First Time in a Relationship

What prompts a couple to become sexually active? Research suggests that a number of factors are involved in this decision. The most important reason appears to be interpersonal in nature—specifically, emotional intimacy and closeness. For example, family studies scholars Scott Christopher and Rodney Cate (1984) asked a group of men and women to rate how important various considerations were in their decisions to have sex for the first time in a premarital relationship. Their analysis revealed four general reasons underlying this decision. The first and most important reason involved *positive affection and communication*. For instance, people considered how much love they felt for the partner, the possibility that the relationship would result in marriage, and their level of commitment or involvement when deciding whether to have sex with the partner. *Arousal and receptivity*—including their own or the partner's level of sexual arousal immediately prior to intercourse and their receptivity to the partner's sexual advances—also played a role in the decision to have sex. A third factor concerned *obligation and pressure*. For example, feelings of obligation to have sex with the partner, as well as the partner's pressure or insistence on having sex, contributed to individuals' decisions about sexual involvement. Finally, people's sexual decisions were influenced by *circumstance*, ranging from the amount of drugs or alcohol they or their partner had consumed to the "specialness" of that particular date. These results suggest that although a number of factors clearly influence the decision to have sex, feelings of love and intimacy play an extremely important role.

Research on why people *refrain* from having sex with a particular partner also highlights the impact of the relationship's emotional tenor. In one study, Lucia O'Sullivan and Michelle Gaines (1998) surveyed a sample of college students who had the opportunity for sexual activity but had felt unsure or ambivalent about actually engaging in the activity. Participants were asked to describe the incidents and to explain in detail their reasons for feeling ambivalent. Analysis of the free responses revealed that the most common reason given by men (35%) and women (49%) for feeling unsure about having sex with someone who clearly wanted them to do so concerned relationship and intimacy issues, including not feeling sufficient levels of commitment and being uncertain about their feelings for the partner.

Although O'Sullivan and Gaines (1998) found no difference in the percentages of men and women who cited relationship factors as causing their ambivalence about sexual participation, other research suggests that emotional intimacy, commitment, and other interpersonal factors may play a greater role in women's than in men's sexual decision making. We have already reviewed evidence, presented in Chapter 4, that women hold less permissive attitudes about uncommitted or casual sex than do men and that women tend to associate sex with love and intimacy more than do men. Similarly, surveys of dating couples reveal that women are more likely than men to specify insufficient commitment as a reason for actually abstaining from sexual intercourse with their current partners (Peplau, Rubin, & Hill, 1977; also see Carroll, Volk, & Hyde, 1985).

Pathways to Sexual Involvement

At some point in their relationships, most couples do choose to become sexually intimate. This intimacy may take several forms, ranging from kissing and light petting to intercourse. In addition, some couples elect to engage in sexual activity relatively early in their relationships, while others wait until they have been together for a longer period of time and perhaps are engaged or even married.

Two teams of researchers, using different methodologies, have documented the different paths that couples follow as they move toward their first acts of sexual intercourse. Anne Peplau and her colleagues (1977) conducted a longitudinal study in which they followed a group of dating couples over a 2-year period and surveyed them periodically about their sexual (and other) experiences. Christopher and Cate (1985) conducted a retrospective study in which they asked a sample of dating couples to think back over their relationships and report about various events and experiences. Despite their differing methods of data collection, the two research teams found strikingly similar results. For example, in both studies, some couples chose to abstain from sexual intercourse entirely and to limit their sexual interactions to nonintercourse activities (e.g., kissing, light petting). These couples, termed *sexually traditional* or *abstaining* by Peplau et al. (1977) and termed *low involvement* by Christopher and Cate (1985), generally believed that love alone did not serve to justify sexual intercourse, that intercourse should be saved for marriage, and that abstinence from intercourse was a sign of the love and respect between the partners. They also tended to hold conservative sexual attitudes and to have lower overall levels of sexual experience than did other couples.

Both research teams also found evidence of the other extreme— that is, couples who elected to engage in intercourse very early in their relationships (sometimes on the first date or after a few dates). *Sexually liberal* (Peplau et al., 1977) or *rapid involvement* (Christopher & Cate, 1985) couples viewed sex without love as acceptable and did not require commitment to have and enjoy intercourse. For these couples, the decision to have intercourse stemmed primarily from physical pleasure and arousal motives rather than from any emotional concerns or relationship factors.

Other types of couple were identified as well. For example, Peplau et al. (1977) described a type of couple they termed *sexually moderate* or *later sex*. Partners in sexually moderate relationships were somewhere in between their traditional and liberal counterparts in terms of their attitudes and behavior. Although they generally chose to wait awhile before engaging in sexual intercourse, they also believed that sexual intercourse was acceptable if the two people loved each other—and they did not need a long-term commitment before becoming sexually involved. Love, rather than commitment per se, was sufficient justification for intercourse.

Christopher and Cate (1985) also described other couple types located between the rapid and low involvement extremes. *Gradual involvement* couples engaged in sexual intercourse when they were considering becoming couples and demonstrated gradual increases in sexual intimacy as their relationships became progressively more committed. For example, as they moved from casual dating to steady dating, they engaged in correspondingly more intimate forms of sexual expression. *Delayed involvement* couples—the most common couple type identified by the researchers—also clearly associated sexual involvement with the level of commitment in their relationships. However, they held more conservative sexual attitudes than did the gradual involvement couples and demonstrated a very different pattern of sexual interaction. Specifically, delayed involvement couples engaged in extremely low levels of sexual activity until the partners made commitments to each other and their relationships; once in steady and monogamous unions, they increased their level of sexual involvement. As noted by Christopher (2001), these couples "resolutely limit their sexual involvement until making a monogamous dating commitment. This level of commitment serves as a sexual watershed once reached, allowing them to explore their sexual involvement as fully as the other coitally experienced couples" (p. 87).

Clearly, commitment and emotional intimacy are intricately connected with sexuality in many dating relationships.

Sexual Influence

Peplau et al.'s (1977) and Christopher and Cate's (1985) studies demonstrated that most dating relationships are characterized by some degree of sexual interaction. Sex, however, does not simply happen; rather, it is something that must be negotiated by the members of the couple. As we discuss next, partners often attempt to influence each other in their quest to have—or to avoid—sexual intimacy.

Several researchers have investigated the ways in which men and women initiate sexual activity or attempt to increase their current level of sexual involvement. Although direct requests are sometimes made, it appears that most individuals prefer to use *indirect* techniques, including sitting closer to the partners and touching, snuggling, kissing, or holding hands with them (Jesser, 1978; McCormick, 1979). For example, Timothy Perper and David Weis (1987) asked women college students to describe in essays the strategies they would use to influence a sexual interaction. Three primary tactics were identified from the respondents' essays. The first included environmental and situational strategies, ranging from dressing in a sexually suggestive or seductive manner, to offering to get the partner a drink, to creating a romantic setting. Verbal strategies were also mentioned, including paying the partner compliments and engaging in romantic or sexually suggestive talk. The third set of strategies was nonverbal; for example, participants wrote about using eye glances, moving close, cuddling, touching, and kissing the partner as a way to initiate a sexual interlude.

More recently, Scott Christopher and Michela Frandsen (1990) asked a group of men and women to think about any sexual encounters that had occurred during their most recent dates and to report about the extent to which they had used a variety of different tactics (identified by the researchers) to influence those encounters. Analysis of participants' responses revealed four general sexual influence strategies. Some participants reported using *antisocial* acts, which involve imposing sexual wishes on a dating partner in socially unacceptable ways. These actions could be direct and overt, including threatening to use force against the partner, actually using force, ridiculing and insulting the partner, and getting angry. Antisocial behaviors also may be covert, including when a person sulks, pleads, acts ill or helpless, or otherwise attempts to make the partner feel guilty for not giving in to his or her sexual demands. Participants also reported using *emotional and physical closeness* behaviors to influence the partner. Examples include expressing affection or love, doing "something special" for the partner, complimenting or flattering the partner, moving physically closer, dropping hints, and communicating feelings about the importance of the relationship. People also invoked *logic and reason* in an attempt to influence sexual outcomes. These techniques ranged from calmly presenting a list of reasons about why the couple should become sexually intimate, to claiming to be knowledgeable about how sexual the relationship ought to be, to asserting authority or even attempting to compromise with the partner. The final sexual influence strategy involved *pressure and manipulation* and included tactics such as using drugs or alcohol to influence the partner, pressuring the partner, being persuasive, persisting in one's efforts, threatening to end the relationship, ignoring the partner's actions, and lying to the partner.

Although men were more likely to report having used pressure and manipulation tactics, no sex differences were found for the other types of sexual influence strategy. In fact, the most common way in which both sexes reported having influenced their sexual encounters was through the use of emotional and physical closeness behaviors. Because this influence strategy was the one most strongly related to the level of sexual activity that actually occurred during the dates, it does appear to be the most successful means of increasing sexual intimacy.

So, how do people successfully *avoid* sexual involvement? One method involves simply avoiding sexual situations entirely. Some of the women who participated in Perper and Weis's (1987) study said that they would avoid sex by keeping away from private settings in which sex might occur. Of course, there are times when an intimate setting cannot be avoided and when one partner issues a sexual invitation that the other partner does not wish to accept. In those circumstances, one of the most common ways in which men and women limit the sexual interaction is by simply ignoring the partner's suggestions, cues, or requests. For example, one person might turn away from the other's attempted kiss or pretend not to hear a compliment or sexually suggestive comment. Men and women also frequently employ logic and reasoning strategies ("We really need to think this over before we decide to take our relationship to that level") to defuse sexual situations and limit sexual involvement (Christopher & Frandsen, 1990).

SUMMARY

Sexuality plays an important role in the attraction process and in the initial stages of romantic relationships. In general, men and women prefer as dates and mates others who possess moderate sexual experience (as opposed to none or extensive sexual experience), and they weigh a number of factors in deciding whether and when to become sexually active with their current partners. Couples follow different pathways to sexual involvement, with some engaging in sex relatively early in their relationships and others preferring to wait until they reach a later stage characterized by high(er) levels of commitment and intimacy. In the process of negotiating the sexual aspects of their relationships, both men and women employ a number of different influence techniques; some are used to increase the level of partners' sexual involvement, whereas others are used to limit sexual intimacy. In

Chapter 6, we turn to a consideration of sexuality as it is experienced by couples in established partnerships, including marriage and cohabiting relationships.

KEY CONCEPTS

Sex appeal (p. 63)
Chastity (p. 66)
Sexually traditional or abstaining couples (p. 69)
Low involvement couples (p. 69)
Sexually liberal couples (p. 69)
Rapid involvement couples (p. 69)
Sexually moderate or later sex couples (p. 69)
Gradual involvement couples (p. 70)
Delayed involvement couples (p. 70)
Indirect sexual influence techniques (p. 70)
Antisocial strategies (p. 71)
Emotional and physical closeness strategies (p. 71)
Logic and reason strategies (p. 71)
Pressure and manipulation strategies (p. 71)

DISCUSSION QUESTIONS

1. How does a person's sexuality (e.g., sex appeal, sexual history) affect his or her desirability as a dating partner?

2. Discuss how attitudes toward chastity have changed over time. How might this change be related to other social changes (e.g., the advent of birth control, media depictions of sexuality)?

3. What factors underlie the decision to have or not have sex with a particular partner for the first time?

4. Discuss the different pathways to sexual involvement that a couple may follow as the partners progress toward the first sexual encounter.

5. Consider the four general strategies that men and women use to influence sexual interactions with their partners. Are there sex differences in the use of these tactics?

RECOMMENDED READINGS

McKinney, K., & Sprecher, S. (Eds.). (1991). *Sexuality in close relationships.* Hillsdale, NJ: Lawrence Erlbaum.

Although somewhat dated, this edited volume contains chapters exploring a number of relational sex issues, including attitudes about the role of sex in close relationships, sexual decision making, sexual communication, sexual violence and coercion, and sexual infidelity.

O'Sullivan, L. F., & Byers, E. S. (1993). Eroding stereotypes: College women's attempts to influence reluctant male sexual partners. *Journal of Sex Research, 30,* 270-282.

This article suggests that women as well as men use various strategies to influence a couple's sexual interactions.

6

Sexuality in Established Relationships

Chapter Outline

We have seen in previous chapters that men and women around the world view marriage and other committed relationships as an appropriate—in fact, the most appropriate—context for sexual activity. In this chapter, we review research on sexuality as it occurs and is experienced within long-term or established relationships. Specifically, we explore what is known about sexual frequency, sexual practices and preferences, sexual satisfaction, and sexual communication within married, cohabiting heterosexual, and homosexual couples. It is important to keep in mind that because more research has been conducted on marital relationships than on other kinds of long-term unions, the conclusions we can draw about sexuality are stronger for that particular type of romantic association.

SEXUAL FREQUENCY

One topic that has received a great deal of attention concerns the frequency with which spouses engage in sexual intercourse. Research conducted over the past 50 years suggests that the average amount of sex that married couples have has not changed much over time. For example, during the late 1940s and early 1950s, pioneering sex researcher Alfred Kinsey and his colleagues (Kinsey, Pomeroy, & Martin, 1948; Kinsey, Pomeroy, Martin, & Gebhard, 1953) asked more than 11,000 men and women living in the United States to indicate how often they engaged in sexual intercourse. They found that young married couples between 16 and 25 years of age reported having sex between two and three times a week on average; slightly older couples (between 26 and 35 years of age) indicated engaging in intercourse about twice a week on average. Another survey conducted two decades later yielded similar frequencies, with young couples (18-24 years of age) reporting sexual intercourse approximately three times a week on average (Hunt, 1974).

Couples surveyed during the 1990s appear to resemble their counterparts from earlier decades in terms of their level of sexual activity. Like Kinsey and his colleagues, sex researchers Robert Michael, John Gagnon, Edward Laumann, and Gina Kolata (1994) conducted a national study of the sexual experiences of men and women living in the United States. One of the questions they asked their participants was to indicate how often they had engaged in sex during the previous 12 months. The possible response options were *not at all, once or twice, about once a month, two or three times a month, about once a week, two or three times a week,* and *four or more times a week.* Although participants were not asked to report the precise amount of sex in which they had engaged during the specified time period, the results were similar to those reported by previous researchers. Specifically, the response option endorsed by the highest percentages of married men (43%) and women (47%) was *a few times a month.* The next most commonly endorsed option was *two or three times a week,* with 36% of married men and 32% of married women reporting engaging in sex that frequently. Very small percentages of married men (1%) and women (3%) said that they had absolutely no intercourse at all with their partners over the past year; similarly, few married men (7%) or women (7%) reported extremely high amounts of sexual activity (i.e., four or more times a week). Taken together, the results of these various research endeavors suggest that most married couples (at least most younger married couples) tend to engage in sexual intercourse approximately one to three times a week.

Before coming to any firm conclusion about sexual frequency in marital relationships, however, it is important to recognize that tremendous variability exists both within and across individual couples. For example, various life events (e.g., job stress, fatigue, health, pregnancy, child care) might temporarily reduce a couple's motivation and ability to engage in sexual activity. Thus, the rate of intercourse for any one couple may fluctuate over time. In addition, researchers find that some married couples tend to engage in sexual activity quite frequently, whereas others engage in sex infrequently if at all (Donnelly, 1993). In one study, social scientist Cathy Greenblat (1983) asked 80 married individuals to retrospectively recall how often they had sexual intercourse each month during their very first year of marriage; reports ranged from 1 (or an average of 12 times during that first year) to 45 (or 540 times that first year). Clearly, some married couples have sex more often than others!

Similarly, certain *types* of couple engage in sexual activity more frequently than do others. In general, surveys reveal that cohabiting heterosexual couples and homosexual male couples tend to have sex (defined as genital contact) more frequently than do married couples, who in turn have sex more frequently than do homosexual female couples (e.g., Blumstein & Schwartz, 1983; Call, Sprecher, & Schwartz, 1995; Rao & DeMaris, 1995). And all of these couple types seem to engage in greater amounts of sexual activity than do single men and women. Recall that Michael et al. (1994) found that very few married men (1%) and women (3%) reported having no sex at all during the previous 12 months. Similarly, very few of the cohabiting men and women who participated in their study indicated having a sexless past year, but 23% of the single men and 32% of the single women reported engaging in no intercourse during the same time. In discussing their results, the authors concluded,

> We find that the critical factor that produces the most sexual activity is being part of a couple, whether it is a marriage or a cohabitation.

Even though married life is not seen as very erotic, it is actually the social arrangement that produces the highest rate of partnered sexual activity among heterosexuals. What seems to produce the highest rates of partnered sex is an easily accessible partner. (p. 118)

Essentially, the state of singlehood is not as conducive to sexual activity as is marriage or cohabitation.

Age and Sexual Activity

Age—both that of the partners and that of their relationship—is intimately connected with a couple's level of sexual activity. Cross-sectional studies, in which individuals from different age-groups or ranges are surveyed about their sexual experiences, generally reveal that older couples engage in sexual intercourse less frequently than do younger couples. For example, sociologists Vaughn Call, Susan Sprecher, and Pepper Schwartz (1995) examined sexual frequency across the life span using data gathered as part of the National Survey of Families and Households (a large-scale research endeavor consisting of personal interviews conducted with a national probability sample of 13,008 people). Their analyses were based on the 6,785 respondents who were married and had a spouse living with them in the household, and the item of interest concerned how often the participants reported engaging in sexual intercourse with their spouse during the past month. The results revealed that the frequency of marital sex was negatively correlated with age. For example, married men and women from 19 to 24 years of age reported having intercourse approximately 12 times a month. Those in their early to mid-30s engaged in sexual activity close to 9 times a month. Respondents from 50 to 54 years of age indicated having intercourse an average of 5.5 times a month, those in their late 60s reported having sex a little over twice a month, and those age 75 years or over engaged in intercourse less than once a month. Thus, increasing age was associated with decreasing levels of sexual activity. However, the authors also noted that although the older respondents definitely had less sex than their younger counterparts, they were far from asexual. About half of married adults between 65 and 74 years of age were still having sex (just not perhaps every month).

The frequency with which a couple has sexual intercourse is associated not only with the partners' chronological ages but also with the age of their relationship. Most studies demonstrate that the longer a couple has been married or has cohabited, the less often the partners have sex (e.g., Rao & DeMaris, 1995; Samson, Levy, Dupras, & Tessier, 1991). This decline seems to be greatest during the first year of marriage, such that newlyweds typically experience high rates of sexual activity during the very beginning phases of their unions and then sharp decreases in activity as they settle into married life. This phenomenon has been termed the "honeymoon effect" (James, 1981). A longitudinal study conducted by researcher William James (1981), who analyzed diaries and calendars kept by 21 newlywed couples, provides evidence for the honeymoon effect. The results revealed that couples had intercourse an average of 17 times during their very first month of marriage but that their sexual activity level declined to about 8 times a month by the end of the first year. Similarly, Greenblat (1983) found that more than two thirds of the men and women in her interview study who were married for more than a year reported that their current rate of sexual activity was lower than the rate they experienced during their first year of marriage.

The lower level of sexual activity seen in older couples (and in older relationships) is undoubtedly due to a number of different factors, including the physical and psychological changes that are associated with the aging process and the loss of sexual novelty that develops from having intercourse with the same partner year after year. Other factors that may contribute to decreased activity over time include pregnancy (and its associated lack of sexual interest), fatigue and loss of privacy due to the presence of children and child care activities, and heavy work schedules (Greenblat, 1983). All of these may conspire to make it difficult for couples to find the time—and the inclination—for sexual activity.

SEXUAL PRACTICES

Another question that has sparked researchers' interest concerns sexual practices or what people do when they are sexually intimate with each other. Michael and colleagues' (1994) national survey revealed that although there are a number of sexual activities from which to choose, the most commonly practiced is vaginal intercourse, with more than 95% of the heterosexual respondents stating that they had vaginal intercourse the last time they had sex. Oral sex, although less common than vaginal intercourse, was also reported by a sizable percentage of respondents. Specifically, about one third of cohabiting men, and one fifth of cohabiting women, reported either giving or receiving oral sex during their last sexual interaction. The numbers were slightly lower for married individuals, with approximately 24% of married men and 17% of married women reporting having participated in this activity during their last sexual event. Other forms of sexual expression occurred far less frequently. For example, only 2% of cohabiting men and women (and even fewer married respondents) reported having engaged in anal intercourse during their last encounter.

Homosexual couples practice many of the same sexual activities as do heterosexual couples but report higher frequencies of particular behaviors. For example, lesbian couples engage in more kissing, caressing, holding, and breast stimulation during sex than do cohabiting or married heterosexual couples (e.g., Blumstein & Schwartz, 1983; Masters & Johnson, 1979). In addition, oral sex and anal sex are more commonly used by homosexual couples than by heterosexual ones. Approximately 40% to 50% of gay male and lesbian couples report usually or always engaging in oral sex during lovemaking, compared with 20% to 30% of heterosexual couples, and gay men are more likely to have anal sex than are heterosexual couples (Blumstein & Schwartz, 1983; Lever, 1995; Michael et al., 1994).

The results of two national surveys conducted by sociologist Janet Lever (1994, 1995) suggest that homosexual couples may also be more experimental than their heterosexual counterparts. For example, many of the lesbian respondents—particularly those in their teens, 20s, and early 30s—had incorporated dildos (43%) or food (35%) into their sexual activities, had engaged in bondage or discipline (25%), or had participated in three-way sex (14%). Similarly, 55% of the gay male respondents had used dildos during sex, 48% had engaged in three-way sex, 24% had participated in group sex, and 10% had experienced sadomasochistic sexual encounters. It is important to note that Lever's question concerned activities during the past 5 years; consequently, we do not know how often participants engaged in these particular behaviors. It is possible that these activities were a common part of her respondents' sexual interactions, but it is also possible that they were tried once and then never again. In either case, her results do suggest that some couple types may be more sexually experimental than others.

SEXUAL PREFERENCES

In addition to exploring what people actually do sexually with their partners, some researchers have examined what people say they would *like* to do—in other words, their sexual preferences. Of all the possible sexual practices on the heterosexual menu, vaginal intercourse seems to possess the most appeal. For example, participants in the national survey conducted by Michael et al. (1994) were given the following list of possible sexual activities:

- Having sex with more than one person at the same time
- Having sex with someone of the same sex
- Forcing someone to do something sexual that he or she does not want to do
- Being forced to do something sexual that you do not want to do
- Seeing other people do sexual things
- Having sex with someone you do not personally know
- Watching a partner undress or strip
- Engaging in vaginal intercourse
- Using a dildo or vibrator
- Having a partner perform oral sex on you
- Performing oral sex on a partner
- Having a partner stimulate your anus with his or her fingers
- Stimulating a partner's anus with your fingers
- Engaging in passive anal intercourse
- Engaging in active anal intercourse (only men received this item)

Participants were asked to indicate how appealing they found each of these sexual activities using a 4-point scale, where 1 represented *very appealing,* 2 represented *somewhat appealing,* 3 represented *not appealing,* and 4 represented *not at all appealing.*

The results indicated that despite the wide variety of acts from which to choose, both sexes found only a small number to be appealing. Specifically, 96% of younger women and 95% of younger men (18-44 years of age) rated vaginal intercourse as either very appealing or somewhat appealing; similarly, 93% of older women and 95% of older men (45-59 years of age) found this particular act to be at least somewhat appealing. In fact, vaginal intercourse was the clear favorite, with all other acts receiving much lower preference ratings. Watching a partner undress was the second most preferred activity, although this particular event was rated as very appealing by more men than women in both the younger (50% vs. 30%) and older (40% vs. 18%) age groups. This was followed by receiving and giving oral sex, with both men and women indicating that it was more appealing to receive than to give this particular sex act. Each of the other behaviors or events seemed to appeal to only a very small percentage of people. For example, less than 5% of women and men said that they found using a dildo or vibrator, watching other people do sexual things, having sex with a stranger, or engaging in passive anal intercourse to be very appealing. No respondents indicated that being forced to do something sexual was very appealing, and none of the women and younger men (and only 1% of the older men) rated forcing someone to do something sexual as very appealing.

Although much less is known about the sexual preferences of homosexual men and women, Lever's (1994, 1995) national surveys yield some insight. For example, her male respondents said that their favorite bedroom acts included hugging, caressing, and snuggling (endorsed by 85%); deep kissing (74%); receiving oral sex (72%); giving oral sex (71%); masturbating a partner (52%); and being masturbated by a partner (51%). Their biggest sexual turn-offs were engaging in insertive anilingus (disliked by 26%) and engaging in receptive anal intercourse (disliked by 14%). Interestingly, however, many men selected these two particular sex acts as turn-ons; fully 29% said that they preferred insertive anilingus, and 43% endorsed receptive anal intercourse. Lever (1994) concluded, "When it comes to anal play, it appears [that gay] men either love it or hate it, and significant numbers are in both camps" (p. 21).

Homosexual women expressed similar sexual preferences. For example, most participants said that they "loved" hugging, caressing, and cuddling (91%); French kissing (82%); caressing a partner's breasts (82%); and sucking a partner's nipples (80%). About 75% identified holding hands, touching a partner's genitals, and having their own genitals touched as appealing practices. Like homosexual men (and like the heterosexual men and women in Michael et al.'s [1994] study), more lesbians prefer receiving oral sex (75%) than giving it (70%). Women reported that their least favorite activity is anal stimulation, with more than half expressing a dislike for anilingus (both giving and receiving) and anal penetration.

Thus, although the sexual menu is varied, most men and women—whether married or cohabiting, homosexual or heterosexual—prefer a limited selection of activities and express many of the same likes and dislikes.

SEXUAL SATISFACTION

Most paired individuals report that they are satisfied with their sex lives (e.g., Blumstein & Schwartz, 1983; Kurdek, 1991b; Lawrance & Byers,

1995). For example, approximately two thirds of the husbands and wives in one national survey reported experiencing a great deal or a very great deal of sexual satisfaction (Greeley, 1991). Similarly, more than half of the married and cohabiting men, and about 45% of the married women, in Michael et al.'s (1994) survey reported that their relationships were "extremely" physically pleasurable. Homosexual men and women appear to be equally satisfied sexually; more than 40% of the gay men (most of whom were partnered) in Lever's (1994, 1995) studies rated their current sex lives as great or good, and more than 30% of the partnered lesbians believed that their sex lives were great.

One of the most important factors associated with sexual satisfaction is how often a couple engages in sexual activity. Couples who have more frequent sex generally report higher levels of sexual satisfaction than do couples who have less frequent sex (e.g., Young, Denny, Luquis, & Young, 1998). For instance, Lever's (1995) survey data revealed a strong relationship between sexual frequency and sexual satisfaction among partnered homosexual women. Nearly all (92%) of the women who had sex 21 to 40 times during the past month rated their sex lives as great, compared with 67% who had sex 11 to 20 times, 44% who had sex 5 to 10 times, and 18% who had sex 2 to 4 times. Basically, the more sex her respondents reported, the more satisfied they were with the quality of their sexual interactions.

Sexual satisfaction is also associated with other factors, including whether the partner(s) experiences orgasm (e.g., Perlman & Abramson, 1982; Pinney, Gerrard, & Denney, 1987; Young et al., 1998), when during the sexual interaction the partners reach orgasm (Darling, Davidson, & Cox, 1991), and the ratio of rewards to costs that the partners receive from their sexual relationship (Byers, Demmons, & Lawrance, 1998). In general, couples tend to experience higher levels of sexual satisfaction when the partners engage in sex frequently, reach orgasm as a result of their activity and at about the same time, and experience more sexual rewards than costs.

SEXUAL COMMUNICATION

Another factor that is closely connected to sexual satisfaction in long-term relationships is communication. Communicative competence—that is, the ability to effectively communicate with the partner about one's sexual needs, preferences, expectations, and attitudes—is very important in established relationships. Not only is effective communication necessary for successfully negotiating the amount and type of a couple's sexual involvement, but it is also essential for maintaining the quality of their sexual relationship over time (Cupach & Comstock, 1990; Metts, Sprecher, & Regan, 1998).

One aspect of sexual communication that has received a great deal of attention from theorists and researchers is the initiation and refusal of sexual requests. In the traditional heterosexual "sexual script," men are expected to initiate sexual activity, whereas women are expected to then accept or refuse these sexual requests (e.g., Gagnon & Simon, 1973; Reiss, 1981). Research on sexual communication within cohabiting and marital relationships indicates that men and women generally follow this script in their actual sexual interactions, with men functioning as the sexual initiators and women serving as the sexual regulators (Blumstein & Schwartz, 1983). In fact, one of the most common wishes expressed by married men (and, not surprisingly, by partnered lesbians) is that their partners would initiate sex more often (Lever, 1995; Schwartz & Rutter, 1998). Over time, of course, women may become more comfortable in initiating sexual activity with their partners; one study revealed a small annual increase in the rate of initiations among wives (Brown & Auerback, 1981).

Regardless of which partner does the initiating, most sexual initiation attempts that occur in long-term relationships are successful; that is, most men and women respond positively to their partners' sexual invitations (Byers & Heinlein, 1989). These positive responses (as well as the initiation attempts) are generally communicated nonverbally and indirectly (Brown & Auerback, 1981; Byers & Heinlein, 1989). It is unusual for individuals to explicitly and verbally request sex from their partners ("Hey, do you want to have sex?"); it is equally unusual for partners to agree to sexual invitations in a verbally explicit manner ("Why yes, I would love to have sex right now"). Rather, a person who desires sexual activity might turn the radio to a romantic soft rock station, pour his or her partner a glass of wine, and glance suggestively in the direction of the bedroom. The partner who receives this indirect invitation might smile, put down his or her book, and engage in other nonverbal behaviors that continue the sexual interaction without explicitly acknowledging acceptance (or even awareness) of the initial invitation.

Sexual *refusals*, however, do tend to be communicated verbally and directly ("Honey, I'm just not in the mood right now; I'm kind of stressed about that dinner party we have to go to"). As noted by communication scholars William Cupach and Sandra Metts (1991), such directness "seems to fulfill simultaneously the goals of averting unwanted persistence of initiation by the partner and of maintaining the face of the rejected individual by offering an account" (p. 103). So, how do couples ultimately resolve situations in which one partner wants sex and the other does not? Research suggests that couples employ several strategies for reaching amicable conclusions to these episodes. For example, they may mutually agree not to have sex ("Yeah, you're right, we really don't have time"), they may agree to postpone sex until a later time ("Since we're running late for the party right now, how about later tonight?"), or they may simply agree to disagree ("Well, I still think we have time, but if you're not in the mood, I guess there's nothing more to say"). Of course, sometimes even the most reluctant partners change their minds. They may become aroused and therefore more interested in the proposed activity, they may be swayed by the arguments offered by their partners, or they may simply decide to accommodate their partners' wishes (Byers & Heinlein, 1989).

Whether initiations, refusals, and other aspects of sexual negotiation influence a couple's level of sexual satisfaction depends to a large extent on the communicative skill of the partners. It is not easy to be an effective sexual communicator. Successful communication about sexuality requires the ability both to *express* information about one's needs, desires, likes, and dislikes and to *solicit and receive* this information in a nonjudgmental and nondefensive manner from the partner (D'Augelli & D'Augelli, 1985). This level of disclosure and intimacy requires a great deal of trust and acceptance and may be difficult for couples to achieve. Many couples do, however, manage to express some aspects of their sexual feelings. In one study (Rubin, Hill, Peplau, & Dunkel-Schetter, 1980), researchers asked dating couples to report how much self-disclosure they experienced on a number of topics, including "my feelings about our sexual relationship." The majority (about three fourths) of men and women indicated having full disclosure on this topic with their partners. Thus, although open and honest communication about sexuality may seem like a difficult goal for couples to reach, it is certainly not impossible. More important, effective sexual communication is vital for maintaining the quality of the sexual relationship.

SEXUALITY AND GENERAL
RELATIONSHIP SATISFACTION

Not surprisingly, how people feel about their sex lives is related to how they feel about their relationships in general. All of the aspects of sexuality we have considered—sexual frequency, practices and preferences, satisfaction, and communication—are associated with the *non*sexual dimensions of a relationship. For example, the frequency with which a couple has sexual intercourse is related to relationship satisfaction. Specifically, the more often partners have sex, the more generally satisfied they are with the relationship (e.g., Call et al., 1995; Donnelly, 1993; Regan, 2000b), the more they enjoy spending time together and sharing activities and hobbies (e.g., Blumstein & Schwartz, 1983; Sprecher, Metts, Burleson, Hatfield, & Thompson, 1995), and the more equitable and fair they perceive their relationship to be (Hatfield, Greenberger, Traupmann, & Lambert, 1982).

Similarly, a large and growing body of research indicates that there is a strong correlation between sexual satisfaction and relationship satisfaction. Heterosexual and homosexual couples who are satisfied with their sexual relationships tend also to be satisfied with other areas of their partnerships (for reviews, see Christopher & Sprecher, 2000; Kurdek, 1991b). In one study, for example, Kelli-An Lawrance and Sandra Byers (1995) asked close to 250 heterosexual men and women who were currently involved in long-term (mostly marital) relationships to rate their sexual relationships and their overall relationships on five 7-point bipolar scales: *good-bad, pleasant-unpleasant, positive-negative, satisfying-unsatisfying,* and *valuable-worthless.* They found a strong association between these two measures. Specifically, the more satisfied participants were with their sexual relationships (i.e., the more they rated them as good, pleasant, positive, etc.), the more satisfied they were with their relationships in general.

Similar evidence for the connection between sexual satisfaction and interpersonal happiness was provided by a study conducted by Donna Henderson-King and Joseph Veroff (1994). These researchers asked 373 newly married African American and Caucasian couples to evaluate both the affective aspects of their marital relationships and the nature of their sexual interactions. Specifically, each participant completed a six-item scale that reflected feelings of affirmation in the relationship, including feeling good about oneself in the relationship and being cared for and valued by the spouse. Representative items included "During the past month, how often did you feel that your husband/wife felt especially caring toward you?," "During the past month, how often did you feel that your husband/wife made your life especially interesting and exciting?," and "During the past month, how often did you feel pleased that you were thought of as a couple?" Participants also completed a two-item scale that assessed sexual joy;

the items were "During the past month, how often did you feel that your sexual life together was joyful and exciting?" and "During the past month, how often did you feel that your husband/wife felt your sexual life together was joyful and exciting?" The researchers examined the correlation between these two measures—affirmation and sexual joy—for men and women as well as for African Americans and Caucasians. All associations were strong and positive, suggesting that regardless of one's sex or racial identity, sexual happiness is related to feeling good about one's relationship.

Of course, these and other correlational findings do not allow us to come to any firm conclusion about causality. That is, does good sex lead to a good relationship, or does a good relationship produce good sex? On the one hand, it certainly seems likely that a happy, well-adjusted person who is basically satisfied with the nonsexual aspects of his or her relationship would have no difficulty in seeking and enjoying sexual interactions with the partner, particularly if that partner is viewed as a source of happiness and well-being. On the other hand, it is equally likely that a person who is satisfied with the sexual aspects of his or her relationship will also tend to feel pleased about other aspects of the relationship. Whatever the direction of causality, most researchers agree that sexuality and relationship satisfaction are intimately connected.

SUMMARY

Sexuality is an important part of marital and other established relationships. The attitudes that partners hold about relational sexuality, the timing and manner of their sexual initiations, the amount of sex that they have, the kinds of sexual activities in which they engage, and how they communicate with each other about their needs, desires, and preferences can have an enormous impact on their level of sexual satisfaction and on their happiness with the relationship in general. In Chapter 7, we examine what happens when couples develop problems with the sexual aspects of their relationships.

KEY CONCEPTS

Sexual frequency (p. 76)
Cohabitation (p. 77)

Sexual satisfaction (pp. 82-83)
Communicative competence (p. 83)
Sexual initiation (p. 84)
Sexual refusal (p. 84)
Sexual script (p. 84)

DISCUSSION QUESTIONS

1. Consider common themes in marital sexual behavior (e.g., frequency, practices, preferences).

2. Contrary to popular myths about the "swinging single," paired individuals often have more sex than do their single counterparts. Why do you think that marriage or cohabitation might be more conducive to sexual expression than is singlehood?

3. Explain how time—duration of a relationship and age of the partners—affects sexual frequency.

4. What factors are associated with sexual satisfaction? Why might sexual frequency be associated with sexual satisfaction (and do you think that this relationship holds even for mediocre or bad sex)? What is the relationship between sexual satisfaction and overall relationship satisfaction?

5. Define the traditional heterosexual sexual script. Do you think that this script has changed over time? Why might it change once a relationship has moved beyond beginning phases and become committed and established?

RECOMMENDED READINGS

Christopher, F. S., & Sprecher, S. (2000). Sexuality in marriage, family, and other relationships: A decade review. *Journal of Marriage and the Family, 62,* 999-1017.

This article reviews the literature on marital sexuality.

Michael, R. T., Gagnon, J. H., Laumann, E. O., & Kolata, G. (1994). *Sex in America: A definitive survey.* Boston: Little, Brown.

This book presents the results of the authors' large-scale survey of the sexual practices and preferences of men and women in the United States. It provides insight into the sexual lives of married, cohabiting, and single people.

Schwartz, P., & Rutter, V. (1998). *The gender of sexuality*. Thousand Oaks, CA: Pine Forge.

This book surveys the literature on men's and women's sexuality. Of particular interest are Chapter 3, which explores norms and attitudes about uncommitted (or nonrelational) sex, and Chapter 4, which examines marital sexuality. The authors also touch on various political debates that have raged over sexuality, including teenage sexuality, sex education, same-sex marriage, and sexual assault.

7

Sex Gone Bad:
Problematic Aspects
of Relational Sexuality

Chapter Outline

In Chapter 6, we considered how the members of couples who engage in frequent and satisfying sexual interactions are likely to experience happiness, feelings of equity and affirmation, and general satisfaction with each other and with the relationship. However, it is important to recognize that there also exists a dark side to relational sexuality. Not only do relational partners often use sex to express their feelings of love and commitment, but they also may withhold, demand, or coerce sex as a way of punishing each other or demonstrating interpersonal power (Christopher & Lloyd, 2000). In sum, sex can serve as both a positive and a negative force in close relationships. In this chapter, we turn to three problematic aspects of sexuality in beginning and established romantic relationships: sexual aggression, sexual dissatisfaction, and sexual infidelity.

SEXUAL AGGRESSION

Most couples manage to successfully negotiate sexual situations and achieve mutually agreed-on sexual outcomes. For some, however, sexual encounters may involve various forms of aggressive behavior. There are two broad categories of sexual aggression (see Christopher, 2001; Muehlenhard, Goggins, Jones, & Satterfield, 1991; Sprecher & McKinney, 1993). The first, *sexual coercion,* involves the use of verbal or psychological manipulation, pressure, or coercion to gain sexual compliance from another individual. Examples include pleading, verbally threatening to end the relationship, making the other person feel guilty for refusing sex, and continuing to persist in the face of the other's objections. Sexual coercion does not involve threats of physical harm or the use of physical force. The second type of sexual aggression is *sexual assault* (also called sexual abuse or sexual violence). Sexual assault reflects "a direct power assertion" (Christopher, 2001, p. 134) on the part of one partner toward the other and involves the threatened or actual use of physical force or bodily harm to obtain sexual contact. Next, we consider social scientific efforts to document the incidence and understand the origins of these two forms of sexual aggression.

Prevalence of Sexual Aggression in Romantic Relationships

Contrary to popular opinion—which tends to portray sexual violence as an act perpetrated by strangers who lurk in dark alleys—sexual aggression between dating partners and spouses is surprisingly common. An early study of undergraduate men, for example, revealed that 26% reported having made forceful attempts at intercourse while on dates that had, in turn, prompted a fighting, crying, or screaming response from their partners (Kanin, 1967). Similarly, 25% of the men in a national survey of college students conducted by Mary Koss, Christine Gidycz, and Nadine Wisniewski (1987) reported using some form of sexual coercion or aggression on a partner, and a much higher percentage of the women surveyed by David Finkelhor and Kersti Yllö (1985) were sexually assaulted by dates (10%) than were assaulted by strangers (3%). Although estimates of marital sexual assault vary (and are difficult to obtain), the results of a national survey conducted in Great Britain by criminologists Kate Painter and David Farrington (1998) revealed that 13% of wives had experienced forced sexual intercourse with their husbands. Sexual violence is, unfortunately, a common occurrence within romantic relationships.

The national survey conducted by Robert Michael and his colleagues (Michael, Gagnon, Laumann, & Kolata, 1994) provides additional evidence that many victims of sexual assault or violence know, and are currently involved in relationships with, their assailants. The researchers began their examination of the topic of forced sex by asking their respondents a series of questions about sexual behavior after puberty, including whether their first experience with intercourse had been forced and whether they had ever been forced "to do something sexually that you did not want to do" by a same- or opposite-sex person. Participants who had been sexually forced were asked how many times this had occurred, what their relationships with the assailants were, and the specific sex acts that had occurred during the incidents. The results revealed that most victims of sexual force were female and that most perpetrators were male. Many more women (22%) than men (2%) said they had experienced forced sexual activity at some time in their lives, and nearly all of the women (and one third of the men) who were forced reported being forced by men.

When we focus only on the responses given by the 204 women who reported being forced by men to engage in sexual activity, we once more find evidence of just how uncommon it is for women to be assaulted by strangers. Nearly all of the women were acquainted with the men who forced them. In fact, the majority (55%) were either in love with or married to these men, many (22%) said they knew the men quite well, and a sizable proportion (19%) stated that they knew the men but not very well. Only 4% of the respondents indicated that their male assailants were strangers who were unknown to them. Thus, most of the forced and unwanted sexual episodes reported by these women occurred within the context of existing, and oftentimes romantic, relationships.

The Origins of Sexual Aggression

The recognition that aggressive sexual episodes occur with some frequency within dating and other romantic relationships has created an interest in discovering the factors that may contribute to sexual coercion and assault. Some researchers have focused on individual-level variables, including sex or gender and personality. For example, when individuals are asked to evaluate date rape scenarios, men generally perceive a higher degree of sexual willingness on the part of the female target than do women. In addition, men typically believe that the female target is more responsible for the assault—and that the male target's behavior is more justified—than do women (e.g., Feltey, Ainslie, & Geib, 1991; Kowalski, 1992; Proite, Dannells, & Benton, 1993). Personality characteristics also are associated with rape perceptions. Men who possess high levels of *hypermasculinity* (a trait dimension reflecting exaggerated adherence to a masculine gender role) have a more positive emotional response to rape depictions and are more likely to have engaged in sexually aggressive behavior than are men low on this attribute (e.g., Beaver, Gold, & Prisco, 1992; Mosher & Anderson, 1986).

Other researchers and theorists have explored social factors that may create an environment that is conducive to sexual aggression within romantic relationships. For example, in their discussion of sexual violence and coercion in close relationships, psychologist Charlene Muehlenhard and her colleagues (1991) noted how the *sexual double standard*, which encompasses normative beliefs that men are sexual, that male sexuality is an uncontrollable and powerful force, and that women often offer token resistance to sex, may contribute to sexual aggression. Similarly, *legal and religious influences* also are implicated in the occurrence of sexual coercion. Some ideologies promote the idea that husbands are entitled to have sex with their wives and that wives have no right to refuse their husbands' sexual requests, and until very recently husbands in some states could not be charged with raping their wives. Other social influences that have been investigated and that are believed to foster sexual coercion in close relationships include *sex role scripts* associated with heterosexual dating situations (e.g., men should control the progression of the relationship and any sexual interactions that occur [see Christopher, 2001]), *socialization processes* that foster the acquisition of rape myths (e.g., Burt, 1980), and *peer group norms* that support and promote exploitative attitudes toward women and the use of coercive sexual strategies (e.g., Kanin, 1984, 1985; Martin & Hummer, 1989).

Sexual aggression does occur between relational partners, and there is a strong and immediate need for additional research on the causes and consequences of this dark side of interpersonal sexuality.

SEXUAL DISSATISFACTION

We have already reviewed research suggesting that most couples experience relatively high levels of sexual satisfaction. Some, however, become distressed or unhappy over the sexual aspects of the relationship. Sexual dissatisfaction can have consequences that extend far beyond the bedroom, including relationship termination (Blumstein & Schwartz, 1983; Cleek & Pearson, 1985).

What causes the members of a couple to become dissatisfied with their sex life? One leading contender is poor sexual communication. In Chapter 6, we discussed how the ability to communicate effectively about sex with one's partner is an essential ingredient in sexual happiness. Indeed, communication researchers William Cupach and Sandra Metts (1991) noted that "sex talk" serves a number of important functions within close romantic relationships, including allowing partners to communicate desires and preferences to each other, to coordinate meanings for sexual behaviors, to negotiate a dyadic sexual script, and to reduce their uncertainty about each other's sexual expectations. Partners who cannot disclose sexual information and/or who are unwilling to listen to sexual disclosures will inevitably end up engaging in undesired and less-than-satisfying activities. At best, they may feel annoyed, embarrassed, or irritated; at worst, they may feel coerced, manipulated, or abused.

Another factor that may contribute to sexual dissatisfaction is incompatibility. For example, one partner may be highly physically attracted to the other and eager to engage in frequent sexual activity. If the other does not reciprocate these feelings—perhaps he or she simply has a lower sex drive or does not find the other quite as sexually desirable—some degree of interpersonal distress is likely to result. There is little empirical research on the actual consequences of mismatched desire and other sexual incompatibilities within ongoing romantic relationships. However, people *believe* that this state of affairs—one partner feeling more sexual desire than the other—produces negative outcomes, including unhappiness, conflict, and relationship termination (Regan, 1998b). In addition, clinical studies reveal that many couples view a partner's sudden loss of desire as a problem that requires therapeutic intervention (see Leiblum & Rosen, 1988; Talmadge & Talmadge, 1986).

In sum, most people are happy with their sex lives, and most are able to deal with any small sexual difficulties that may arise during the course of their relationships. However, a high level of sexual dissatisfaction, particularly when it reflects or is caused by poor sexual communication or sexual incompatibility, may result in distress, emotional upset, or even relationship dissolution.

SEXUAL INFIDELITY

One of the primary beliefs that people hold about marital and other forms of a long-term committed relationship is that they should be *sexually exclusive*. That is, the majority of men and women living in cultures around the world expect married or committed partners to engage in intercourse and other sexual activities only with each other. And most people appear not only to believe this proscription but also to follow it. When Michael et al. (1994) asked participants to indicate how many sex partners they had had during the past year, the responses men and women gave clearly demonstrated "how likely people are to remain faithful to their sexual partners, whether or not they were married" (p. 101). Specifically, 95% of the married men and women, 75% of the never-married but cohabiting men and women, and 82% of the divorced and now cohabiting men and women had engaged in sexual activity with one person (the partner) over the past 12 months. In fact, the people who reported multiple sex partners were, for the most part, single with no primary romantic partner. The researchers concluded, "Despite the popular myth that there is a great deal of adultery in marriage, our data and other reliable studies do not find it. Instead, a vast majority are faithful while the marriage is intact" (p. 89).

However, although most people are sexually faithful to their partners, infidelity or *extrarelational sex* does occur. There are many reasons why an individual might engage in sexual activities with someone other than his or her primary partner. After reviewing the literature, sociologists Pepper Schwartz and Virginia Rutter (1998) identified seven factors that are implicated in sexual infidelity. The first is *emotional incompatibility* between the romantic partners. Spouses who stay in a loveless marriage for the sake of the children or for economic or social reasons might seek affairs or one-night stands to obtain the passion, excitement, and affection they used to receive from each other. A second reason why spouses stray concerns *boredom*; people sometimes engage in affairs for purely recreational motives. They may love their partners and even find their relational sex lives to be highly pleasurable, but at the same time they may feel a need for sexual adventure. A third motive for infidelity is *sexual incompatibility.* One partner who desires sex more than the other, or who wishes to engage in activities that the other does not enjoy or want to try, may pursue sex outside the relationship. People also engage in extrarelational sex out of *anger* or as a way to punish the partner for emotional slights or other "bad" behavior. As noted by Schwartz and Rutter, "Anger makes extrarelational sex more likely in two ways: It makes making love to your partner difficult, thereby fueling a sense of deprivation; it also makes having sex outside the relationship seem like a good way to get even" (p. 153). Anger also reduces feelings of guilt or shame; hiding behind anger, the unfaithful partner can excuse, rationalize, or justify the sexual transgression.

Sometimes, of course, people have affairs or casual sexual encounters simply because they meet individuals whose attentions are so flattering, and who are so attractive and exciting, that they succumb to temptation. *Flattery,* which Schwartz and Rutter (1998) defined as the notice or attention of an especially attractive or successful suitor, can cause people in even the most stable, positive, and successful relationships to stray. Extrarelational sex can also be motivated by a conscious, or even an unconscious, *desire to end the relationship.* A person might have an affair, a one-night stand, or some other sexual liaison precisely so that the partner will find out and terminate the relationship. Men and women who use this strategy either are uncertain about whether they really want to leave their primary relationships or are unable to face talking directly with their partners about their feelings; by having affairs, they create a situation that will make their partners angry and indirectly force the issue. *Love* (for the extrarelational partner) is the seventh and final reason for infidelity identified by Schwartz and Rutter. Some affairs grow out of long-term friendships or coworker relationships; the individuals involved already have a strong affection and love for each other, and over time their feelings lead to a sexual relationship. Alternatively, two people might fall suddenly and madly in love with each other, with their passion culminating in an affair.

Just as infidelity may stem from a variety of motives and serve a number of different functions in people's lives, it is also associated with a great many outcomes—both positive and negative. Affairs, one-night stands, and other forms of extrarelational sexual encounters certainly can produce beneficial outcomes for the individual, including sheer physical pleasure, a sense of excitement and adventure, a feeling of personal growth, and the formation of an intense physical and/or emotional connection with the extrarelational partner (see Bringle & Buunk, 1991). In general, however, most research indicates that the negative consequences of infidelity far outweigh any potential benefits. For example, the partner who engages in extrarelational sexual activity often experiences guilt and conflict about deceiving the other partner and violating moral or personal standards about exclusivity and fidelity as well as anxiety and fear about sexually transmitted diseases, pregnancy, getting caught by the other partner, and so on (Bringle & Buunk, 1991; Spanier & Margolies, 1983). Infidelity can also produce negative interpersonal outcomes. The cheated-on partner may experience jealousy, anger, and feelings of betrayal as well as self-doubt and disappointment (Buunk, 1995; Charny & Parnass, 1995), and the relationship itself might not survive. Indeed, infidelity is one of the leading causes of relationship termination (e.g., Amato & Rogers, 1997; Atkins, Baucom, & Jacobson, 2001; Betzig, 1989). In sum, sexual infidelity is a potent and often quite destructive force in romantic relationships.

SUMMARY

As we have seen in this and previous chapters, sexuality can produce both positive and negative outcomes for romantic partners. Sexual aggression, dissatisfaction, and infidelity occur with varying degrees of frequency within committed love relationships. Each of these sexual phenomena produces a number of adverse consequences for the partners and their relationship.

KEY CONCEPTS

Sexual aggression (p. 91)
Sexual coercion (p. 91)
Sexual assault (p. 91)
Hypermasculinity (p. 93)
Sexual double standard (p. 93)
Sex role scripts (p. 93)
Sexual exclusivity (p. 95)
Infidelity (p. 95)
Extrarelational sex (p. 95)

DISCUSSION QUESTIONS

1. In what ways can sex serve as a positive force in romantic relationships? As a negative force?

2. Discuss the factors that may encourage sexual aggression in dating and other romantic relationships.

3. Evaluate this statement: "Decreased sexual expression between partners is a sign that their relationship is in trouble."

4. Consider the consequences of sexual infidelity for romantic relationships.

RECOMMENDED READINGS

Christopher, F. S., & Lloyd, S. A. (2000). Physical and sexual aggression in relationships. In C. Hendrick & S. S. Hendrick (Eds.), *Close relationships: A sourcebook* (pp. 331-343). Thousand Oaks, CA: Sage.

Christopher, F. S., Owens, L. A., & Stecker, H. L. (1993). An examination of single men's and women's sexual aggressiveness in dating relationships. *Journal of Social and Personal Relationships, 10,* 511-527.

Muehlenhard, C. L. (1988). "Nice women" don't say yes and "real men" don't say no: How miscommunication and the double standard can cause sexual problems. *Women and Therapy, 7,* 95-108.

Muehlenhard, C. L., Goggins, M. F., Jones, J. M., & Satterfield, A. T. (1991). Sexual violence and coercion in close relationships. In K. McKinney & S. Sprecher (Eds.), *Sexuality in close relationships* (pp. 155-175). Hillsdale, NJ: Lawrence Erlbaum.

These works examine the "dark" side of relational sexuality, including sexual aggression, coercion, and violence.

PART III

MATE SELECTION
AND MARRIAGE

The first two sections of this textbook examined issues of love and sexuality. Both of these topics are intimately connected with human mating relationships. We experience and express the majority of our sexual desires and behaviors within the context of mating relationships, and we feel affection, companionate love, passionate love, intimacy, and other emotions for our potential and actual mates. This section of the text focuses on mate selection and marriage, two fundamental features of human mating.

Chapter 8 discusses theoretical approaches to understanding the dynamics of human mating relationships. Chapter 9 focuses on mate preference or the desires that guide men's and women's choice of a long-term partner, and Chapter 10 focuses on the process of attraction and courtship—how people actually obtain a mate. Chapter 11 presents theories designed to explain how mating relationships progress and change over time, and Chapter 12 considers conflict and dissolution. Chapter 13 discusses mate choice, including types of mating systems that exist, marriage and cohabitation, and changes in the nature of marriage over time.

8

General Theories
of Mate Selection

Chapter Outline

There are a number of ways in which social and behavioral scientists attempt to make sense of human mating dynamics. In general, these approaches tend to fall into two broad theoretical frameworks. The first of these frameworks emphasizes the way in which mating dynamics are influenced by social forces created by and residing within the contemporary environment. The second targets evolutionary forces that arose in the ancient past and that form part of our species' heritage.

SOCIAL CONTEXT THEORIES: THE WORLD THAT IS

Social context frameworks focus on proximal mechanisms—that is, forces located in the contemporary social, cultural, and historical milieu—that may influence mate preferences, attraction strategies, choices, and relationship outcomes.

Social exchange or equity models of relationship development and maintenance represent one such framework (e.g., Blau, 1964; Murstein, 1970, 1976; Walster, Walster, & Berscheid, 1978; for a review of social exchange models relevant to mating, see Sprecher, 1998). According to these models, the process of mate selection and relationship formation resembles a marketplace in which people attempt to maximize their rewards and make social interaction as profitable as possible by exchanging their own assets—beauty, health, intelligence, a sense of humor, kindness, wealth, status, and so on—for desirable attributes in a partner. A person's own value as a potential partner is presumed to influence the extent to which he or she is able to attract and retain a high-value partner. Because people seek the best possible value in a potential mate but are constrained by their own assets, this process is assumed to result in the pairing of individuals of roughly equal value. That is, "wealthy" individuals who possess a great many desirable characteristics, or who have high amounts of a few particularly valuable attributes, will be able to attract and pair with others of equally high value. "Poorer" persons, or those who have fewer assets to offer a potential mate, inevitably will form liaisons with less valuable and less expensive others.

Exchange theorists argue that mating mistakes are costly. For example, in his discussion of the early stages of marital choice, Bernard Murstein (1970) noted that although an individual may run less risk of rejection if he or she seeks a less desirable partner (low cost), the rewards of such a conquest are correspondingly meager (low profit); at the same time, the increased likelihood of rejection (high cost) associated with seeking a partner who is substantially more desirable than oneself (high profit) renders this enterprise equally risky. Consequently, an accurate perception of one's own qualities and what one has to contribute or offer to a relationship is believed to be extremely important.

Other social context theories focus on sex differences in (heterosexual) mating relationships. For example, *social role* theorists (e.g., Eagly, 1987; Eagly & Karau, 1991) posit that people develop expectations for their own and others' behavior based on their beliefs about sex-appropriate behavior and attributes. Such beliefs and expectations are assumed to arise from the distribution of men and women into different social roles in natural settings; specifically, the sexes are believed to possess attributes suited for the roles each typically occupies. For men, these roles continue to be primarily occupational and economic; for women, these roles are traditionally domestic. Consequently, sex differences in romantic preferences and choices are caused in part by the tendency of people to behave in a manner consistent with their sex roles. To the extent that people prefer others to behave in accordance with existing sex role stereotypes, traditionally "male" characteristics and attributes—including having a high-paying job, accruing resources, and displaying assertiveness, ambition, strength, and other "masculine" traits—may be valued more by women than by men when considering and selecting a potential mate. Conversely, traditionally "female" characteristics and attributes—including expressing nurturance, displaying emotional warmth, and being concerned with one's physical appearance—may be valued more by men than by women.

Other social forces that also may shape men's and women's mating behavior include *social and cultural scripts* (e.g., Gagnon & Simon, 1973; Reiss, 1967, 1981, 1986; Simon & Gagnon, 1986) and *social learning processes* (e.g., Hogben & Byrne, 1998; Mischel, 1966). In Western cultures, for example, it is not considered appropriate to establish a sexual or romantic relationship with a child or an underage partner, and laws have been enacted to prevent individuals from doing so. Like social role theory, script and social learning theories have been used to account for sex differences in mating behavior. For example, the different patterns of reinforcement and punishment that men and women receive for their sexual behavior, coupled with the existence of normative beliefs about male and female sexuality (e.g., men are sexual creatures who eagerly seek sexual experience, women are sexual gatekeepers who restrict sexual access), may encourage men to adopt positive attitudes toward sexual involvement during the early or beginning stages of romantic relationships. Those same social forces may encourage women to refrain from sexual activity until more committed relational stages have been reached.

All of these contemporary social mechanisms—scripts, social learning processes, sex-based beliefs and expectations, and social exchange—undoubtedly contribute to men's and women's mating preferences, behavior, and outcomes.

EVOLUTIONARY MODELS: THE WORLD THAT WAS

> *The mind is a set of information-processing machines that were designed by natural selection to solve adaptive problems faced by our hunter-gatherer ancestors.*
>
> —Cosmides and Tooby (1997, p. 1)

Evolutionary models of human mating are derived from the theoretical principles of evolutionary psychology, encapsulated in the preceding quotation. Specifically, according to noted evolutionary theorists Leda Cosmides and John Tooby (1997; also see Tooby & Cosmides, 1992), evolutionary psychology is concerned with the design of the human mind or the neural circuits we possess that process information. Evolutionary psychologists conceive of the mind as composed of many specialized processing systems. For example, we possess neural circuitry that is specialized for use in mate selection, just as we possess neural circuitry for language acquisition and for food selection. In addition, evolutionary psychologists agree that the human mind (all of our neural circuitry) was designed by the processes of natural and sexual selection originally articulated by naturalist Charles Darwin (1859, 1871). Relatedly, the human mind is believed to be designed to solve adaptive problems or recurrent issues in human evolutionary history that had implications for reproduction and survival. One of the most significant of these adaptive problems involved the selection, attraction, and retention of a suitable mate. Finally, evolutionary psychology is oriented toward our species' distant past. The human mind was designed to solve adaptive problems that existed eons ago and that affected the daily lives of our earliest ancestors. With these principles in mind, evolutionary models of mating consider the ways in which mating behavior might be influenced by evolved psychological heuristics that were selected because they overcame obstacles to reproduction located in the human ancestral past and therefore maximized reproductive success.

Several factors are believed to affect partner preferences, choices, and relationship outcomes (see Buss & Kenrick, 1998; Cunningham, Druen, & Barbee, 1997; Gangestad & Simpson, 1990; Regan, 2002). When considering a potential romantic partner, *emotional fitness* is presumed to be of paramount importance. Evolutionary models recognize that the human biological design favors the formation of enduring relationships and few sex differences in long-term mating behavior. Specifically, because human offspring are characterized by a period of dependency that extends well beyond infancy, successful pairbonding and child rearing in the ancestral past depended for both sexes on the ability to select a mate who could and would provide sustained social and emotional support. Those who selected emotionally fit partners achieved greater reproductive success than those who did not; hence, the former's genes survived. As a result of this genetic legacy, contemporary men and women are presumed to be particularly desirous of a long-term partner who possesses prosocial personality characteristics that indicate an ability and a willingness to emotionally commit to the reproductive partner, the reproductive relationship, and any resulting offspring.

In addition to dispositional attributes and emotional fitness, a potential partner also must be evaluated in terms of his or her *physical or genetic fitness.* Evolutionary models suggest that reproductive success is dependent, for both sexes, on selecting a sexually mature healthy individual who is capable of reproduction, who will pass on "good" genetic material to any resulting offspring, and who is physically able to contribute to the reproductive relationship, the partner, and the offspring. Insofar as physical appearance served as an external indicant or "honest advertisement" of underlying genetic fitness, reproductive status, and health in the ancestral environment (e.g., Fisher, 1958; Gangestad, 1993), appearance attributes are believed to play an important role in the mating decisions of both sexes today.

A third class of adaptively significant features includes those interpersonal attributes that promote the successful formation and maintenance of a committed pairbond. An appropriate mate is one who not only possesses emotional and physical fitness but also demonstrates *relational fitness*—the ability and motivation to become exclusively attached to one particular individual, to ignore the temptations posed by other individuals, and to confine reproductively relevant behaviors (e.g., emotional, sexual, economic, social) to the primary relationship. A number of characteristics are indicative of relational fitness, including mutual attraction or love, exclusivity, and similarity between partners. Those early humans who chose to pursue and establish a relationship with an individual who did not reciprocate their feelings of attraction, who did not confine his or her sexual and emotional activities to the primary relationship, and/or whose characteristics were not compatible with their own would have experienced lower levels of reproductive success than would those men and women who selected a more appropriate partner. Thus, contemporary men and women are presumed to prefer as a mate an individual who loves them passionately (and with whom they are themselves in love), who is willing to form an exclusive (i.e., monogamous) partnership, and who resembles them along important demographic, personality, and attitudinal dimensions.

The final feature category that may have served to promote reproductive success in the ancestral environment concerns *social fitness.* In the ancestral environment, men and women who based their reproductive decisions at least partly on social fitness considerations—that is, who selected as mates individuals with strong ties to the existing community, with some degree of status or position within that community, and with the ability to provide tangible resources in the form of food, shelter, and physical protection—would have enjoyed a higher degree of reproductive success than would men and women who chose to ignore or undervalue social fitness. Consequently, contemporary humans are presumed to prefer mates who possess attributes that reflect the ability to successfully negotiate the social hierarchy.

Sex Differences in Mate Selection

Although all men and women are assumed to be desirous of mates who possess emotional, physical, relational, and social fitness, some evolutionary models posit sex differences in preferences for particular partner attributes. *Parental investment-based* evolutionary models (e.g., Buss & Schmitt, 1993; Kenrick, Sadalla, Groth, & Trost, 1990) posit that women, who invest more direct physiological resources in their offspring than do men (e.g., contributing body nutrients during pregnancy and lactation), will be more sensitive to resource limitations and thus particularly attentive to reproductive partners' social fitness (e.g., status, ability to provide resources). Men, on the other hand, are assumed to be constrained by access to women who can produce viable offspring and thus should be relatively more sensitive than women to characteristics that reflect physical fitness, including health and reproductive capacity.

Interestingly, although men and women are assumed to differ with respect to the emphasis they place on particular partner attributes, they are believed to hold similar standards and to be relatively equally selective with respect to their partners. Specifically, because human males as well as females invest heavily in offspring, mating mistakes— including selecting a partner who is unable to provide resources, who is capricious and emotionally unstable, or who is infertile and unhealthy—are extremely costly to both sexes in the long-term relational context. Thus, parental investment theories posit that both men and women will be highly—and equally—discriminating in their choice of long-term partners.

SUMMARY

The preferences, choices, and behaviors that men and women demonstrate as they enter, maintain, and terminate mating relationships undoubtedly are influenced by both contemporary and distal mechanisms. As becomes evident in Chapter 9, each of the aforementioned theories and perspectives sheds some light on mating dynamics.

KEY CONCEPTS

Social context frameworks (p. 101)
Social exchange or equity models (p. 102)
Social role theory (p. 102)
Social and cultural scripts (p. 103)
Social learning processes (p. 103)
Evolutionary models (p. 104)
Emotional fitness (p. 104)
Physical or genetic fitness (p. 105)
Relational fitness (p. 105)
Social fitness (pp. 105-106)
Parental investment-based models (p. 106)

DISCUSSION QUESTIONS

1. In what ways does the process of mate selection resemble a "social marketplace"? Do we always pay attention to our own and our potential partners' "bargaining power"?

2. How do social roles, sociocultural scripts, and social learning processes contribute to sex differences in sexual and romantic behavior?

3. Consider how various attributes (e.g., emotional fitness, physical vitality, resources, status) may have contributed to personal survival and reproductive success in the ancestral environment.

4. How do parental investment models explain modern-day sex differences in partner preferences?

RECOMMENDED READINGS

Hogben, M., & Byrne, D. (1998). Using social learning theory to explain individual differences in human sexuality. *Journal of Sex Research, 35,* 58-71.

These authors examine sexuality (in particular, sex differences in sexual attitudes and behavior) from the perspective of social learning theory.

Oliver, M. B., & Hyde, J. S. (1993). Gender differences in sexuality: A meta-analysis. *Psychological Bulletin, 114,* 29-51.

In the introduction to this article, the authors review a number of theories (both social contextual and evolutionary) that have been used to predict and explain sex differences in mating behavior.

Sprecher, S. (1998). Social exchange theories and sexuality. *Journal of Sex Research, 35,* 32-43.

This article presents an overview of social exchange models that can be applied to human mating dynamics.

9

Mate Preferences

In Chapter 8, we explored two major theoretical frameworks that have been used to explain and predict men's and women's mating preferences, attitudes, choices, and behaviors. This chapter examines research that speaks to the utility of each of these frameworks. Specifically, we examine what is known about the attributes, traits, and characteristics that people actually prefer and seek in their dates and mates.

METHODOLOGIES

There are several different methods for exploring mate preferences. By far the most common methods used involve self-report. For example, many of the early (and some of the more recent) investigations employed a *ranking procedure* in which participants ordered or organized features in terms of their importance or desirability (e.g., Hill, 1945; Regan & Berscheid, 1997). Other researchers have chosen to use a *rating procedure* in which participants evaluate the importance or desirability of features with Likert-type scales (e.g., Wiederman & Allgeier, 1992). Still others have used a *percentile ranking procedure* in which participants indicate how much of a particular characteristic they would like a potential partner to possess relative to other same-sex peers (e.g., Kenrick, Groth, Trost, & Sadalla, 1993; Regan, 1998d). These three self-report methods are illustrated in Exhibit 9.1.

Some researchers have chosen to employ *content analyses* of personal ads in an attempt to identify the attributes people seek from their partners (e.g., Davis, 1990; Deaux & Hanna, 1984). And finally, some researchers have examined the importance of particular attributes *experimentally* by manipulating the features that a target individual possesses and examining the impact of this manipulation on participants' perceptions (e.g., self-reported desire to date the target [Graziano, Jensen-Campbell, Todd, & Finch, 1997; Townsend & Levy, 1990]). As discussed later, some of these methods may provide a more accurate picture of mate preference than do others.

EMPIRICAL EVIDENCE

The mate preference literature is enormous and encompasses a myriad of studies, all of which generally indicate that men and women overwhelmingly prefer a long-term partner who possesses intelligence, emotional stability, an honest and trustworthy disposition, an exciting overall personality, and a physically attractive appearance. In two of the first documented examinations of mate preference, both conducted during the late 1930s and early 1940s, social scientists Harold Christensen (1947) and Reuben Hill (1945) asked college students at their respective universities to rank order a list of characteristics in terms of their importance in a romantic partner. The two most important attributes, according to both samples of participants, were "dependable character" and "emotional stability." Men and women also emphasized a "pleasing disposition" and "mutual attraction or love." Less important attributes included "similar political background" (unimportant to men and women in both samples), "good cook/housekeeper" (unimportant to women), and "good financial prospect" (unimportant to men). Other researchers have since replicated

Exhibit 9.1   Three Self-Report Methods of Determining Mate Preferences

Instructions

We are interested in exploring the attributes that people seek in a long-term romantic partner—a steady date, a spouse or domestic partner, someone with whom you might cohabit and/or raise children. Below, you will find a list of attributes or characteristics that you might want a long-term romantic partner to possess. After you read over the entire list, please evaluate these characteristics using the three different methods described below. Take your time and think carefully about your ratings.

Scoring

Column 1: *Rank order.* Read over the entire list of attributes and rank order them from most to least important (1:*most important characteristic to me,* 2: *second most important characteristic to me,* etc.).

Column 2: *Rating scale.* Rate the importance of each attribute to you in this type of partner using the following scale:

1	2	3	4	5	6	7	8	9
Not at all important								Extremely important

Column 3: *Percentile ranking.* Indicate how you would like your partner to rank on each attribute, as compared with other men or women, using the following scale:
My perfect partner is above _____% of other men (women) on this attribute.
Note: Scores can range from 0 to 99. For example, a score of 50 means that your partner is above 50% and below 49% of others on this characteristic (exactly average). A score of 35 means that your partner is above 35% and below 64% of the population (below average). A score of 80 means that your partner is above 80% and below 19% of all other men (women) on this attribute (above average).

Characteristic:	Column 1: Rank Order	Column 2: Importance	Column 3: Percentile
Intelligent	_____	_____	_____
Kind and understanding	_____	_____	_____
Emotionally stable	_____	_____	_____
Honest and trustworthy	_____	_____	_____
Physically attractive	_____	_____	_____
Good sense of humor	_____	_____	_____
High social status	_____	_____	_____
Similar to you (e.g., interests, values)	_____	_____	_____
Good housekeeper	_____	_____	_____
Sexually inexperienced	_____	_____	_____

Exhibit 9.2   Top 10 Desired Characteristics in a Marriage Partner

Men	Women
Good overall personality	Honesty and trustworthiness
Honesty and trustworthiness	Kindness and compassion
Attractive appearance	Good overall personality
Intelligence	Intelligence
Good health	Attentive to one's partner
Kindness and compassion	Good sense of humor
Good sense of humor	Self-confidence
Self-confidence	Good health
Attentive to one's partner	Attractive appearance
Easygoing nature	Easygoing nature

SOURCE: From Regan, P. C., & Berscheid, E. (1997). Gender differences in characteristics desired in a potential sexual and marriage partner. *Human Journal of Psychology and Sexuality, 9,* 25-37. Copyright © 1997 by The Haworth Press, Inc. Adapted with permission.

NOTE: In this study, men and women were asked to rank order (from most to least desirable in a marriage partner) a list of attributes similar to the ones used by Christensen (1947), Hill (1945), and other early mate selection researchers. This table shows the top 10 most desired characteristics, arranged in order from most to least appealing. As can be seen from the results, men and women tend to desire similar attributes in a marriage partner, although there is also evidence that men rank external attributes (e.g., health, appearance) higher than do women.

these results using the same or very similar lists of features (e.g., Hudson & Henze, 1969; McGinnis, 1958; Regan & Berscheid, 1997). Exhibit 9.2 illustrates these findings.

More recently, social psychologist Pamela Regan (1998d) asked men and women to indicate their ideal mate preferences for a larger variety of characteristics. For both sexes, the "perfect" long-term romantic partner was someone who possessed a great deal of the following attributes, in order of importance:

1. Characteristics related to physical appeal

First and foremost, participants desired a mate who was physically appealing. Specifically, both men and women emphasized a physically attractive, sexy, and healthy appearance when evaluating a long-term romantic partner.

2. Characteristics related to interpersonal skill and responsiveness

Only slightly less important than physical appeal were attributes related to social skill and interpersonal responsiveness. Men and women emphasized the importance of a good sense of humor, friendliness, and attentiveness to the needs of others. In addition, they sought someone who was relaxed in social settings and who possessed an easygoing and amiable disposition.

3. Characteristics related to intellect

Intellect and other mental qualities were also considered very important by the participants. Both men and women sought a partner who was intellectually gifted—who possessed intelligence, enjoyed intellectual pursuits, was educated, and was knowledgeable about the arts.

4. Characteristics related to family orientation

Finally, the perfect mate also needed to want children and to possess a relatively high level of religiosity and other "hearth and home" attributes.

In addition to exploring what people seek in potential partners, some researchers have begun to examine the attributes that people seek to *avoid* when selecting dates or mates. For example, social scientists Michael Cunningham, Anita Barbee, and Perri Druen (1996; also see Ault & Philhower, 2001; Rowatt et al., 1997) argued that the extended time commitment involved in human reproduction requires that individuals evaluate their partners not only in terms of the positive qualities they offer but also in terms of whether their negative qualities can be endured. Research on these undesirable partner attributes or *social allergens* reveals that men and women are repulsed by people who consistently *violate social norms and rules of conduct,* including drinking too much alcohol, gambling, cheating at games, gossiping about others, arriving late all the time, and lying. In addition, they dislike partners who are *oversexed*—that is, who brag about sexual conquests or skills, constantly talk about or mention previous relationship partners, or gaze longingly at other men or women. People also seek to avoid partners who *display bad habits* (e.g., have poor table manners, stand too close or stare inappropriately, use a loud speaking voice) or who are *profane or "punk-like"* (e.g., use a lot of profanity, have a lot of tattoos or body piercings). In sum, individuals seek potential mates who not only fulfill their desires but also manage to avoid doing the things that repulse them.

Not only do men and women desire—and seek to avoid—similar features when considering a potential mate, but they are equally discriminating as well. Psychologist Douglas Kenrick and his colleagues (1993) asked a sample of young adults to indicate their minimum mate selection standards or the lowest amount of various characteristics they would consider acceptable when selecting a marriage partner. Their results revealed that neither men nor women would consider marrying someone unless he or she were above average (the 50th percentile) on nearly all attributes. In fact, summed across all characteristics, men's minimally acceptable mate scored at the 56th percentile, whereas women's minimally acceptable partner scored at the 60th percentile. In addition, there was only one significant sex difference: Women expressed higher minimum standards with respect to characteristics related to social status than did men. Regan (1998a) reported similar results. When it comes to selecting a long-term mate, both sexes appear to be highly selective.

INDIVIDUAL AND GROUP DIFFERENCES

We have seen that men and women have similar preferences with respect to their long-term romantic partners. In fact, there are only two attribute categories on which men and women demonstrate consistent differences: physical appearance and social status. Specifically, when considering a potential date or marriage partner, men tend to emphasize physical attractiveness more than do women, and women tend to emphasize social or economic position more than do men (for a review, see Feingold, 1992). For example, Susan Sprecher, Quintin Sullivan, and Elaine Hatfield (1994) asked a large national sample of men and women to indicate how willing they would be to marry someone who possessed a variety of characteristics. They found that men were significantly less willing than women to marry someone who was "not good-looking," whereas women were significantly less willing than men to marry a partner who was "not likely to hold a steady job" and who "would earn less than you." *Neither* sex, however, was very willing to marry an individual with these attributes. Thus, it is not the case that attractiveness is *un*important to women or that social status does *not* matter to men; rather, both sexes appear to value each of these two attributes, but to different degrees.

Culture is another variable that appears to be associated with romantic partner preferences. Although men and women from around the world value the same core group of dispositional features (e.g., emotional stability, honesty and trustworthiness, openness, a dependable character), robust cultural differences exist. For example, adults from collectivist cultures, such as China and India, tend to value "practical" characteristics (e.g., good housekeeper, money-mindedness) and demographic similarity (e.g., same religion, caste) in a potential spouse or long-term partner more than do adults from individualist cultures (Buss, Abbott, et al., 1990; Goodwin & Tang, 1991; Sprecher & Chandak, 1992). The emphasis placed on these particular constellations of features is understandable when we consider that many collectivist cultures have a history of (and still practice) arranged marriage. Selecting a partner based on practical considerations and demographic similarity increases the likelihood that the partners will be compatible, that the marriage will function smoothly, and that the couple will receive approval and support from their families and other social groups. Culture appears to be a much more powerful correlate of mate preference, in fact, than does sex or gender (see Goodwin, 1999).

DO WE ALWAYS GET WHAT
WE WANT? THE ISSUE OF COMPROMISE

A very important issue that must be addressed when interpreting research on mate preference concerns compromise. Most researchers interested in exploring partner preferences focus on what people want—that is, on the characteristics or attributes they seek in potential, and often idealized, partners. However, one of the realities of human existence in general—and certainly of human mating—is that, to quote a famous rock group's lyrics, "you can't always get what you want." In other words, although we might ideally want to date or marry someone with a particular set of features, we might not be able to attract someone with those attributes. Perhaps the desired partner is so attractive that he or she has many mating choices and we are merely one among many possible options. Perhaps we simply do not meet the desired partner's ideals. Maybe we are already paired with someone else and therefore not free to select a partner. Regardless of the reason, the bottom line is that we cannot always obtain the kind of partner we ideally desire. And so we must compromise.

The ability to make compromises in the arena of sex, love, and mating is extremely important. For example, if most people were completely unwilling to deviate from their ideal standards—that is, if they absolutely refused to consider less than perfect partners and to enter into less than ideal mating relationships—then little actual mating would take place; instead, everyone would be stuck in mating limbo waiting for that "perfect someone" to come along. Because a great deal of mating does occur, it is obvious that some degree of compromise must characterize the process of mate selection. Recognizing this, a few researchers have begun to explore when and how people make those compromises.

One of the first studies that provided evidence for the fact that people can and do alter their mating standards was conducted by psychologist James Pennebaker and his colleagues (1979). This creative field study took place over a 3-hour period in a number of bars and taverns located near a college campus. Specifically, at three preselected times—9:00 p.m., 10:30 p.m., and midnight (half an hour before closing)—the researchers entered the various establishments and asked a sample of randomly selected men and women to indicate how attractive they found the other bar patrons present at each of those times. Participants evaluated both same-sex and opposite-sex patrons. The researchers' results indicated that, as closing time neared, the perceived attractiveness of opposite-sex (but not same-sex) bar patrons increased significantly. In other words, the men got handsomer (according to the women) and the women got prettier (according to the men) as closing time approached. Assuming that the bar patrons actually did not alter their appearances over the course of the evening, and assuming that one goal of the participants was to select a potential mate from the existing pool, these results suggest that men's and women's mating standards are not set in stone but rather are actually quite flexible. When we think we are running out of time to select a mate, the available alternatives become more attractive.

Researchers have also found evidence that people moderate their mate preferences to take into account their own desirability or *mate value*. For example, in one study, Regan (1998d) asked a group of men and women to identify how much intelligence, attractiveness, humor, and so on they desired in a perfect romantic partner and then to estimate how much of each attribute they themselves possessed. She found a strong and positive correlation between ideal preferences and mate value. For example, women who thought that they possessed high amounts of attributes related to intellect, interpersonal skill and responsiveness, and social status demanded equally high levels of these desirable attributes from their potential partner, whereas women who believed that they had lower levels of those characteristics expected correspondingly lower levels from their potential partner. Similarly, men who possessed a strong family orientation (e.g., desire for children and related "hearth and home" attributes) preferred a long-term partner with the same high level of these characteristics. In addition, the greater a man estimated his own social status to be, the less willing he was to compromise on that dimension with respect to a potential romantic partner. The fact that people seem to link their expectations to their own mate value provides support for the principles of social exchange we discussed in Chapter 8 as well as additional evidence for the important role played by compromise in mate selection.

People also appear willing to moderate their preferences by making "trade-offs" among various sets of features. For example, Cunningham and colleagues (1997) found that both men and women selected partners who combined physical attractiveness with a pleasing personality over partners who possessed the combination of physical attractiveness and wealth or the combination of a pleasing personality and wealth. Similarly, Lauri Jensen-Campbell, William Graziano, and Stephen West (1995) reported that women preferred as dates men who possessed high levels of both agentic (e.g., active, assertive, bold, talkative) and agreeable (e.g., considerate, cooperative, kind, sympathetic) features over men who were agentic and disagreeable, nonagentic and agreeable, or nonagentic and disagreeable. And in a more recent study, Joanna Scheib (2001) found that women who were asked to imagine that they were selecting a husband overwhelmingly chose a less attractive man with a good character (e.g., dependable, faithful, kind and understanding, mature, patient) over a more attractive man with a less desirable character.

In sum, research indicates that men and women are willing to compromise their ideal mate standards by paying attention to external factors (e.g., selection time) that affect mate choice, by taking into account their own mate value, and by selectively choosing one characteristic or combination of characteristics over others.

DO WE ALWAYS KNOW WHAT WE WANT? THE ISSUE OF SELF-REPORT

No discussion of this topic area would be complete without a consideration of whether the self-report methodologies that most researchers use adequately capture people's mate preferences. There is some evidence that self-report methodologies may contribute to a misleading view of men's and women's mating desires. For example, sex differences are greater in self-report paradigms than in behavioral research paradigms (see Feingold, 1990). The results of a study conducted by Sprecher (1989) provide a compelling illustration of this phenomenon. In her study, men and women received information about an opposite-sex target who was presented as possessing high or low levels of three attributes: physical attractiveness, earning potential, and expressiveness. After rating the target's desirability as a dating partner, participants then were asked to indicate which of these factors they believed had influenced their evaluations. Men reported being more influenced than women by the target's physical appearance. Recall that this is the first of the two major sex differences commonly reported in the literature (i.e., men value physical attractiveness more than do women in potential romantic partners). However, the experimental data revealed that men and women were equally affected by the manipulation. That is, the physically attractive target was overwhelmingly preferred as a dating partner by both men and women. Similarly, women believed more than did men that their evaluations had been affected by the target's earning potential. This is the second major sex difference often found in the literature (i.e., women value social status and resource attributes more than do men in potential mates). As before, however, there was no actual sex difference in the impact of that variable on perceptions of the target. These results suggest that men and women may be differentially aware of (or motivated to reveal) the factors that influence their perceptions and evaluations of potential mates—an important consideration to keep in mind when evaluating research on partner preferences.

SUMMARY

In this chapter, we have explored the preferences and desires that people have for their dates, mates, and other long-term romantic partners. As was predicted from both of the theoretical frameworks we reviewed in Chapter 8, men and women generally prefer partners who possess a constellation of positive characteristics, ranging from internal or dispositional traits (e.g., intelligence, emotional stability, humor), to interpersonal attributes (e.g., friendliness, sociability), to physical features (e.g., attractiveness), to social variables (e.g., status). In addition, they seek to avoid certain particularly repellant features, and they seem willing to modify their preferences as a function of various factors, including their own mate value. In Chapter 10, we turn to a consideration of the ways in which people go about fulfilling their desires and obtaining the type of mate they seek.

KEY CONCEPTS

Self-report methodologies (pp. 109-110)
Content analyses (p. 110)
Social allergens (p. 113)
Mate value (p. 116)

DISCUSSION QUESTIONS

1. Compare and contrast the various methodologies available for examining mate preferences. Which one do you think provides the most accurate view of people's desires? Which one provides the least accurate view?

2. Consider what is known about men's and women's partner preferences. How does the empirical evidence support or contradict the social context and evolutionary theories that we reviewed in Chapter 8?

3. Discuss cultural differences and similarities in mate preference. How do cross-cultural similarities support an evolutionary view of human mating?

4. Collect a sample of personal ads. What do people seek in a potential partner? What do they advertise? Make a list. Are there any similarities among your sample of writers? How do the preferences contained in the ads compare with research from self-report studies of mate preference?

5. Make a list of all the attributes, behaviors, and characteristics that you find repellant in a romantic partner. Compare your list with the "social allergens" identified by Cunningham and colleagues (1996, 1997). Are there any similarities? Any differences?

RECOMMENDED READINGS

Deaux, K., & Hanna, R. (1984). Courtship in the personals column: The influence of gender and sexual orientation. *Sex Roles, 11,* 363-375.

Jensen-Campbell, L. A., Graziano, W. G., & West, S. (1995). Dominance, prosocial orientation, and female preferences: Do nice guys really finish last? *Journal of Personality and Social Psychology, 68,* 427-440.

Kenrick, D. T., Groth, G. E., Trost, M. R., & Sadalla, E. K. (1993). Integrating evolutionary and social exchange perspectives on relationships: Effects of gender, self-appraisal, and involvement level on mate selection criteria. *Journal of Personality and Social Psychology, 64,* 951-969.

Regan, P. C., & Berscheid, E. (1997). Gender differences in characteristics desired in a potential sexual and marriage partner. *Journal of Psychology and Human Sexuality, 9,* 25-37.

Wiederman, M. W., & Allgeier, E. R. (1992). Gender differences in mate selection criteria: Sociobiological or socioeconomic explanation? *Ethology and Sociobiology, 13,* 115-124.

The authors of these articles use different methodological approaches to investigate mate preferences.

Langlois, J, H., Kalakanis, L., Rubenstein, A. J., Larson, A., Hallam, M., & Smoot, M. (2000). Maxims or myths of beauty? A meta-analytic and theoretical review. *Psychological Bulletin, 126,* 390-423.

This meta-analysis reveals that physical attractiveness is as important a social asset for men to possess as it is for women to possess. The authors argue that theories emphasizing sex differences (e.g., parental investment-based evolutionary frameworks) may be less accurate than others in explaining the social impact of physical attractiveness.

10

Attraction and Courtship

Chapter Outline

Most animal species perform courtship rituals designed to attract and secure the attention of a reproductive partner. For example, the male African widowbird performs an elaborate hopping display in which he fans his magnificent 18-inch tail and skims over the ground using exaggeratedly slow wingbeats. The male sage grouse puffs his chest, raises his white neck feathers, spreads his tail, lifts his wings, and makes a loud popping noise by expelling air from a specialized sac in his throat. The male bowerbird builds a structure to attract his mate, decorating it with flowers and bits of glass and painting the walls with a mixture of saliva and chewed-up fruits and grass. We humans also perform various behaviors in the process of courting a potential mate (although perhaps not as colorful as those exhibited by our animal counterparts).

INITIAL ENCOUNTERS:
COMMUNICATING ROMANTIC INTEREST

Researchers have identified a repertoire of facial expressions, gestures, and other nonverbal behaviors that serve as signals designed to communicate attraction and romantic interest to a potential partner. For example, in one study, psychologists Naomi McCormick and Andrew Jones (1989) examined the nonverbal flirting behavior of heterosexual couples. Trained confederates, working for the researchers, observed 70 pairs of unmarried men and women interacting in bars, taverns, and cocktail lounges. Each couple was watched for a period of 15 minutes, and their nonverbal behaviors were coded. The results revealed that men and women engaged in a number of flirting behaviors designed to communicate romantic interest. One of the most common behaviors displayed by both sexes was that of moving closer to the potential partner and gazing into his or her eyes. Other acts included smiling, laughing, and displaying other positive facial expressions along with such grooming activities as self-touching, smoothing one's hair, tightening one's abdomen, arching one's back, and stretching.

Similar results were reported by anthropologist David Givens (1978), who observed male-female pairs of college students in initial encounters ranging from having coffee together for the first time after class to conversing for the first time at a cafeteria table. Typical nonverbal behaviors displayed by both men and women included facing the partner, gazing directly at the partner as well as in a downward direction, abundant smiling, and such "automanipulation" behaviors as clasping the hands, covering the mouth, and touching the cheek or neck. Givens posited that these nonverbal actions contain a mix of friendliness and submissiveness that conveys "an interest in the partner that is coupled with covert denials of aggressiveness and threat" (p. 355). Such behaviors serve as a potent signal that romantic overtures will be well received.

Research also reveals that interpersonal touch is another powerful communicator of attraction. Men and women in one investigation were asked to provide a detailed description of their most recent flirtation episode (Abrahams, 1994). A second group of participants then rated these accounts in terms of how flirtatious they appeared to be. Accounts rated as highly flirtatious tended to contain references to interpersonal touch, including specific actions such as "I began to rub my fingers up her arm," "I then lightly hit her with a pillow, which led to a pillow fight that ended in us holding each other," "I lightly touched him on the shoulder," and "I moved my head closer to his [and] we put our arms around each other." Other researchers have similarly found that interpersonal touch communicates attraction, interest, liking, and intimacy (Burgoon, Buller, Hale, & deTurck, 1984).

Smiling, touch, and other nonverbal actions are not the only means by which men and women convey romantic interest to potential mates. Social scientists Jerrold Downey and Katharina Damhave (1991) set out to explore people's perceptions of what constitutes flirting. Participants in their study were asked to read a number of hypothetical scenarios involving an interaction between themselves and a stranger. These scenarios differed along three dimensions: location (school hallway or restaurant bar), amount of effort expended by the stranger (makes inadvertent eye contact vs. goes out of his or her way to approach), and type of comment made by the stranger (pays a compliment vs. asks for the time). For each scenario, participants indicated whether they believed that the stranger was flirting with them or not. The results revealed significantly higher percentages of "yes" (i.e., flirting) responses when the stranger was in the restaurant bar as opposed to the school hallway (61% vs. 49%), when the stranger made an effort to go out of his or her way as opposed to making inadvertent and non-effortful eye contact (68% vs. 41%), and when the stranger paid a compliment as opposed to asking for the time (83% vs. 26%). Not surprisingly, given this pattern of results, the scenario that produced the highest percentage of "yes" responses (74%) was that involving a stranger who went out of his or her way to compliment the target while in the "flirt-friendly" setting of a restaurant bar.

In sum, researchers have identified a wide array of nonverbal and verbal actions that are used by men and women to convey romantic interest.

Does Flirting Work?

The real question, of course, is whether or not these flirting behaviors actually "work." Do smiles, touches, effortful approaches, and sincere compliments do what they are designed to do—that is, prompt romantic interest and overtures from potential mates? To answer this question, psychologist Monica Moore (1985) unobtrusively observed 40 women (ranging in estimated age from 18 to 35 years) in four different social settings: a local singles bar, a university snack bar, a university library, and a meeting at a university women's center. Women were selected for observation only if they were surrounded by at least 25 other people and if they were not accompanied by a man. During each hour-long observational period, both the type (e.g., smiling, sustained gazing, hair flipping, head tossing) and the number of flirting behaviors demonstrated by each woman were recorded.

There were a number of interesting results. First, Moore (1985) found that women's flirting behavior was context specific. That is, women in the singles bar (the most likely setting in which to meet a mate) flirted significantly more frequently than did women in the other three settings. In addition, women in the snack bar flirted more than did women in the library, who in turn flirted more than did women in the women's center (the least likely setting to meet a mate, assuming a heterosexual sample). Second, Moore found that women in the singles bar increased their rate of flirtatious display over the observational period; they flirted more as the hour passed. However, flirting behavior was constant (i.e., did not change over time) in the other three contexts. Third, and perhaps most important, the results revealed that women's flirting behaviors actually were quite effective at eliciting interest from potential mates. Specifically, regardless of the setting the women who engaged in the most flirting behavior were also those who were approached most often by men. Thus, flirting does appear to work!

THE FIRST DATE

After an initial encounter, and assuming the successful communication of romantic interest, two people may further their relationship by embarking on an "official" romantic interaction—the first date. Given the existence of the traditional (heterosexual) sexual script (see Chapter 6), it is not surprising that both men and women believe that it is more socially appropriate for a man to initiate a date than for a woman to do so (Green & Sandos, 1983). Compared with women, men also report a greater willingness to initiate dates and a higher frequency of actual relationship initiations (Clark, Shaver, & Abrahams, 1999; Green & Sandos, 1983; McNamara & Grossman, 1991; Spreadbury, 1982).

These results notwithstanding, there is some evidence that many heterosexual men would like women to take a more active role in relationship initiation than the traditional script would seem to allow. In one survey (Muehlenhard & Miller, 1988), for example, more than 200 undergraduate men indicated their preferences with regard to three different approaches a woman might make to initiate a date: *asking directly* for a date, *hinting* for a date, and simply *waiting* for the man to ask her out. The majority preferred the more direct approaches. Specifically, 44% said that they preferred a woman to ask for a date, and 53% indicated that they preferred a woman to hint for a date. Only 3% of the men surveyed stated that they preferred a woman to adopt the passive and indirect approach of simply waiting to be asked out. In addition, provided that they liked the woman, nearly all of the men believed that the strategies of directly asking (99%) and hinting (93%) would result in a date. Few men (4%) believed that waiting would result in a date, even if they themselves liked the woman and wanted to go out with her. The initiation of a dating relationship clearly requires active efforts on the part of both individuals.

So, what prevents men—and women, for that matter—from pursuing dates with individuals to whom they are attracted? One of the primary reasons why people fail to initiate dating relationships concerns their fear of being rebuffed by the objects of their affection. Jacquie Vorauer and Rebecca Ratner (1996) asked a sample of 291 men and women whether a fear of rejection had ever been a "significant obstacle" to their pursuing a romantic relationship with another individual. The majority (76%) responded affirmatively, suggesting that the experience of fearful inhibition is quite common. The researchers then asked a second set of participants to imagine themselves in the following situation:

> You are at a party; currently, you are not seriously romantically involved with anyone. Early in the evening, you are introduced to a single person who could be a potential romantic partner. You learn from a brief conversation that you have a lot in common. In your opinion, the two of you are equally physically attractive. Toward the end of the evening, you find yourself alone in the kitchen with the person. You talk with each other for a while. Neither of you explicitly expresses a romantic interest in the other, or an interest in seeing the other again. You head back to join the group in the living room. (pp. 491-492)

After reading the scenario, men and women indicated which of two possible alternatives explained their own and the other person's inaction: lack of romantic interest or fear of being rejected. Interestingly, the results provided strong evidence for *pluralistic ignorance*, a phenomenon in which people observe others behaving similarly to themselves but attribute their own behavior and that of the others to very different underlying causes. In this case, participants attributed their own failure to make a romantic overture to fear of rejection (74%); however, they assumed that the other person's inactivity was caused by a lack of interest (71%). This attributional bias may create a dynamic that impedes a potentially rewarding romantic relationship from even starting. The researchers summarized the process as follows:

> Individuals who are romantically interested in one another hesitate to make their feelings explicit because they fear that they will be rejected. However, even though both people are engaging in the same "waiting" behavior, they apply different explanations to their own and the other person's conduct. They see their own failure to make initiatives as stemming from a fear of rejection, but attribute the other person's inaction to a lack of interest. These unwarranted negative inferences about the other person's feelings subsequently exacerbate individuals' hesitation to take the risk of conveying their affection, leading them to give up on the relationship prematurely. (p. 484)

Thus, it is no wonder that women want men to make the first move when it comes to initiating a first date and that men wish that women would make the first move more often!

What Happens During a First Date?

What occurs during a "typical" first date between a man and a woman? In an effort to answer this question, psychologists John Pryor and Thomas Merluzzi (1985) asked a sample of undergraduate students to list the "typical things that occur when a male and a female decide to go on a first date" (p. 365). Participants were instructed to generate events that happen in the "getting a date" stage as well as events that happen during the date itself. The following event sequence was viewed as typical during a first date initiation:

Step 1: Notice each other (with the man noticing the woman first).

Step 2: Get caught staring at each other.

Step 3: Smile.

Step 4: Find out about the other person from friends.

Step 5: Create ways in which to "accidentally" run into each other.

Step 6: Get introduced by a friend.

Step 7: The woman says "hello" and the man begins the conversation.

Step 8: Make an attempt during conversation to find common interests.

Step 9: The man asks the woman for her phone number.

Step 10: The man phones the woman later to ask her out, beginning the conversation with "small talk" and then making arrangements for the date.

Both men and women generated this same type of sequence. Their scripts for the actual first date were similarly identical:

Step 1: The man arrives to pick up the woman for the date.

Step 2: The woman greets the man at the door.

Step 3: They make conversation.

Step 4: The woman introduces her date to her parents/roommates, and the two leave the house/apartment/dormitory.

Step 5: They discuss where they will go on their date.

Step 6: They talk about common interests (i.e., make "small talk").

Step 7: They go to a movie.

Step 8: The man buys refreshments at the movie.

Step 9: They then go get something to eat/drink and continue their conversation.

Step 10: The man takes the woman home.

Step 11: The man walks the woman to her door.

Step 12: They exchange complimentary views of the evening.

Step 13: If interested, the man asks to call again/the woman hopes the man asks to call again.

Step 14: They kiss.

Step 15: They say "good night" and thank each other for the evening.

Step 16: The man returns home.

In this study (Pryor & Merluzzi, 1985), both men and women agreed on the sequencing of events. However, more recent research suggests that men and women may possess slightly different first date scripts. For example, although the "good night kiss" remains a fixed feature of this particular social interaction, heterosexual men often expect greater sexual involvement than do heterosexual women on a first date (Mongeau & Johnson, 1995). Indeed, there is evidence that men and women may pursue different goals when initiating a romantic relationship. Catherine Clark, Phillip Shaver, and Matthew Abrahams (1999) asked a large sample of undergraduates to describe what goals they had pursued in the initiation of their two most recent successful romantic relationships. The primary goal identified by the researchers concerned love; most men (84%) and women (81%) said that they sought to obtain a loving, caring, serious relationship. Other relatively common goals mentioned by equal numbers of both sexes included fun (cited by 18% of the men and 16% of the women) and learning (e.g., to experience dating, learn more about the other person [cited by 16% of the men and 18% of the women]). Only one sex difference was found. Far more men (30%) than women (8%) identified sexual intimacy—including kissing, intercourse, and just "following hormones"—as the reason why they sought to initiate a dating relationship.

The different expectations that men and women may bring to their initial romantic interactions may result in misunderstanding and miscommunication. For example, a woman who wishes to communicate her feelings of affection and liking for a new dating partner may smile at him and engage in other nonverbal displays. The woman's partner, whose goal may be one of sexual intimacy, may misinterpret her behavior as indicating sexual attraction. Indeed, researchers have found that men are much more likely than women to perceive a number of interpersonal cues as signaling an interest in sex (e.g., Abbey, 1982; Abbey & Melby, 1986; Zellman & Goodchilds, 1983). For example, a study conducted by Robin Kowalski (1993) revealed that men imputed a higher desire for sexual intercourse than did women to a woman who was described as engaging in common dating behaviors such as accepting a man's invitation for a date, having dinner with him, maintaining eye contact with him, smiling at him, allowing him to pay for dinner, and complimenting him. Perhaps not surprisingly, other researchers have found that women are more likely than men to report having had their friendliness toward someone of the opposite sex mistakenly perceived as a sign of sexual interest (Abbey, 1987). Clearly, knowledge of the different ways in which men and women perceive interpersonal cues, along with direct and open communication of dating goals and desires, is essential between partners during the early stages of a romantic relationship.

BEYOND THE FIRST DATE: INITIATING A ROMANTIC RELATIONSHIP

Only a very small portion of the first dates and other initial encounters that we have with potential partners actually will evolve into stable romantic relationships. What strategies do men and women use when trying to move relationships beyond those beginning stages? To explore this question, communication scholar James Tolhuizen (1989) asked men and women who had been or who were involved in a serious dating relationship to describe the things they said or did to intensify their relationship and change it from "one of casual dating to one of serious and exclusive dating" (p. 418). Analysis of participants' free responses revealed that the most common strategy was to *increase contact*; more than 39% of the participants reported increasing the frequency and duration of their contact and interaction with the partner. Another commonly used method was *relationship negotiation* or direct discussion of the relationship, feelings between the partners, and the future of the relationship (29%). Participants also sought *social support and assistance* from individuals in their social networks, usually by asking for advice on how to proceed in intensifying the relationship (26%). Other strategies included *increasing the partner's rewards* (18% [e.g., paying compliments, doing favors]), *making a direct bid* for a more serious relationship (17% [e.g., directly requesting a more exclusive or serious relationship]), giving the partner *tokens of affection* (16% [e.g., giving gifts, cards, or other items that symbolize feelings of affection for the partner]), providing *verbal expressions of affection* (14% [e.g., declaring feelings of love, caring, or affection for the partner]), and *accepting a direct bid* for a more serious relationship (10% [e.g., agreeing to a direct request for a more exclusive relationship]). Not surprisingly, men and women differed slightly in the types of strategies they reported. Men were significantly more likely to report using verbal expressions of affection and making a direct relationship bid, whereas women were more likely to report using relationship negotiation and accepting a direct relationship bid.

Similar results were reported by Clark and colleagues (1999), who asked a large group of undergraduates to describe the strategies they used when initiating a romantic relationship. Participants reported engaging in a variety of behaviors to propel a relationship through its beginning stages. One of the most common categories of strategy involved *emotional disclosure*. For example, the majority of participants said that they talked in person (94%), talked on the phone (54%), and spent time (85%) with the partner. *Direct and forward action* was also mentioned frequently. Specifically, participants reported asking the other person directly to be their girlfriend or boyfriend (63%) and touching (64% [e.g., kissing, hand holding]). As in Tolhuizen's study, participants also clearly used their social networks to promote the relationship. Approximately 86% reported that third parties helped to initiate and intensify the relationship by engaging in such activities as discovering whether a potential partner was available and/or interested, by introducing the two people, and by going out with them as the relationship began to develop.

In sum, men and women enact a number of behaviors as they attempt to shape their initial encounters with a potential date or mate into a more enduring relationship.

PATHWAYS TO COMMITMENT

As noted earlier, many relationships do not stand the test of time despite the best efforts of the couples to promote or intensify their development. Some relationships, however, will survive beyond the initial exchanges and continue along a path toward commitment. A number of different courtship patterns or trajectories to commitment have been identified. In one early study, social scientist Catherine Surra (1985) asked a sample of young newlywed couples to retrospectively report on how the partners' commitment to each other had changed from the time they first met to the day of their wedding. Specifically, husbands and wives were instructed to estimate the chance of marriage (on a scale ranging from 0% to 100%) that they felt characterized their relationship from the date it began, during the subsequent months of courtship, and up until the wedding day (which naturally received a "chance-of-marriage" rating of 100%). These estimated chance-of-marriage values were placed on a graph that provided a pictorial view of each couple's pathway to commitment.

Surra (1985) then coded monthly chance-of-marriage values for each participant and derived a number of additional variables from the graphs, including length of courtship (number of months from the beginning of the relationship to the wedding day), degree of acceleration (number of months it took for the couple to move from a low [25%] to a high [75%] chance of marriage), number of turning points (upturns and downturns in the graph), and length of stage of involvement (number of months the couple spent in the casually dating, seriously dating, and engaged stages of involvement).

Analysis of the monthly chance-of-marriage values and the derived variables revealed four different courtship paths or trajectories to marital commitment. Couples on an *accelerated* courtship trajectory moved rapidly and smoothly to marriage, spent relatively little time dating prior to engagement, and experienced a higher index of upturns (turning points characterized by increased commitment) than did other couple types. *Accelerated-arrested* couples also experienced a high number of upturns, which Surra (1985) hypothesized may provide momentum to the courtship process. The courtship of these couples was characterized by an even more rapid trajectory to marriage. Specifically, accelerated-arrested couples devoted very little time to dating, preferring to become engaged very quickly and then spending most (nearly 60%) of their courtship in this stage. Couples on a *prolonged* trajectory to marital commitment demonstrated the reverse pattern; that is, they spent 65% of their courtship seriously dating and only 22% of it engaged. The *intermediate* courtship type fell somewhere in between the two accelerated types and the prolonged type in the smoothness and rapidity of its progression toward commitment.

Essentially, Surra's (1985) research demonstrated that there is no one path toward permanence; couples may achieve commitment in a variety of ways.

SUMMARY

During initial romantic encounters, men and women engage in a number of behaviors designed to attract a potential mate. Eye contact, smiling, interpersonal touch, and other flirtatious behaviors all serve to convey romantic interest. Following these initial interactions, many individuals may further the relationship by embarking on a first date. Research indicates that a first date often involves a series of scripted behaviors and action sequences, in some instances including the communication of sexual attraction and the willingness to engage in some form of sexual contact (e.g., good night kiss). After a first date or series of initial encounters, one or both partners may attempt to intensify the relationship or propel it to a state of greater permanence through engaging in various affectional and communicative behaviors. Assuming that the relationship does, in fact, endure beyond these beginning stages, a couple may progress along one of several different pathways to commitment. In Chapter 11, we consider the actual processes that serve to move couples along their courtship trajectory.

KEY CONCEPTS

Flirting behavior (p. 122)
First date (p. 124)
Heterosexual sexual script (p. 124)
Pluralistic ignorance (p. 126)
First date script (pp. 127-128)
Accelerated courtship pattern (p. 131)
Accelerated-arrested courtship pattern (p. 131)
Prolonged courtship pattern (p. 131)
Intermediate courtship pattern (p. 131)

DISCUSSION QUESTIONS

1. Describe the nonverbal behaviors that people use to signal their romantic interest. Does flirting "work"?

2. In what ways might pluralistic ignorance contribute to missed dating opportunities?

3. Create your own "first date" script. How does the typical first date script identified by researchers differ from—or resemble—your own? What do you think explains the difference between men's and women's first date scripts? How would the theories we reviewed in Chapter 8 explain this sex difference?

4. In what ways might perceptions about sexual interest and intent contribute to interpersonal conflict and miscommunication?

RECOMMENDED READINGS

Pryor, J. B., & Merluzzi, T. V. (1985). The role of expertise in processing social interaction scripts. *Journal of Experimental Social Psychology, 21*, 362-379.

Rose, S., & Frieze, I. H. (1989). Young singles' scripts for a first date. *Gender & Society, 3*, 258-268.

Rose, S., & Frieze, I. H. (1993). Young singles' contemporary dating scripts. *Sex Roles, 28*, 499-509.

These three articles examine men's and women's expectations about the events that occur during a first date.

Cate, R. M., & Lloyd, S. A. (1992). *Courtship.* Newbury Park, CA: Sage.

This book explores the topic of courtship, including the events that take place during courtship, the relation between courtship and later relational outcomes (e.g., marriage), and problematic aspects of courtship (e.g., violence).

11

Relationship Development

Chapter Outline

In Chapter 10, we discussed how initial encounters with potential partners can lead to the establishment of a more permanent relationship. We also considered the behavioral strategies that men and women use to communicate romantic interest to a partner and to intensify the relationship and propel it along its developmental trajectory. In this chapter, we review a variety of theories that have been proposed to explain exactly how romantic relationships progress and develop over time.

THE SEQUENCE OF RELATIONSHIP DEVELOPMENT

Early theories of relationship development proposed that couples move through a sequential series of stages that are characterized by increasing amounts of commitment and involvement. Each stage was assumed to revolve around a particular developmental issue whose resolution propelled the couple into the next stage. Although largely supplanted by process-oriented theories, these *stage models* represent an important first step toward understanding relationship progression.

Filter Theory

Based on a longitudinal study of the experiences of dating couples, Alan Kerckhoff and Keith Davis (1962) proposed that various "filtering factors" operate during the process of mate selection. According to *Filter Theory*, specific filters come into prominence at different phases of courtship. First, potential partners are screened or evaluated in terms of their similarity on *social attributes*, including religion, education, and social class. People who are deemed to be too different with respect to these social attributes are filtered out from the field of potential mates. At that point, possible partners are screened with respect to similarity on attitudes and values or *value consensus*. As before, those who are judged to be too dissimilar are filtered out. Finally, partners are evaluated on *need complementarity* or whether they possess complementary or compatible traits, behavioral characteristics, or interpersonal styles. In reviewing the data collected from their sample of couples, the authors concluded the following:

> These findings are interpreted as indicating that a series of "filtering factors" operate in mate selection at different stages of the selection process. Our data generally support the idea that social status variables (class, religion, etc.) operate in the early stages,

consensus on values somewhat later, and need complementarity still later. (p. 303)

The notion that different aspects of the "fit" between two partners would become important at different times in their courtship makes implicit sense. During early courtship stages, demographic similarity might be of utmost importance in promoting a couple's relational growth. Later, as the couple begins to enter more committed or involved stages of courtship, similarity on underlying values and belief systems, and compatibility with regard to interpersonal styles, might become more important in determining whether or not the relationship continues. However, although conceptually interesting, subsequent research generally has not supported this model of relationship development (e.g., Levinger, Senn, & Jorgensen, 1970; for a review, see Levinger, 1983).

Wheel Theory

Sociologist Ira Reiss (e.g., 1960, 1980) also proposed one of the first developmental models of mate selection. According to the *Wheel Theory of Love*, the "mate-selecting process" involves four sequential but highly interrelated stages. During the initial stage, called *rapport*, potential partners assess the extent to which they feel at ease with, understand, and feel free to talk with each other. The process of establishing and feeling rapport is facilitated by similarity; Reiss suggests that we are most able to feel rapport with those who resemble us on key social and cultural variables (e.g., religious upbringing, educational background). Feelings of rapport, in turn, increase the likelihood that individuals will begin a process of mutual *self-revelation* in which they reveal or disclose varying degrees of information about their values and belief systems to each other. These acts of self-revelation, in turn, contribute to *mutual dependency*, such that each partner becomes dependent on the other to fulfill his or her habits or obtain certain goals. For example, Reiss (1980) wrote, "One needs the other person as an audience for one's jokes, as a confidant(e) for the expression of one's fears and wishes, as a partner for one's sexual needs, and so forth" (p. 127). When these goals or habits are not fulfilled, the person will experience frustration and loneliness; consequently, these habits tend to perpetuate a relationship. The fourth and final stage in the development of love relationships is called *intimacy need fulfillment*. Here, the partners evaluate whether their relationship and their interactions with each other satisfy basic intimacy needs, including love, sympathy, and support. These needs, as they are fulfilled, "express the closeness and privacy of the relationship" (p. 128).

Stimulus-Value-Role Theory

Another popular theory of romantic relationship development was proposed by Bernard Murstein (e.g., 1970, 1976). *Stimulus-Value-Role Theory* suggests that couples progress through three stages in mate selection. During the *stimulus* stage, the potential mates perceive each other's external attributes, physical appearance, and behavior, and each evaluates his or her own attributes in terms of how attractive they might be to the partner. Based on this comparison, the individuals estimate the likelihood that their attraction will be reciprocated and that future interaction with the other will be rewarding. If this estimate is favorable (i.e., if each believes that the other will like him or her and find his or her attributes desirable and that additional interaction will be rewarding), then the individuals are propelled into the next stage. During the *value* stage, the partners appraise their compatibility on various values and attitudes. This process of value appraisal allows them to continue to assess the potential benefits or rewards of the relationship. During the final *role* stage, the partners evaluate themselves and each other for suitability in various roles (e.g., spouse, parent). These stages are seen as relatively distinct; for example, Murstein (1987) asserted that stimulus information is gathered during the first encounter, that value information is collected during the second to seventh encounters, and that role assessments are made during and after the eighth encounter. However, he also noted that individuals make stimulus, value, and role assessments of each other throughout the entire courtship process; each factor simply becomes more prominent during a particular stage.

Although historically interesting, stage models of relationship development have fallen out of scientific favor for a number of reasons. First, stage theorists do not agree on the number, the sequence, or even the characteristics of the various stages of courtship. Second, not all relationships progress through the same stages. Third, couples differ in the rate at which they pass through particular courtship stages (e.g., Cate, Huston, & Nesselroade, 1986; Huston, Surra, Fitzgerald, & Cate, 1981; Surra, 1985). And finally, a number of process models have been developed that seem to capture more accurately the how and why of relationship progression.

THE PROCESS OF RELATIONSHIP DEVELOPMENT

The majority of theorists now agree that romantic relationships develop gradually over time rather than by passing through a series of discrete stages. *Process models* suggest that relationship development is fueled by sometimes imperceptible changes in intimacy, self-disclosure, and other interpersonal processes that occur between partners.

Self-Disclosure and Intimacy

Irwin Altman and Dalmas Taylor (1973) proposed one of the first process models of relationship progression. *Social Penetration Theory* targets self-disclosure as the fuel that propels couples along their developmental trajectory. Specifically, romantic partners are believed to become progressively more committed to each other as they increase both the *depth* (degree of intimacy) and *breadth* (number of areas) of their self-disclosure. At first, relationships are characterized by superficial shallow exchanges in which the partners reveal relatively impersonal information (low depth) along very few dimensions (low breadth). Meeting for the first time at a college party, for example, Jen and Paul might exchange information about their majors, their musical preferences, and the food being served by the host of the party. If these initial disclosures are rewarding and if each believes that future interactions will also be rewarding, then presumably they will progress to more intimate exchanges in which they reveal increasingly intimate, emotional, and detailed personal information about themselves along a greater number of dimensions. Following their enjoyable conversation at the party, Jen and Paul might begin to meet a few times a week for coffee. During these interactions, Paul might disclose his ambivalent feelings about his parents and their expectations about his future career. Jen, in turn, might reveal the problems she is experiencing with her roommate and her secret desire to spend a year hiking in the Himalayas.

Other theorists have subsequently expanded this theory by proposing that it is not only the depth and breadth of self-disclosure that propel a couple's relationship along its courtship path but also how responsive each partner is to the other's disclosures. According to

Intimacy Theory (Reis & Patrick, 1996; Reis & Shaver, 1988), responses that leave the partner feeling validated, understood, cared for, accepted, and nurtured promote the growth of intimacy and the subsequent development of the relationship. In the preceding example, Jen's acknowledgment of Paul's statements about his parents, her expressions of sympathy, her responsiveness and willingness to continue the conversation, and her reciprocal disclosures all serve to communicate that she understands the situation and that she respects Paul's point of view. This, in turn, will increase Paul's sense of trust and security and will promote intimacy and the development of the relationship. To the extent that Jen fails to reciprocate ("Let's talk about something else"), challenges ("I've never had those feelings about my own parents"), or dismisses ("Hey, I didn't come here to listen to you whine about your personal problems") Paul's revelations, intimacy will decrease and the relationship may stall or be compromised. Thus, it is not simply the act of disclosing information or making personal revelations that contributes to relationship development. Rather, _reciprocal_ disclosures that contribute to _feelings of intimacy_—in other words, disclosures that reflect mutual perceptions of understanding, caring, and validation—are what encourage and sustain the growth of romantic relationships.

Many of these theoretical statements have received empirical support. For example, self-disclosure and intimacy appear to be integrally connected with both relationship satisfaction and stability. Research conducted with dating and married couples generally reveals that people who self-disclose, who perceive their partners as self-disclosing, and who believe that their disclosures and confidences are understood by their partners experience greater need fulfillment, satisfaction, and love than people whose relationships contain lower levels of intimacy and disclosure (e.g., Morrow & O'Sullivan, 1998; Prager & Buhrmester, 1998; Rosenfeld & Bowen, 1991). In one study, for example, Brenda Meeks and her colleagues (Meeks, Hendrick, & Hendrick, 1998) asked 140 couples to complete a variety of measures, including a relationship satisfaction scale, a self-perceived self-disclosure index that assessed participants' tendency to disclose to the partner, a partner-perceived self-disclosure scale that reflected participants' evaluations about their partners' level of self-disclosure, a self-reported perspective-taking scale designed to assess participants' general awareness of and ability to understand the partner, and a partner-perceived perspective-taking scale that assessed participants' perceptions of the partner's perspective-taking abilities.

The correlational analyses revealed strong positive associations between relationship satisfaction and the other measures for both men and women. Specifically, participants who believed that they themselves self-disclosed and that their partners also self-disclosed tended to be very satisfied with the relationship. Similarly, participants who believed that they were able to take the partner's perspective and that the partner was able to take their perspective were very satisfied. In sum, mutuality—of disclosure and perspective taking—was strongly correlated with overall relationship satisfaction.

In fact, men and women often consciously use self-disclosure and expressions of intimacy as strategies for intensifying and maintaining their romantic relationships. For example, communication researchers Stephen Haas and Laura Stafford (1998) asked a convenience sample of men and women involved in committed (homosexual) romantic relationships to report on the behaviors that they used to maintain their relationships. Although participants generated a number of maintenance strategies, one of the most commonly cited was self-disclosure. Specifically, 57% of the sample specified open and honest communication about thoughts and feelings, including disclosures about the relationship, as an effective way in which to maintain the romantic relationship. Less "deep" communication, akin to "small talk," was mentioned by close to 25% as a means by which the relationship is maintained. Research conducted with heterosexual samples corroborates these findings (for a review, see Dindia, 2000).

The process of revealing oneself to another, particularly when accompanied by reciprocity and validation, appears to play an essential role in the progression of romantic relationships.

Social Exchange

Many theories of relationship development are grounded in principles of _social exchange_ (e.g., Adams, 1965; Hatfield, Utne, & Traupmann, 1979; Homans, 1961; Walster, Walster, & Berscheid, 1978). These theories focus on the exchange of rewards and costs that occurs between partners in ongoing mating relationships. Although a number of social exchange theories exist, each with its own particular terminology and "take" on the process of relationship development, all share a few basic assumptions (some of which we reviewed in Chapter 8).

Principle 1: Maximize rewards, minimize costs. The first assumption is that individuals seek to maximize their rewards and minimize their costs in any given relationship. *Rewards* are anything that the individual considers valuable; they can range from the concrete and tangible to the abstract and intangible. For example, Robert's marriage with Vicki may provide him with a number of concrete benefits that he values, including financial security, sex, children, and the social profit that comes from having an attractive and intelligent partner. This relationship also may provide Robert with a variety of less tangible rewards, including love, emotional support, and the fulfillment of life goals involving marriage and fatherhood. *Costs* are those things that the individual considers to be unrewarding or that involve time, effort, compromise, or lost opportunity. To maintain his relationship with Vicki, for instance, Robert contributes to the housework, shares parenting tasks, listens supportively to Vicki's complaints about her new coworker, and spends vacations with his (greatly detested) in-laws.

Of course, what is rewarding or costly for one person might not be rewarding for another. Fresh-baked cookies are rewarding to a child but distinctly costly to an adult trying to stay on a diet; an invitation to the opera might fill some with glee, while it fills others with dismay; and a foot massage might be pleasing when offered by a loved one but creepy if offered by a casual business associate. In addition, two individuals in a relationship might not agree on the value of a particular reward or cost. For example, Robert may place greater worth on the housework he does than Vicki places on Robert's housework.

Principle 2: Relationships are dynamic. The second assumption shared by social exchange theories is that relationships themselves are dynamic; they change over time. Relational partners are assumed to engage in a continual process of evaluation whereby they assess each other's gains and losses, profits and expenditures, and rewards and costs. This means that a relationship that is seen as equitable and satisfying at one point in time may come to be viewed as less equitable and satisfying (and even as inequitable and dissatisfying) as the gains and losses of each partner change over time. This happens, in part, because of the shifting nature of rewards and costs. A particular event, behavior, or occurrence may become less rewarding and/or more costly as it occurs repeatedly or as the relationship progresses. Two people caught up in the thrill of a new love might find sexual activity to be highly rewarding and not at all costly. Over time, as they become used to each other and the novelty of their passion decreases, they may come to view sexual activity as less rewarding.

Principle 3: Evaluations influence relationship development. Third, social exchange theories assume that the result of each partner's cost-benefit evaluation determines the course of the relationship. For example, two strangers might meet at a party. Following their initial contact, each person evaluates the immediate outcomes of that interaction and makes a prediction about the outcomes of future interactions. If these evaluations and predictions are positive ("What a fun conversation; she seemed to really like me, and we have so much in common"), then the individuals are likely to continue down the path to romantic involvement. If the evaluations and predictions are negative ("He didn't listen to a thing I said; we have nothing in common, and what's with those clothes?"), then the two are unlikely to maintain anything other than a superficial relationship; they may even cease to interact altogether.

Principle 4: Evaluations influence relationship satisfaction. A fourth (and related) assumption is that the partners' perceptions of the outcomes they obtain from the relationship are strongly linked with their level of satisfaction. Exchange frameworks posit that people will be most satisfied with a relationship when the ratio between the benefits derived from the relationship and the contributions made to the relationship is similar for both partners, that is, when they perceive the relationship to be characterized by *equity*:

$$\frac{\text{Vicki's benefits}}{\text{Vicki's contributions}} = \frac{\text{Robert's benefits}}{\text{Robert's contributions}}$$

It is the ratio of benefits to contributions that determines equity rather than the exact number that each partner receives or makes. Thus, a relationship in which one partner receives more benefits than the other may still be equitable so long as he or she makes a correspondingly higher number of contributions.

Principle 5: Inequity causes distress. A final assumption of this theoretical framework is that people who find themselves in an inequitable relationship—who are underbenefited or overbenefited relative to the partner—will experience distress and seek to restore equity. Equity can be restored to a relationship in a number of ways. For example, a woman who believes that her steady dating partner contributes much more to the relationship than she herself does may attempt to restore *actual equity*. She may increase her own contributions (e.g., by making an effort to return his phone calls more promptly, by paying him more compliments) and/or decrease her own benefits (e.g., by asking him to fix fewer things around her apartment). Alternatively, she may try to restore *psychological equity*. She may, for instance, convince herself that equity actually does exist ("It's not like I'm taking advantage of our relationship; he likes fixing things, and he already owns all the tools"). And finally, if the distress caused by the inequity should prove too great, then she can simply *end the relationship*.

Empirical Evidence. Some of the principles set forth by social exchange theories have received empirical support. For example, there is evidence that the nature of rewards and costs shifts over time and within relationships. Sociologist Diane Felmlee (e.g., 1995) has conducted research on what she labels "fatal attractions." Her work demonstrates that a partner's attributes that are seen as particularly attractive, rewarding, and valuable at the beginning of a relationship can later come to be viewed as unpleasant, costly, and detrimental to the relationship. For example, a woman who values her lover's "spontaneous and carefree" nature may later perceive that same attribute as an annoying "flightiness." A man who is attracted to his dating partner's "refreshing innocence" may later find that it has become an irritating "lack of maturity."

We also know that people differ in terms of what they consider costly and/or rewarding; in particular, there appear to be several sex differences. In one study, Constantine Sedikides, Mary Beth Oliver, and Keith Campbell (1994) investigated the perceived benefits and costs of romantic relationships in a sample of heterosexual college students. Participants were reminded that romantic relationships are likely to result in both benefits and costs and then were asked to list the five most important benefits they had enjoyed, and the five most serious costs they had incurred, as a result of all the romantic relationships they had personally experienced. Analysis of these lists revealed a variety of *benefits*, including the following:

- Companionship or affiliation (cited by 60% of the total sample)
- Sexual gratification (46%)
- Feeling loved or loving another (43%)
- Intimacy (42%)
- Relationship expertise or knowledge (40%)
- Self-growth and self-understanding (37%)
- Enhanced self-esteem (32%)
- Exclusivity (32%)
- Feeling secure (28%)
- Social support from the partner's friends or relatives (22%)
- Feelings of happiness or elation (16%)
- Learning about the other sex (12%)

Although men and women reported experiencing similar kinds of benefits from their romantic relationships, significantly more men (65%) than women (26%) cited sexual gratification as a particularly important benefit. Conversely, significantly more women (49%) than men (14%) specified enhanced self-esteem (including higher self-respect and self-confidence) as a romantic relationship benefit.

Participants also generated a number of different *costs*, including the following:

- Loss of freedom to socialize (cited by 69% of the total sample)
- Loss of freedom to date (68%)
- Time and effort investment (27%)
- Nonsocial sacrifices, such as falling grades (24%)
- Loss of identity (22%)
- Feeling worse about oneself (22%)
- Stress and worry about the relationship (20%)
- Fights (16%)
- Increased dependence on the partner (13%)
- Monetary losses (12%)
- Loss of privacy (10%)
- Loss of innocence about relationships and love (9%)

As before, there were sex differences. More men than women cited loss of freedom to socialize (77% vs. 61%) and to date (83% vs. 56%) as particularly heavy costs associated with their romantic relationships, and more men than women specified monetary losses (18% vs. 6%) as a dating burden. More women than men mentioned loss of identity

(29% vs. 14%), feeling worse about themselves (29% vs. 14%), and increased dependence on the partner (23% vs. 3%) as important costs they had experienced in their relationships.

In a second study, the authors asked another sample of men and women to rank order the list of benefits and costs generated by the first group of participants in terms of their perceived importance; these results confirmed and extended those of the first study. Specifically, women in the second study viewed intimacy, self-growth and self-understanding, and enhanced self-esteem as more important benefits than did men, whereas men in the second study perceived sexual gratification and learning about the other sex as more important benefits than did women. Also in the second study, women regarded loss of identity, increased dependence on the partner, feeling worse about oneself, and loss of innocence about relationships and love as greater costs to romantic involvement than did men, who considered monetary losses and time and effort investment to be more serious costs than did women.

Other researchers, rather than exploring perceptions of costs and benefits, have tested the theoretical prediction about the association between equity and relationship satisfaction. People clearly *believe* that equity is an important determinant of relationship quality, *expect* to experience distress if confronted by inequity in close relationships, and *believe* that equity should be restored to inequitable relationships (e.g., Canary & Stafford, 1992; Dainton & Stafford, 1993; Haas & Stafford, 1998). For example, sociologist Susan Sprecher (1992) asked a large sample of men and women college students to imagine that they were in a long-term romantic relationship that had recently become inequitable. Participants first imagined that the inequity benefited their partner, that is, that the relationship was one of *underbenefit* for themselves: "You feel that you are contributing more (in love, effort, time, emotions, tasks) than your partner is. In other words, you feel that you are currently getting a worse deal than your partner is" (p. 60). They then were asked to imagine the opposite situation—a relationship that was inequitable due to *overbenefit* for themselves. For each scenario, participants indicated how they would respond emotionally to the inequity. The results revealed that men and women expected to become distressed—to experience increased anger and depression and decreased happiness, contentment, satisfaction, and love—in response to underbenefiting inequity. In addition, although participants did not expect to experience a great deal of distress in response to overbenefiting inequity, they did expect their feelings of guilt to increase. Clearly, inequity is believed to be associated with some form of emotional distress and dissatisfaction.

However, there is mixed evidence about whether equity and satisfaction actually are correlated in ongoing romantic relationships. Some studies find that equity is associated with a higher degree of satisfaction than is inequity (for a review, see Sprecher & Schwartz, 1994). Others find that inequity—specifically, overbenefit—is related to higher levels of satisfaction than is equity (as we might expect from Sprecher's [1992] belief study). Yoshinori Kamo (1993), for example, examined the relationship between perceived fairness in the allocation of household chores and self-reported marital satisfaction in a sample of American and Japanese couples. Among American couples, being overbenefited (believing that the spouse does more than his or her fair share of tasks around the house) was positively associated with marital satisfaction—for both husbands and wives. The same result was found for Japanese wives; that is, the more Japanese wives believed that they benefited from the relationship in terms of household task allocation, the more satisfied they were with their marriages.

Although the evidence in support of the social exchange framework is mixed, these theories nonetheless provide insight into how the exchange of rewards and costs between romantic partners can promote relationship development and continuity.

Interdependence

We have seen that the exchanges between partners—their disclosures and revelations, their contributions and benefits—can propel a relationship toward increasing closeness (or, alternatively, toward dissolution). *Interdependence frameworks* also focus on partners' exchanges, their perceptions of rewards and costs, and the process by which they evaluate and regulate the relationship (see Holmes, 2000). In addition, these models add to our understanding of relationship development in two important ways. First, interdependence models distinguish between relationship satisfaction and relationship stability. They recognize that a highly satisfying relationship may ultimately prove unstable and that a deeply unsatisfying one can endure for a lifetime. Second, these frameworks propose that relationship outcomes are affected not only by what happens between the partners but also by external forces that can serve to cement or weaken the partners' bond.

For example, sociocultural taboos against divorce may prevent an unhappily married couple from terminating their relationship; legalization of same-sex marriage may enable another couple to publicly acknowledge the commitment the partners have to each other; and parental interference may heighten (or extinguish) the passion between two young lovers.

Interdependence Theory. John Thibaut and Harold Kelley's (1959) *Interdependence Theory* proposes that two people involved in a relationship are interdependent with respect to the outcomes of their behavior; that is, the thoughts, feelings, and actions of one partner influence his or her own outcomes as well as those of the other partner. Because each partner generally cannot achieve his or her best possible outcome at the same time, some degree of compromise is necessary for both partners to obtain at least minimally satisfactory outcomes. Thus, as their relationship develops, the partners are likely to coordinate their behaviors to achieve mutually rewarding outcomes ("We'll spend this vacation doing what you want, and next year we'll do what I want"). This process of coordination is called *transformation of motivation* and is assumed to produce satisfaction and to enhance commitment to the relationship.

The fact that partners experience a transformation of motivation and achieve beneficial outcomes is not enough, however, to guarantee that their union will be satisfying or that it will endure. Interdependence Theory proposes that relationship partners rely on two standards when evaluating the outcomes they are receiving from a relationship. The first, called *comparison level* (CL), is the standard against which a partner evaluates the attractiveness of a relationship or how satisfactory it is. The comparison level is determined by the individual's expectations about the level of outcomes (rewards and costs) that the relationship ought to provide, and it is influenced by personal experience as well as general knowledge of outcomes commonly experienced in that type of relationship. To the extent that the outcomes the person actually experiences in the current relationship meet or exceed what is expected (outcomes > CL), he or she is likely to view the relationship as attractive and to be satisfied; to the extent that the outcomes fall short of expectations (outcomes < CL), dissatisfaction is likely to result. Thus, it is possible for someone who benefits immensely from a relationship to nonetheless be unhappy—if he or she expects more. Conversely, it is possible for someone who appears to be in a highly unrewarding relationship to be relatively satisfied—if he or she believes things could be worse.

The second standard on which partners rely when evaluating their interpersonal outcomes is called the *comparison level for alternatives* (CLalt). CLalt is the standard the partners use in determining whether or not to remain in the relationship, and it reflects the outcomes the partners believe they could obtain from available alternatives to the current relationship. If a person's current outcomes meet or exceed his or her expected outcomes in alternative relationships (outcomes > CLalt), then the relationship is likely to endure. If current outcomes fall below perceived alternative outcomes (outcomes < CLalt), however, then the relationship will be unstable and may dissolve. Thus, an unhappy relationship may persist if there are no acceptable alternatives, and a blissful union may dissolve in the face of a particularly appealing alternative (see Figure 11.1).

In sum, this theory predicts that the most stable relationships will be those in which partners do not expect a great deal (have a low CL) but actually get quite a lot (receive many positive outcomes) from the relationship (and consequently experience high levels of satisfaction) and have very few attractive alternatives to the relationship (have a low CLalt). These factors work together to produce a high level of *dependence* on the relationship; the partners need the relationship to obtain the outcomes they desire, and they have no other viable options for attaining those desired outcomes. Their dependence, in turn, promotes the stability and endurance of their union.

Interdependence Theory reminds us that satisfaction and stability are not necessarily one and the same and that relationships develop as a function of changes in the partners' needs, motives, and expectations as well as shifts in the surrounding social context.

Extensions of Interdependence Theory: Cohesiveness and Commitment. Other theorists have elaborated on the basic principles of Interdependence Theory. For example, George Levinger's (e.g., 1965, 1976) *Marital Cohesiveness Model* posits that the strength of the bond between partners is a function of two basic factors: the various inducements to remain in the relationship and the inducements to leave it (see Figure 11.2). *Inducements to remain* include all of the sources of *attractions* to the marriage and the spouse, which range from affectional rewards (e.g., love, companionship, sexual enjoyment), to socioeconomic rewards (e.g., income, material possessions, social prestige), to

Figure 11.1   Thibaut and Kelley's Interdependence Theory. Interdependence Theory predicts that relationships will endure to the extent that the partners are highly dependent upon each other and the relationship for desirable outcomes. Dependence is a function of satisfaction with the relationship (which is highest when people's actual outcomes meet or exceed the outcomes they expect to obtain or their comparison level) and the comparison level for alternatives (or what is believed to be available from other relationships or partners). Thus, both internal (satisfaction) and external (quality and quantity of alternatives) forces determine whether a relationship will continue.

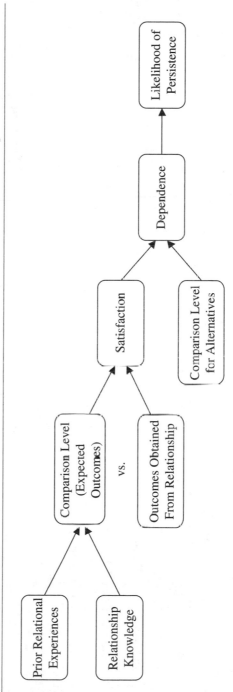

Figure 11.2   Levinger's Marital Cohesiveness Model. Like Interdependence Theory, the Marital Cohesiveness Model proposes that both internal and external factors determine whether a relationship will endure over time. Highly cohesive relationships are the most likely to last. Cohesiveness (the strength of the relational bond between partners) is determined by the level of rewards and costs experienced in the relationship, which produces attraction; by the number of costs associated with terminating the relationship, or barriers; and by the presence or absence of acceptable alternatives to the relationship.

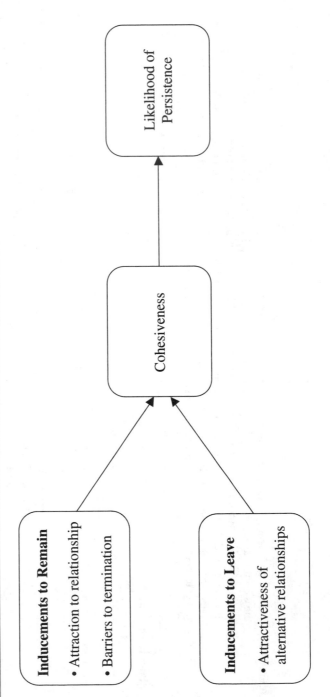

Inducements to Remain

• Attraction to relationship

• Barriers to termination

Inducements to Leave

• Attractiveness of alternative relationships

Cohesiveness

Likelihood of Persistence

Figure 11.3 Rusbult's Investment Model. Like Interdependence Theory and the Marital Cohesiveness Model, the Investment Model recognizes that the outcomes an individual obtains in his or her relationship, as well as the perceived quality of alternatives to that relationship, are important contributors to relationship stability. Specifically, this model proposes that people will feel committed to their relationships to the extent that they feel satisfied, believe that they have few good alternatives to the relationship, and have invested important resources in the relationship. This feeling of commitment, in turn, influences whether or not a relationship will last.

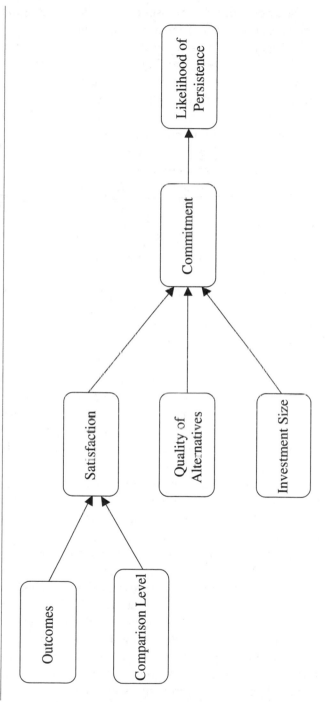

similarity between the spouses on important demographic dimensions. Other inducements to remain in a relationship include the restraints or *barriers* against its dissolution. Barriers derive from the social structure in which people live and from the social contracts into which they enter. For example, feelings of obligation to the partner, the marriage, and existing children; moral proscriptions stemming from religious values; and external pressures from kin, community, and social institutions all may serve as potent barriers to termination. *Inducements to leave* the relationship include the various attractions or rewards that can be obtained from alternative relationships (including no relationship at all). Essentially, this model proposes that "marital strength is a function of bars as well as bonds" (Levinger, 1965, p. 20). Thus, the bond between two people is likely to be cohesive (strong and stable) to the extent that they experience high attraction to the relationship, many barriers to terminating the relationship, and low attraction to alternative relationships.

Another extension of Interdependence Theory was proposed by Caryl Rusbult (1983; see also Rusbult & Buunk, 1993). Her *Investment Model* proposes that commitment, defined as the individual's feelings of attachment to the partner and his or her intention and desire to remain in the relationship, is a function of three factors: (a) the person's level of *satisfaction* with the relationship, which is a function of rewards and costs (outcomes actually experienced) and comparison level (the level of outcomes people believe they deserve); (b) the perceived *quality of alternatives* to the relationship or the degree to which the individual believes that important needs could be met outside the relationship (e.g., by specific others, by friendships, by hobbies and other activities, by no relationship at all); and (c) the size of the person's *investment* in the relationship, which refers to the ways in which he or she is connected to the partner and bound to the relationship (these can be of a direct [e.g., time, emotional energy, personal sacrifice] or indirect [e.g., mutual friends, shared memories, shared possessions] nature) (see Figure 11.3). Thus, this model proposes that partners will feel committed to their relationship to the extent that they feel satisfied (i.e., their relationship provides abundant rewards, does not involve heavy costs, and closely matches their beliefs and assumptions about an ideal partnership), they believe they have few and/or poor-quality alternatives to the relationship, and they have invested important resources in the relationship that serve as powerful inducements for its continuation. Commitment, in turn, influences whether or not the relationship will endure.

Empirical Evidence. There is strong support for many of the basic propositions just outlined. Both Interdependence Theory and the Investment Model propose that relationship satisfaction will be greater to the extent that partners' actual outcomes exceed their expectations (outcomes > CL). Research supports this contention. For example, Marianne Dainton (2000) gave people currently involved in romantic relationships a list of everyday behavioral strategies that can be used to maintain or promote a relationship. These maintenance activities encompassed five general dimensions: *positivity* (e.g., behaving in a cheerful and optimistic manner), *openness* (e.g., engaging in self-disclosure or direct discussion of the relationship), *assurances* (e.g., providing messages stressing commitment to the partner and the relationship), *social networks* (e.g., relying on common friends and affiliations), and *sharing tasks* (e.g., being equally responsible for accomplishing tasks that the couple faces). For each activity, participants were asked to consider their partners' behavior and to indicate the extent to which their current relationships compared, either favorably or unfavorably, with their expectation levels. They also completed a measure of relationship satisfaction. The results revealed a strong and positive correlation between expectation fulfillment and satisfaction, the more an individual perceived his or her partner as using the various maintenance behaviors relative to his or her expectations, the more satisfied the individual was with the relationship.

Other aspects of these theories also have received support. In particular, research reveals that both the internal characteristics of a relationship (e.g., satisfaction, perceptions of rewards and costs, investment level) and the external forces surrounding the partners (e.g., availability and quality of alternatives, presence or absence of societal barriers to divorce) influence whether the relationship continues and the well-being of the partners (e.g., Attridge & Berscheid, 1994; Drigotas, Rusbult, & Verette, 1999; Kurdek, 2000; Rusbult, Johnson, & Morrow, 1986; Rusbult, Martz, & Agnew, 1998). Clearly, interdependence models provide a compelling view of relationship development.

SUMMARY

Recognizing that only a very few relationships survive beyond initial interactions and first dates, social and behavioral scientists have devoted a great deal of time and effort to understanding the how and why of relationship development. In their quest, they have proposed a number of theoretical frameworks. Those who adopt a stage approach have charted the phases or stages of relational progression. Others have focused on the processes—self-disclosure and intimacy, exchange of rewards and costs, interdependence—that occur between partners and that fuel relationship development. Regardless of the framework used, researchers and theorists acknowledge that relationships are dynamic entities that fluctuate over time as a result not only of changes in the partners but also of alterations in the social environment and in the properties of the relationship itself.

KEY CONCEPTS

Stage models of relationship development (p. 135)
Filter Theory (pp. 135-136)
Social attributes (p. 135)
Value consensus (p. 135)
Need complementarity (p. 135)
Wheel Theory (pp. 136-137)
Rapport (p. 136)
Self-revelation (p. 136)
Mutual dependency (p. 136)
Intimacy need fulfillment (p. 136-137)
Stimulus-Value-Role Theory (p. 137)
Stimulus stage (p. 137)
Value stage (p. 137)
Role stage (p. 137)
Process models of relationship development (p. 138)
Social Penetration Theory (p. 138)
Depth of disclosure (p. 138)
Breadth of disclosure (p. 138)
Intimacy Theory (p. 139)
Social exchange theories (pp. 140-143)
Rewards (p. 141)
Costs (p. 141)
Equity (p. 142)
Actual equity (p. 143)
Psychological equity (p. 143)

DISCUSSION QUESTIONS

1. What are the basic premises of stage models of relationship development? Why have these models fallen out of favor?

2. Think about your current (or a previous) romantic relationship. Explain how your relationship developed using Social Penetration Theory and Intimacy Theory.

3. Identify and describe the five basic assumptions of social exchange models of relationship development.

4. Discuss the concept of inequity and identify the ways in which theorists say that people can restore equity. Have you ever been in an inequitable relationship? How did you respond to the inequity? Does your response support theoretical assumptions or not?

5. Evaluate the following three statements from the perspective of Interdependence Theory:

   Statement 1: "A rewarding marriage is a happy marriage."

   Statement 2: "If he/she were really unhappy, then he/she would leave."

   Statement 3: "A good relationship will last forever."

RECOMMENDED READINGS

Berscheid, E., & Reis, H. T. (1998). Attraction and close relationships. In D. T. Gilbert, S. T. Fiske, & G. Lindzey (Eds.), *The handbook of social psychology* (4th ed., pp. 193-281). Boston: McGraw-Hill.

Holmes, J. G. (2000). Social relationships: The nature and function of relational schemas. *European Journal of Social Psychology, 30,* 447-495.

These reviews present several theories of relationship development, with an emphasis on process models.

12

Conflict and Dissolution

The process of relationship development is not always smooth. Inequity, inappropriate disclosures, lack of intimacy and mutuality, and other events may create tension between the partners and impede the progress of their relationship. In this chapter, we examine the topic of conflict, including the events that occur during conflict and how couples manage conflict. We also consider relationship dissolution—from the sequence of events involved in breakups to the ways in which people commonly respond to the demise of romantic relationships.

CONFLICT

Conflict and disagreement are extremely common occurrences in even the most intimate and close romantic relationships. Community surveys, for instance, reveal that nearly all married couples report having "unpleasant disagreements" at least some of the time, with most reporting average frequencies of one to three disagreements per month (McGonagle, Kessler, & Schilling, 1992). In addition, as couples progress from casual dating to more intimate forms of romantic involvement (e.g., steady dating, engagement, marriage), they often experience an increase not only in their levels of love and commitment but also in the amount of conflict in their relationships (e.g., Braiker & Kelley, 1979). In sum, conflict appears to be part and parcel of most dating and mating relationships.

What Happens During Conflict? The Role of Attributions

As anyone who has ever had a disagreement with a loved one knows, partners not only act and react to each other during conflict, but they also experience emotions and thoughts, express beliefs, make attributions, and come to conclusions. Research now suggests that these affective and cognitive processes play a crucial role in conflictual interactions. As noted by Bruce Orvis, Harold Kelley, and Deborah Butler (1976), partners in even the most ideal relationship often place different (and sometimes contradictory) interpretations on each other's behavior. In their seminal article on attributional conflict in young couples, these social scientists identified several basic attributional "facts" about interpersonal conflict.

The first fact is that during conflict, *attributional processes become activated* as each partner seeks to understand the cause of the conflict and of the other's behavior.

> "I thought he loved me. So why did he forget our anniversary?"
> Julia wonders.
> "Why isn't she speaking to me?" Richard thinks. "What's going on? Did I do something wrong?"

When the relationship is progressing smoothly, partners do not ask why; agreement does not need explaining. It is only when an unpleasant—or unexpected—event occurs that the flow of the relationship is interrupted and partners begin to actively search for an explanation.

The second fact is that *the attribution process is selective*. During conflict, partners can—and do—quickly and easily bring to mind information that serves their own personal interests. In addition, partners often genuinely believe that they possess an accurate understanding of the causes of each other's behavior and believe that their own behavior is justified.

> "He deserves the silent treatment for not remembering our anniversary. I always remember to do nice things for him, like the time I planned that huge surprise party. He knows how important this day is to me. I bet he's still mad because I threw out his ratty old T-shirt; this is just his petty way of getting back at me," Julia fumes.
>
> "Is she still upset about that comment I made? She knows I was only kidding. How many times do I have to apologize? I hate this silent treatment crap; it's so childish. I wish she'd just grow up and tell me when she's mad. At least I have the decency to communicate openly about my feelings," Richard sighs with exasperation.

Orvis and his colleagues (1976) noted that attributions can serve conflicting personal interests and still meet the criteria of plausibility because "ordinary events, including interpersonal behavior, readily lend themselves to different interpretations. . . ., [and] the everyday attributor has great freedom to select from many different kinds of information and causes" (p. 380). In other words, faced with an unpleasant or unexpected interpersonal event, the individual has at his or her mental fingertips an array of seemingly plausible explanations, any one of which may promote or further his or her own agenda.

The third fact is that *the attributions that partners make during times of conflict can create "attributional conflicts"*—disagreements about the causes of behavior—that usually are irresolvable. Partners often disagree, not only about the ostensible conflict of interest but also about the reasons for their behavior.

> "I'm mad because you forgot our anniversary. How could you? And don't give me any lame excuses; I know how you operate, and I know that this is your way of getting back at me for throwing out that stupid T-shirt," Julia yells.
>
> "What? You've got to be kidding me. I'm not mad about the T-shirt. I forgot because I'm under a lot of pressure at work; you know how that new project has sucked up all my time. The

deadline is getting closer, and I'm the one whose job is on the line. I can't believe you think I would deliberately do something like this!" Jason argues.

Both partners in our example agree that Richard forgot their anniversary. However, they disagree about the reasons for this event. Richard honestly believes that he forgot because he is under extreme pressure at work. Julia just as firmly believes that he forgot because he is upset that she threw out his old T-shirt and therefore is punishing her. As noted by Orvis and his colleagues (1976), the multiple interpretations that can be given to any one behavior, the relative inability of each partner to prove that a particular causal explanation is correct, and the continuing conflict of interest itself all "make it improbable that the actor and the partner can come to see eye-to-eye in the matter" (p. 381). During conflict, then, partners often find themselves with both a source of initial disagreement and an additional source of conflict regarding attributions. Richard and Julia may end up arguing not only about the forgotten anniversary but also about the putative reasons for the original conflict.

The fourth fact is that *"meta-attributions"—explanations for explanations—may arise and create additional problems* for the partners. The researchers proposed that partners often evaluate the credibility of the attributions that are made for a particular behavior (Orvis et al., 1976). When an individual gives a causal explanation that is not credible, that is illogical, or that seems particularly unconvincing, the partner may wonder why it was given.

"He just hired an assistant," Julia thinks. "And his boss said he could extend the deadline if he needed to. So why would he use that as his excuse for missing our anniversary? It doesn't make any sense. I just know he's still upset about the T-shirt. If he's not, then something else must be going on."

The issue of why a certain attribution was made may raise serious doubts about the giver of the attribution (e.g., his or her candor, trustworthiness, honesty, or perceptiveness) and about the future of the relationship, and it may become yet another source of conflict between partners.

Recent investigations of the moment-by-moment thought processes that occur between romantic partners during conflict episodes support many of the observations initially made by Orvis and his colleagues

(1976). In one study, for example, married couples visited a "family interaction lab" that was created by researchers Alan Sillars, Linda Roberts, Kenneth Leonard, and Tim Dun (2000). The lab resembled a combination living room and dining room, and each couple spent 15 minutes in this setting discussing a current unresolved disagreement they had. The spouses then went into separate rooms to view the videotape of the couple's interaction. The videotape was designed to stop playing after each 20-second interval; when it did, participants reported what they remembered thinking and feeling at the time into a microphone.

Analysis of these spontaneous thoughts revealed that individuals tended to treat their own inferences as objective observations (e.g., "He's attacking me," "She's lying"). They seemed unaware of the possibility that they might be mistaken in their assumptions and/or conclusions. Similarly, participants' thoughts showed little evidence of complex perspective taking. For example, only 3% of their codable thoughts had a mutual or relational focus (i.e., showed awareness of the interdependence between each partner's behavior), and only 5% of their thoughts focused on how the partner might be interpreting the situation. Furthermore, when participants did attempt to identify or acknowledge the partner's perspective, they tended to view that perspective in simplistic and undifferentiated terms (e.g., "He thinks he's right," "She knows I'm sick of talking about this"). Negative thoughts and feelings also occurred much more frequently than did positive ones. And finally, both husbands and wives displayed a tendency to view their own communication during the conflict more favorably than that of their partner. Specifically, both spouses attributed positive acts (e.g., collaboration and cooperation, disclosure and openness, soliciting information, attending to the partner) more often to themselves than to the partner, and both attributed negative acts and intentions (e.g., confrontation, avoidance and withdrawal, topic shifting, stonewalling, lying, insincerity) more often to the partner than to themselves. The researchers concluded,

A surprisingly high proportion of thoughts were negatively valenced, and there was minimal evidence of attention to the inherent complexity and ambiguity that exists in the communicative process. Participants showed a tendency to construe their own and their partner's communicative acts as objectifiable behaviors with unequivocal meaning. Presumably, this is part of the problem that occurs when interaction does not go smoothly—people treat their inferences as objective observations. (Sillars et al., 2000, p. 496)

Taken as a whole, these data suggest that people's perceptions, attributions, and thoughts during conflict often are subjective, simplistic, and self-serving. Knowing this, couples should strive for accuracy, for objectivity, and for empathic understanding of each other's positions during times of duress and disagreement.

Attributional Styles

In addition to exploring the attributional processes that occur during conflict, researchers have identified the types of attributions that romantic partners make for each other's behavior and whether these attributional styles are associated with important relational events such as satisfaction and stability. In their exhaustive review of the marital attribution literature, Thomas Bradbury and Frank Fincham (1990) concluded that there is a clear association between attributional styles and marital satisfaction. Partners in nondistressed relationships explain positive behavior as being due to the internal disposition of each other and believe that the cause of the behavior will be stable over time and globally influential in a variety of marital situations (see Figure 12.1a). A nondistressed spouse attributes negative partner behavior to external circumstances or the partner's temporary state, believes that it will be unstable over time, and believes that it will be specific to that one marital area. By enhancing the impact of positive events and minimizing the impact of negative events, this particular attributional pattern promotes relational well-being.

Distressed partners demonstrate the opposite attributional pattern. Specifically, they attribute each other's positive behaviors to situational (rather than dispositional) causes, assume that these causes are unstable and unlikely to be repeated, and believe that these causes are operative in one specific situation rather than in many or all marital situations (see Figure 12.1b). Essentially, a distressed spouse views a partner who does something positive as "having acted unintentionally and with less positive and more negative intent, having little control over the cause of the event, being influenced by a temporary state rather than by a persisting trait, behaving involuntarily, being motivated by selfish concerns, being less deserving of praise, and having a less positive attitude toward the respondent" (Bradbury & Fincham,

Figure 12.1a The Attributional Style of Nondistressed Couples. After reviewing the marital attribution literature, Thomas Bradbury and Frank Fincham (1990) concluded that there is a clear association between marital satisfaction and attribution styles. People in satisfying or nondistressed relationships tend to attribute positive spouse behaviors to internal, stable, and global causes. They tend to attribute negative spouse behaviors to external, unstable, and specific causes. This attributional pattern enhances the impact of positive events and minimizes the impact of negative events, and therefore promotes marital well-being.

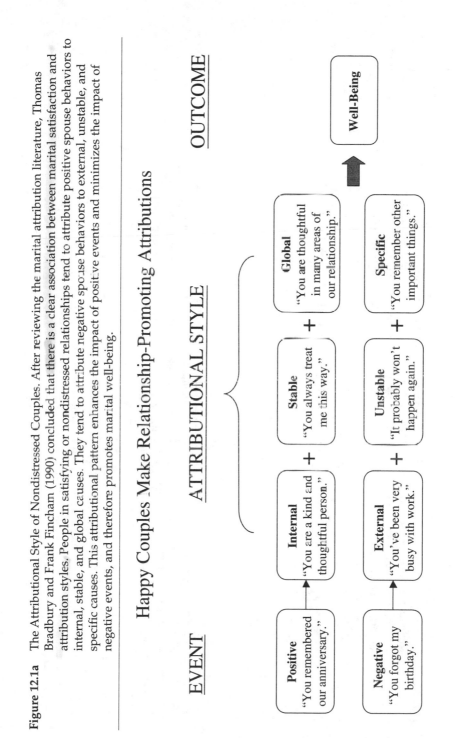

Happy Couples Make Relationship-Promoting Attributions

EVENT   ATTRIBUTIONAL STYLE   OUTCOME

Positive
"You remembered our anniversary."

Internal
"You are a kind and thoughtful person."

Stable
"You always treat me this way."

Global
"You are thoughtful in many areas of our relationship."

Negative
"You forgot my birthday."

External
"You've been very busy with work."

Unstable
"It probably won't happen again."

Specific
"You remember other important things."

Well-Being

Figure 12.1b The Attributional Style of Distressed Couples. People in distressed marriages demonstrate the opposite attributional pattern. They attribute positive spouse behaviors to external, unstable, and specific causes, and they attribute negative spouse behaviors to internal, stable, and global causes. This attributional pattern diminishes or discounts the impact of positive events and accentuates the impact of negative events, thereby promoting relational distress.

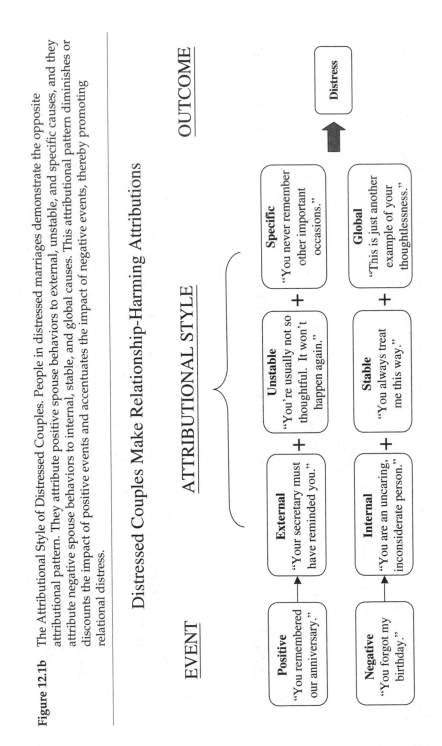

Distressed Couples Make Relationship-Harming Attributions

EVENT

ATTRIBUTIONAL STYLE

OUTCOME

Positive
"You remembered our anniversary."

External
"Your secretary must have reminded you."

Unstable
"You're usually not so thoughtful. It won't happen again."

Specific
"You never remember other important occasions."

Negative
"You forgot my birthday."

Internal
"You are an uncaring, inconsiderate person."

Stable
"You always treat me this way."

Global
"This is just another example of your thoughtlessness."

Distress

1990, p. 5). Conversely, a distressed spouse attributes negative behaviors to the partner's enduring dispositional characteristics; these causes are believed to be stable over time and are perceived as globally influential across marital situations rather than as specific to one or a few situations. By discounting positive events and accentuating the impact of negative ones, this attributional pattern promotes relational distress.

Conflict Resolution

Whether conflicts promote relational satisfaction or produce interpersonal distress depends, in part, on how the conflict is managed by the partners. For example, research generally reveals that relationship satisfaction is strongly associated with the use of "positive" conflict resolution strategies. Men and women whose partners employ *reason* (problem solving and the use of rational argument [e.g., presenting alternatives, seeking solutions to the problem]), *assertion* (direct expression of opinions or wants [e.g., clearly stating one's position, redirecting the conversation to the issue or topic, emphasizing points by gesture or eye contact]), or *partner support* (acknowledgment of the partner's views [e.g., actively listening or questioning, expressing clear agreement with the partner, making compromises or concessions]) are happier and more satisfied than individuals whose partners make less use of these strategies (e.g., Noller, Feeney, Bonnell, & Callan, 1994).

"Negative" conflict resolution strategies are associated with interpersonal distress and dissatisfaction (Noller et al., 1994). Negative strategies include *coercion,* defined as seeking control through the use of force (e.g., blame, threats, sarcasm, physical or verbal aggression); *manipulation,* defined as attempting to gain compliance by indirect or false means (e.g., providing misleading information, attempting to make the partner feel guilty or defensive, feigning sincerity or various mood states); and *avoidance,* characterized by a physical and/or emotional retreat from the situation (e.g., changing or avoiding the topic, avoiding eye contact, minimizing the situation by joking).

Another potentially destructive conflict style is the *demand-withdraw pattern* of communication in which one partner desires change and approaches the other partner about it while the other partner withdraws from the issue or conflict. Demand-withdraw consistently has been linked with marital dissatisfaction and instability (e.g., Heavey, Christensen, & Malamuth, 1995; Noller et al., 1994). There also is a robust sex difference with respect to this pattern; research with married couples demonstrates that women typically demand and men typically withdraw (Christensen & Heavey, 1990; Gottman & Levenson, 1988). However, laboratory examinations of actual conflictual interactions between couples reveal that it is not so much the sex of the spouse that predicts the occurrence of demand or withdraw responses but rather whose issue is being discussed and the relative power distribution between partners (e.g., Heavey, Layne, & Christensen, 1993; Sagrestano, Christensen, & Heavey, 1998). For example, husbands—like wives—tend to adopt a demand orientation when discussing issues that are important to them. In addition, the less powerful (and often less satisfied) partner is generally the one who demands change, whereas the more powerful partner is generally the one who attempts to avoid the issue and maintain the status quo. Because women often have less marital power than do men, this may explain why women are more likely to demand and men to withdraw.

Is there a secret to resolving conflict? Obviously, no one strategy will work well for all couples. However, we can glean some hints from the available literature. First, successful conflict management requires open and honest communication in which both partners clearly express their opinions, positions, and wants. Second, the partners should remain focused on the issue or situation at hand. Third, each partner must attempt to understand the other's perspective and try to recognize his or her own contribution to the interaction and the partner's responses. Fourth, the partners should try to express positive affect whenever possible and to suppress (or at least not reciprocate) negative feelings and expressions. Finally, the partners' goal should be to reach an equitable solution rather than a win-lose one, and both must be willing to compromise and negotiate in service of that goal.

RELATIONSHIP DISSOLUTION

Conflict, distress-maintaining attributions, and negative conflict resolution strategies certainly can contribute to unhappiness and the demise of a relationship. However, even stable and satisfying relationships end. The recognition that relationship dissolution is both common and potentially detrimental to the well-being of the partners has created a need to understand this aspect of relationship development.

Why Do Relationships End?

People often end relationships because they become disillusioned with their partners and their relationships. Social scientist Ted Huston and his colleagues (Huston, Caughlin, Houts, Smith, & George, 2001) found that divorce was associated with declining feelings of love, lowered rates of affectionate behavior, increasing ambivalence about the marriage, and the growing conviction that one's spouse is not responsive. The various theories we reviewed in Chapter 11 suggest a number of additional reasons why relationships might end, including changes in the factors that initially promoted relationship development. For example, self-disclosure can fuel the progression of a romantic relationship as the partners learn new things about each other and experience increased intimacy. Self-disclosure also increases the risk, however, that an individual will reveal something about himself or herself that the other finds unappealing. In addition, researchers find that the disclosure of negative thoughts, feelings, and behaviors may produce unhappiness and contribute to relationship dissolution (Gottman & Levenson, 1992).

Changes in the social environment— specifically, in the nature of available alternatives to the current relationship—may also result in termination. Caryl Rusbult and colleagues (Rusbult, Zembrodt, & Gunn, 1982) asked a sample of young adults to think of a time when they became dissatisfied with a romantic relationship and to describe their response to that situation. Their results revealed that men and women who believed that the available alternatives would be "better" and more satisfying than the current partner and relationship were more likely to choose to end that relationship. Other researchers similarly find that divorce rates increase when the existing social environment conspires to create abundant opportunities for remarriage (e.g., high geographic mobility rates, imbalanced sex ratios that result in many marriage prospects [Secord, 1983; South, 1995; South & Lloyd, 1995]).

These are only a few of the many factors that can promote relational distress and contribute to the demise of the association between two people.

How Do Relationships End?

Several models of romantic relationship termination have been proposed. For example, relationship scholar Steve Duck (1982) suggested that relationships undergo four phases of disengagement and dissolution. The first phase, the *intrapsychic* phase, begins when one partner (or both partners) crosses a threshold of what Duck called "unbearable dissatisfaction" with the current state of the relationship. During this phase, the individual privately focuses on the partner's behavior and identifies any causes of dissatisfaction with the partner. In addition, the individual assesses the internal dynamics of the relationship, evaluates the negative aspects of being in the relationship, considers the costs of withdrawing from the relationship, and assesses positive aspects of any available alternatives to the relationship. This cognitive activity is essentially private and generally is not directly expressed to the partner. In essence, an individual in this beginning phase of relationship dissolution asks himself or herself, "Am I happy? Are things between us okay? Will I be better off by myself or with so-and-so?" Once a person comes to the mental realization that leaving the relationship might be better than staying in it and resolves to confront the partner about this issue, the second phase is engaged.

During the *dyadic* phase, the focus becomes interpersonal. Here, the person must confront the partner with his or her dissatisfaction, express his or her discomfort, and present his or her own view of the relationship. The partner, in turn, may question the individual's views, provide alternative explanations for events, present his or her own view of the relationship, and so on. This interpersonal process is likely to be difficult and to produce stress and even anger as the two partners face their differences of opinion and negotiate their respective roles. Together, the partners must make a choice between repairing the relationship or allowing its demise; in so doing, they weigh the pros and cons and consider alternative forms of the relationship. If the partners decide that the relationship cannot be repaired, then the final steps of the dyadic phase "involve preparation for the post-dissolution state: essentially this means starting to create the 'public story' about the causes and course of the disengagement" (Duck, 1982, p. 24).

The third phase of dissolution, the *social* phase, centers on the public and social repercussions of dissolving the relationship. The partners are faced with the tasks of dealing with their own "newly single" status (not an easy situation in a social world that values couplehood) and subsequent doubts about their own futures. In addition, they must explain the situation to friends, family, neighbors, and others in the social network and must face the judgment and possible disapproval of those social entities. The social phase concludes when

Figure 12.2 Baxter's Model of Disengagement Strategies. Research conducted by Leslie Baxter (1985) suggests that the ways in which people disengage from a relationship vary along two primary dimensions. The *direct/indirect* dimension concerns whether the individual makes his or her desire to end the relationship clear to the partner. The *self-/other-oriented* dimension concerns the degree to which the individual focuses on protecting the self or the partner. These two dimensions combine to form four categories of disengagement strategy.

Direct

Openly acknowledge a desire to end the relationship with little effort to protect partner.

•Fait accompli
•Attributional conflict

Openly acknowledge a desire to end the relationship while protecting partner's self-esteem.

•State-of-the-relationship talk
•Negotiated farewell

Self-Oriented ─────────────────────────── **Other-Oriented**

End the relationship without an explicit declaration and with a focus on one's own needs.

•Withdrawal
•Cost escalation

End the relationship without an explicit declaration and without harming the partner.

•Pseudo de-escalation
•Fading away

Indirect

169

each partner creates and distributes publicly a story about the relationship's demise; these stories attribute blame and provide causal explanations for the breakup and often are used by the partners to save face.

The stories or accounts created during the social phase may be quite different from the ones produced by the ex-partners during the final phase, the *grave-dressing* phase. Here, each individual is concerned with coming to terms with the breakup and moving on. As noted by Duck (1982),

> Once the main psychological "work" of dissolving a personal relationship is over, the problem remains of what to do with the memories associated with it. The processes here remind me of grave-dressing: the attempt to neaten up the last resting place of the corpse and to erect public statements of its form, contribution, and importance. Much of the activity of getting over a relationship concerns simplification, rationalization, and beautification of the course, themes, and outcomes of the relationship while it still flourished. (p. 27)

Essentially, the persons involved engage in a retrospective analysis of the relationship and its death; this allows them to create an acceptable personal story (as opposed to a public account that attributes blame for the breakup) about the course of the relationship and to tidy up the memories associated with it.

Disengagement Strategies

In Duck's (1982) model, the dyadic phase involves choosing between repair and dissolution. If the decision is to dissolve the relationship, then the partners must then decide how to go about fulfilling that goal. A number of researchers have investigated the means or tactics, called *disengagement strategies,* that people use when attempting to end a relationship. A series of studies conducted by Leslie Baxter (1985) suggested that disengagement strategies vary along two basic dimensions. The first, called *indirectness versus directness,* refers to the extent to which the person's desire to exit the relationship is made clear to the partner. Direct strategies explicitly make clear the desire to end the relationship, whereas indirect strategies do not. The second dimension is called *other-orientation versus self-orientation* and indicates the degree to which the disengager (the person attempting to end the relationship) tries to avoid hurting the partner. Other-oriented strategies demonstrate a desire to avoid embarrassing or manipulating the partner; self-oriented strategies display concern for the self at the expense of the partner. These two dimensions combine to form four categories of disengagement strategy, illustrated in Figure 12.2.

The first category encompasses strategies that are *direct and other-oriented*. In using the "state of the relationship talk," one or both partners explicitly acknowledge their dissatisfaction and desire to end the relationship—and they do so in a face-saving context of mutual discussion and agreement to exit: "I'm so glad that we decided to talk things over. We really do want different things in life. I agree that we should break up." The "negotiated farewell" is a similar strategy that involves an explicit communication that formally ends the relationship and that allows each partner to share responsibility for the breakup: "We went out to dinner and talked about our situation. We both realized that it wasn't anyone's fault, and we decided to end the relationship." Both of these strategies directly and openly express the goal of termination in a manner that saves face both for the disengager and the partner.

The second category contains strategies that are *direct and self-oriented*. Here, the disengager explicitly states his or her desire to end the relationship and makes little to no effort to avoid hurting, embarrassing, or manipulating the partner. Examples of these strategies include "fait accompli" and "attributional conflict." Fait accompli occurs when the disengager declares that the relationship is over with no opportunity for discussion or compromise: "I don't care what you say. It's over between us. End of discussion." Attributional conflict is a strategy in which both partners wish to end the relationship but cannot agree on why the breakup is necessary and thus blame each other (often bitterly) for its occurrence: "It's all your fault!" "No, it's your fault!" People who use these strategies openly call for the termination of the relationship but often accomplish that goal at their partner's expense.

The third category contains those strategies that are considered *indirect and self-oriented*. Here, an individual attempts to end the relationship without explicitly stating that goal and with an overwhelming concern for his or her own feelings and needs (as opposed to those of the partner). "Withdrawal" involves reducing the frequency and/or intimacy of contact with the partner without telling the partner the real reason for the disengagement (i.e., the desire to end the relationship): "I have a lot of work to do this weekend. I'm going to have to cancel our plans for Saturday, and I don't expect to have much free time on Sunday. In fact, this whole week is going to be really busy.

You should just go ahead and make plans without me." A second indirect/self-oriented strategy is that of "cost escalation," which occurs when the person wishing to exit the relationship attempts to increase the relationship costs of the partner, thereby driving him or her away: "Maybe if I act really mean, he/she will go away." People who use these strategies are avoiding any explicit discussion of relationship termination while at the same time focusing on their own needs and feelings.

The fourth category contains *indirect and other-oriented* strategies that attempt to accomplish a breakup without an explicit declaration and without excessive harm to either partner. One example is "pseudo-deescalation," when one or both partners (falsely) declare that they desire a transformed but less close relationship rather than a final and complete separation: "It's not like we won't see each other ever again. I mean, we can still be friends." Another is "fading away," when both partners implicitly understand that the relationship is over (but never directly say anything about this state of affairs): "She went back to school yesterday. Neither of us said anything, but I could tell that it's over."

Baxter (1985) pointed out that the process of relationship disengagement is multifaceted and complex and that it is possible for one person to use numerous strategies when attempting to end a specific relationship. In addition, it is probable that there are particular strategies that might produce beneficial (or at least less distressing) outcomes for the partners. For example, direct strategies that acknowledge the relationship's demise might be easier for individuals to bear than are indirect strategies that leave them wondering about their romantic futures. Similarly, strategies that take into consideration the feelings of the person who is being left, and that allow both partners to participate in the breakup process, are likely to produce more positive outcomes than are strategies that do not.

Reactions to the End of a Relationship

People respond to the demise of a relationship in a number of ways. How they respond depends to some extent on the nature of the relationship itself. Based on the theories of relationship development we reviewed in Chapter 11, we could predict that people who receive many rewards relative to costs from their partner, who are satisfied with and invested in their relationship, who have been involved with the partner for some time and feel highly committed to him or her, and who believe that they have few viable alternatives to the relationship will experience a great deal of distress at the relationship's demise.

Some research supports this contention. Psychologists Patricia Frazier and Stephen Cook (1993) surveyed 85 men and women who recently had experienced the breakup of a dating relationship. Participants provided information about the ended relationship and the ex-lover, including relationship *satisfaction* (e.g., how satisfied they were with the partner in a variety of areas), perceived *closeness* of the relationship, and perceived *alternatives* (e.g., how easy it would be to find another partner). In addition, participants indicated how *stressful* the breakup had been for them and the extent to which they believed they had *recovered* from the breakup, and they completed a 15-item scale of *current emotional adjustment*. They also took a *self-esteem* inventory and a measure of *perceived social support from friends*.

The results indicated that individuals who had been more satisfied with their partner, whose relationships had been closer, and who believed it would be more difficult for them to find another romantic partner reported experiencing greater stress at the breakup. Interestingly, participants' levels of satisfaction, closeness, and perceived alternatives were *not* significantly related to the extent to which they believed they had recovered from the breakup or their current emotional adjustment—but their self-esteem and perceived level of social support were.

These results provide a ray of light for men and women experiencing breakups. If the relationships were close and satisfying, then the breakups will probably be painful; however, a positive self-image and a supportive group of friends and family may help to heal the wound and speed the recovery process.

Accounts: Why things turned out this way. Although people's reactions to breakups can vary widely, one thing that most people do when faced with the loss of a relationship is to try to understand what went wrong and why the relationship foundered. In fact, the models of relationship dissolution reviewed earlier in the chapter specifically posit that the final stages of breakup occur when the ex-partners achieve a sense of understanding and a feeling of closure about the relationship's end. An important element in this recovery process is the making of *accounts*. Accounts are explanatory scripts that present the plot, introduce the characters and their patterns of interaction, and tell the why of the breakup. Like a novel, play, or some other type of dramatic presentation, accounts tell a story—in this case, that of the relationship and its demise.

According to account scholars John Harvey, Ann Weber, and their colleagues (e.g., Harvey, Weber, Galvin, Huszti, & Garnick, 1986; Weber, 1998), people create accounts for a variety of reasons. First, account making allows individuals to reduce or eliminate the uncertainty and ambiguity that frequently accompany breakups:

> He says, "I know why things didn't work out. It was because I got too wrapped up in work. And so she found someone else. There's no doubt in my mind that this is what killed our marriage."
> She says, "It's not like any one specific thing destroyed our relationship. It was more like a lot of little things that built up over time. I guess eventually I just fell out of love with him."

Accounts are not always accurate, and the individuals involved may create vastly different accounts of the same situation. Nonetheless, accounts allow their creators to satisfy a need for control and simple understanding.

Second, accounts fulfill what Harvey, Weber, and their colleagues termed a "social presentational" function that may protect and enhance the individual's self-esteem. During and after a breakup, people often are motivated to present the stories of their relationship to significant others. By influencing the interpretations that others have of the individual and the events of the breakup, accounts may result in social support, help, sympathy, and other beneficial outcomes. Thus, the husband who tells his best friend that "all is forgiven" and that he accepts responsibility for driving his unfaithful wife into the arms of another man projects an image of charity and martyrdom that may produce esteem-boosting expressions of admiration and respect from his friend. The unfaithful wife who confesses her "weakness" and tells her best friend what a "horrible person" she is projects an image of need and dependence that may result in the provision of nurturance, affection, and support: "So you made a mistake," the friend reassures her. "You're only human. I love you anyway."

And third, accounts serve as a potent vehicle for emotional release. In telling the story of the relationship's demise, individuals may experience a cathartic purging of feelings of guilt, anger, depression, loneliness, insecurity, and confusion: "Here's what happened to me, and here's how I feel about it," the wounded party cries, giving voice to thoughts and pent-up emotions that he or she might not have had the opportunity to express during the breakup itself.

In sum, assembling one's own account of a broken relationship—what happened, why the partnership failed, what went wrong or right—may help to provide the account maker with the tools he or she needs for a successful recovery—emotional release, cognitive understanding, and closure.

SUMMARY

Conflict and disagreements are part and parcel of close relationships. Whether a relationship survives conflict (or whether partners survive termination) is to a large extent determined by how that conflict (or termination) is managed. People who communicate their own needs and feelings clearly and who acknowledge and support those of their partners are more likely to resolve conflict (or accomplish termination) in a manner that benefits both themselves and their partners.

KEY CONCEPTS

Attributions (p. 158)
Attributional conflict (p. 159)
Meta-attribution (p. 160)
Attributional styles (pp. 162-165)
Positive conflict resolution strategies (p. 165)
Reason (p. 165)
Assertion (p. 165)
Partner support (p. 165)
Negative conflict resolution strategies (p. 165)
Coercion (p. 165)
Manipulation (p. 165)
Avoidance (p. 165)
Demand/withdraw pattern (pp. 165-166)
Phases of relationship dissolution (pp. 168, 170)
Intrapsychic phase (p. 168)
Dyadic phase (p. 168)
Social phase (p. 168)
Grave-dressing phase (p. 170)
Disengagement strategies (p. 170)
Indirect vs. direct dimension of relationship disengagement (p. 170)

Other vs. self-orientation dimension of relationship disengagement (pp. 170-171)
Accounts (p. 173)

DISCUSSION QUESTIONS

1. Orvis, Kelley, and Butler (1976) identified several attributional events that occur during times of conflict. Using an example from your own life, describe these attributional events.

2. Compare the attributional styles typically demonstrated by "happy" and "unhappy" couples. How does each style contribute to relationship satisfaction and well-being?

3. Identify three "positive" and three "negative" strategies for managing or resolving conflict. Think of a situation in which you or someone you know has made use of one or more of these strategies. What was the outcome? Was the strategy effective?

4. How do relationships end? Describe the four phases of relationship termination proposed by Duck (1982). Consider a time when you (or someone you know) ended a romantic relationship. Did these phases occur?

5. What is an account? Why do people create accounts when experiencing relationship dissolution?

RECOMMENDED READINGS

Bradbury, T. N., & Fincham, F. D. (1990). Attributions in marriage: Review and critique. *Psychological Bulletin, 107,* 3-33.

Orvis, B. R., Kelley, H. H., & Butler, D. (1976). Attributional conflict in young couples. In J. H. Harvey, W. J. Ickes, & R. F. Kidd (Eds.), *New directions in attribution research* (Vol. 1, pp. 353-386). Hillsdale, NJ: Lawrence Erlbaum.

These authors present evidence that the way in which couples think about their own behavior and their partner's behavior is associated with relationship adjustment.

Braiker, H. B., & Kelley, H. H. (1979). Conflict in the development of close relationships. In R. L. Burgess & T. L. Huston (Eds.), *Social exchange in developing relationships* (pp. 135-168). New York: Academic Press.

This chapter presents some of the first empirical data gathered on the role of conflict in romantic relationship development.

13

Marriage

Chapter Outline

We have seen that most couples experience conflict and disagreement and that many relationships end before they reach levels of even moderate commitment. However, it is also the case that some romantic relationships continue to develop until they reach a state of relative permanence; the partners become "steady" dates, they move in together, they form a domestic partnership, or they marry. In this chapter, we examine research on mate choice and on marriage, cohabiting relationships, and other forms of committed long-term relationship.

MATING SYSTEMS ACROSS CULTURES

The norms or general "rules" that govern mate selection and reproduction differ across cultures. Cultural anthropologists, ethnographers, and other social scientists have identified several mating systems that occur (with varying degrees of frequency) in human societies around the world. These include *polygyny,* which literally means "many females" and refers to a mating system in which men marry multiple women; *polyandry* ("many males"), which is defined as a system in which women pair with multiple men; *monogamy,* which encompasses both *monogyny* ("one female") and *monandry* ("one male") and refers to a system in which two individuals pairbond; and *polygynandry* ("many females and males," also called *cenogamy*), which is defined as group marriage or a system in which husbands and wives share the same spouses (Fisher, 1989; Goodwin, 1999).

Some marriage arrangements are more prevalent than others. One of the most comprehensive sources of cross-cultural information on mating systems is the *Ethnographic Atlas.* The *Atlas* contains data on a variety of sociocultural features (e.g., economy, living arrangement, family organization, mode of marriage, kinship terminology, community size) that characterize more than 1,100 human societies located in Africa, the Mediterranean, Eurasia, the Pacific, North America, and South America. In 1967, ethnologist George Murdock presented information on a subset of 862 of those societies in a special edition of the journal *Ethnology.* Examination of this information, summarized in Table 13.1, reveals that polyandry is much less common than either polygyny or monogamy. For example, only four societies (less than 1%) explicitly endorse a mating system based on a single woman marrying multiple husbands. Monogamy, either between a man and a woman who marry and then live within an extended family or between a man and a woman who marry and then form a single independent family, is the predominant mating system in 137 societies (16%). By far, the most common form of marital arrangement is polygyny; a total of 713 (approximately 83%) of the societies included in the *Atlas* permit this mating arrangement. Polygyny is common in 379 of those societies and is practiced on a limited basis within the remaining 334 societies.

In all but a handful of human societies, then, women practice monandry; a woman marries one man at a time (although in polygynous societies, her spouse may have multiple wives). Similarly, although the data at first glance suggest a high frequency of polygyny, a closer look reveals that men also tend to practice monogyny; they marry one woman at a time. Based on his own analysis of the *Atlas* data, Pierre van den Berghe (1979) reported that only about 10% of the men in polygynous societies actually have more than one wife. Thus,

Table 13.1   Prevalence of Mating Systems Across 862 Human Societies

Mating System	Number and Percentage of Practicing Societies
Polygyny	713 (82.7)
General, within extended families	202 (23.4)
General, within independent nuclear families	177 (20.5)
Occasional or limited, within independent nuclear families	174 (20.2)
Occasional or limited, within extended families	160 (18.6)
Monogamy	137 (15.9)
Within independent nuclear families	72 (8.4)
Within extended families	65 (7.5)
Polyandry	4 (0.5)
Within independent nuclear families	3 (0.3)
Within extended families	1 (0.1)
Unclassified	8 (0.9)

SOURCE: These frequencies were tabulated by the author from raw data presented in the *Ethnographic Atlas* (Murdock, 1967, pp. 170-231).
NOTE: Percentages are in parentheses.

the most frequent type of marital union is that of one man and one woman. As noted by evolutionary scientists Martin Daly and Margo Wilson (1983),

> Polygynous unions remain rarer than monogamous ones . . . even within those societies that permit them. This is hardly surprising given male-male competition for wives and the pressures that are engendered when any substantial number of men are consigned to involuntary celibacy. Hence it is usually only a minority of wealthy, powerful men who have the means to acquire and maintain multiple wives. (pp. 282-283)

In her discussion of human marriage patterns, anthropologist Helen Fisher (1989) also concluded that the formation of a relationship between one man and one woman (monogamy), is "the primary marriage pattern for both men and women" (p. 333). She went on to suggest—based on an examination of marriage, divorce, and remarriage rates across cultures—that human mate selection and reproduction are perhaps best understood as demonstrating a pattern of *serial pairbonding* or *serial monogamy* whereby men and women marry successive individual partners over their life spans (as opposed to marrying one partner for the duration of their life spans or many partners at a single time).

So, is one form of marriage "better" or more "natural" than another? In considering this question, Fisher (1992) suggested the following:

> Is monogamy natural? Yes. There certainly are exceptions. Given the opportunity, men often opt for multiple spouses to further their genetic lines. Polygyny is also natural. Women join harems when the resources they can garner outweigh the disadvantages. Polyandry is natural. But co-wives fight. Co-husbands argue too. Both men and women have to be cajoled by riches to share a spouse. Whereas gorillas, horses, and animals of many other species *always* form harems, among human beings polygyny and polyandry seem to be optional opportunistic exceptions; monogamy is the rule. Human beings almost never have to be cajoled into pairing. Instead, we do this naturally. We flirt. We feel infatuation. We fall in love. We marry. And the vast majority of us marry only one person at a time. Pair-bonding is a trademark of the human animal. (p. 72)

THE NATURE OF MARRIAGE

Definitionally, *marriage* is a long-term mating arrangement that is socially sanctioned and that typically involves economic, social, and reproductive cooperation between the partners. Although customs surrounding the marriage ceremony vary widely from culture to culture, all known human societies practice and endorse this type of long-term pairing (Daly & Wilson, 1983; Goodwin, 1999). Thus, marriage is a human universal.

One of the primary "laws"—albeit an unwritten one—of marriage is the tendency for men and women to marry spouses who resemble them on a number of dimensions. Called *homogamy* or *assortment*, this tendency for similar individuals to pairbond has been documented extensively. For example, researchers have found positive correlations between marital partners on characteristics such as age, race, ethnicity, education level, socioeconomic status, religion, and physical attractiveness as well as on a host of personality traits and cognitive abilities (e.g., Berscheid & Reis, 1998; Buss, 1985; Murstein, 1980). Regardless of our preferences, we seem ultimately to pair with similar others.

International surveys indicate that marriage rates have declined around the world (Lester, 1996). The United States, in particular, has experienced a sharp decrease, with the number of unmarried adults nearly doubling over the past two decades (U.S. Bureau of the Census, 1994, 1998). Nonetheless, most unmarried men and women express a desire to marry, expect to marry at some point in their lives, and hold positive attitudes about the state of marriage (Frazier, Arikian, Benson, Losoff, & Maurer, 1996; Hobart, 1993). In addition, marriage is a common life event for most individuals, with 9 of 10 people estimated to marry at least once (Tucker & Mitchell-Kernan, 1995).

Types of Marriage

Most social and behavioral scientists believe that two general varieties of marriage exist. *Traditional* marriages are those in which the spouses allocate roles and responsibilities on the basis of sex (e.g., Luepnitz, 1988; Rubin, 1976; Turner, 1970). The husband's role encompasses traditional "male" activities and traits. For example, he controls the economic aspects of family life and has the authority to make decisions for the entire family. The wife's role encompasses traditional "female" activities and traits. For example, she is responsible for domestic tasks, including management of the house and children. Traditional relationships often involve little direct or overt expression of emotion between the spouses. Rather, each partner relies on relatives and same-sex friends for companionship and affection (Peplau, 1983). Television "sitcoms" that were popular during the late 1950s through the 1970s showcased this type of marriage. *The Donna Reed Show, Father Knows Best, I Love Lucy, All in the Family,* and similar shows depicted marriages in which the husband worked outside the home and functioned as the sole "breadwinner," primary disciplinarian, and decision maker for the family, whereas the wife stayed at home, raised the children, and took care of domestic tasks such as cooking the family meals, shopping, and cleaning.

A second type of marriage, and one that is increasingly common, is the *egalitarian, peer,* or *equal-status* marriage (e.g., Gilbert, 1993; Scanzoni, Polonko, Teachman, & Thompson, 1989; Schwartz, 1994). Unlike traditional relationships, in which tasks and roles are divided along gender lines, egalitarian marriages are characterized by shared roles and responsibility in all aspects of married life. Both the husband and the wife are assumed to be capable of displaying—and expected to contribute to the relationship—social support and caregiving, affection and emotion, sexuality, financial resources, parenting skills, and domestic labor. Television highlighted this kind of union in 1980s programs such as *The Cosby Show* and *Roseanne*. Sociologists Pepper Schwartz and Virginia Rutter (1998) noted that true peer marriages are relatively rare: "The potential for power sharing, obligation sharing, and resource sharing in marriage is real, though not commonly enacted. Pairs with the ambition of egalitarianism often fall short, into the 'near peer' category" (p. 157). These "near peer" marriages usually involve a husband who helps with child care and household labor, and a wife who provides financial resources and makes economic decisions, to a greater degree than would be expected in traditional marriages. Although truly egalitarian marriages may still be relatively uncommon, there is some evidence that partners who achieve them experience high levels of companionship and mutual respect as well as low levels of anger and conflict. In sum, "equity has its rewards" (p. 158).

Housework and Happiness

Regardless of the type of marriage a couple has, and no matter how strongly the partners endorse the concept of an equal-status relationship, it is likely that their division of household labor will reflect traditional sex roles. Early studies—those conducted during the 1950s and 1960s—revealed a strict division of labor. Husbands specialized in "outside" tasks, including mowing the lawn, shoveling snow, and maintaining the car, whereas wives specialized in "inside" tasks, including cooking and cleaning (e.g., Blood & Wolfe, 1960). Research conducted four or five decades later demonstrates that the same task division continues to characterize modern marriages (Biernat & Wortman, 1991; Blair & Lichter, 1991; Wilkie, Ferree, & Ratcliff, 1998).

In addition, although both sexes have a tendency to overestimate the amount of time they spend engaged in housework (Press & Townsley, 1998), there is overwhelming evidence that married women spend more time on domestic tasks than do married men (Brines, 1994; South & Spitze, 1994). Even in dual-earner marriages (in which both the husband and wife work and make economic contributions to the family), women average approximately twice as many hours per week on housework as do men (Blair & Johnson, 1992 ; Robinson, 1977). As a result, women have fewer hours per day of "free time" (Robinson, Yerby, Fieweger, & Somerick, 1977).

Interestingly, although marriage might seem to place an unfair burden on women, research indicates that so long as each partner *believes* that the division of labor is fair, he or she is likely to be satisfied with both the division of labor and married life in general (e.g., Lennon & Rosenfield, 1994; Major, 1993). In fact, marriage usually is associated with personal happiness for both sexes. Married couples often report more happiness, and less loneliness and stress, than do unmarried, separated, divorced, or widowed people (e.g., Coombs, 1991; Demo & Acock, 1996; Tornstam, 1992), and married men and women appear to be equally satisfied (Feeney, Peterson, & Noller, 1994).

This does not mean, however, that marriage produces a state of perpetual bliss. Longitudinal studies generally find that satisfaction declines steadily throughout marriage (e.g., Johnson & Bradbury, 1999; Kurdek, 1998; Vaillant & Vaillant, 1993). Specifically, most couples begin their married lives with a "honeymoon" period characterized by high amounts of satisfaction and well-being, which then progressively decline and finally stabilize somewhere between the 4th and 6th years, assuming that the partners stay together. For example, Ted Huston, Susan McHale, and Ann Crouter (1986) conducted a series of interviews with a sample of newlywed couples over a 1-year period beginning shortly after their weddings and ending around their first anniversaries. Partners rated their level of love for each other and completed a 10-item measure of marital satisfaction. In addition, they indicated how satisfied they were with the frequency with which various positive events occurred in the marriage (e.g., partner expressing approval). The results revealed declines in all measures over time. Specifically, both husbands and wives became increasingly dissatisfied with the level of positivity in their relationships, reported lower amounts of marital satisfaction, and felt less love for their spouses after 1 year of married life. Interestingly, wives reported more dissatisfaction than did husbands, both during the honeymoon period and 1 year later, and the same pattern was found for feelings of love (i.e., wives felt less love at marriage and after 1 year than did husbands).

Similar results were reported more recently by psychologists Benjamin Karney and Thomas Bradbury (1997), who conducted a longitudinal study in which they asked the members of 60 newlywed couples to rate their satisfaction with their marriages, their spouses, and their relationships with their spouses over a 4-year period. The overall satisfaction of both husbands and wives declined linearly over time, with scores decreasing between 3% and 4% per year.

It might be tempting to conclude from these and related studies that marriage inevitably produces unhappiness for one or both spouses. Such a conclusion, however, would be erroneous. In discussing their findings, Huston and colleagues (1986) made the following point:

> The changes in subjective evaluation over the first year of marriage reveal a consistent pattern. Husbands and wives were less satisfied with their patterns of interaction, less in love, more ambivalent, and less satisfied with the married life in general. . . . These results do not mean, however, that these couples were unhappy, disillusioned, and dissatisfied with their lot. After a year of marriage, they were less euphoric than they were shortly after marriage, but their responses still fell on the positive side of the continuum for each variable. (pp. 121-122)

In addition, the couples in Karney and Bradbury's (1997) study also remained highly content. Their scores, at each of the assessment times over the 4-year period, were well above average. Thus, although happiness may decline during a marriage, it does not inevitably change into *un*happiness.

HAS MARRIAGE CHANGED OVER TIME?

Modern marriages are a bit different from their historical counterparts. We have already seen some evidence that the traditional division of labor is not quite so strictly upheld by contemporary husbands and wives and that a new type of egalitarian or peer marriage may be on the rise (or at least available as an option for couples). Another change in the nature of marriage concerns the age at which people marry for the first time. Data collected by the U.S. Bureau of the Census (1998) reveal that age at first marriage is rising, with greater numbers of men and women delaying marriage until their mid- to late 20s. For example, in 1958, the mean age at first marriage was approximately 23 years for men and 20 years for women. Two decades later, in 1978, the age at first marriage had increased to around 24 for men and 22 for women—a life span delay of 1 to 2 full years. By 1998, men were marrying for the first time at around 27, and women were waiting to marry until they were 25.

Another dramatic change in the nature of marriage concerns the growing emphasis that most men and women place on personal happiness. Love and affection, rather than economic security, reproduction, or any other factor, have become the primary basis for marriage in Western cultures. Survey data reveal that the majority of young men and women refuse to even consider marrying unless they are in love with their partner and view loss of love as an adequate reason for terminating a marriage (Simpson, Campbell, & Berscheid, 1986). There is evidence of a similar trend occurring around the world. Cultures with a strong tradition of arranged marriage, including China, Africa, Russia, and the Middle East, increasingly are adopting a matrimonial system based on love and individual choice (e.g., Xu & Whyte, 1990; for reviews, see Goodwin, 1999; Hatfield & Rapson, 1996).

There is also a change—specifically, an increase—in the likelihood of marital disruption. In the United States, more than half of all first marriages end in divorce or permanent separation (Castro-Martin & Bumpass, 1989; Michael, Gagnon, Laumann, & Kolata, 1994), and other countries are experiencing a similar rise in the divorce rate (Kumagai, 1995; Lester, 1996). Various factors are implicated in divorce. Surveys conducted within the United States reveal that divorce is associated with the spouses' ages; specifically, the risk of marital dissolution decreases with increasing age at first marriage (Heaton, 1991). The education levels of the spouses are also related to their likelihood to divorce. Research suggests that both very high (Kposowa, 1998; Maneker & Rankin, 1997) and very low (Kurdek, 1991a) levels of education are associated with an increased likelihood of marital disruption. Ethnic or racial differences in divorce likelihood exist as well. For example, African Americans have a higher divorce rate than do other ethnic/racial groups living in the United States (Dickson, 1993; Kposowa, 1998).

Other researchers have identified certain common grounds for divorce that exist across cultures. One of the most potent of these causes is infidelity. Evolutionary scientist Laura Betzig (1989) examined reasons for divorce in a sample of 160 societies. Infidelity or adultery was the most common cause of conjugal dissolution, mentioned in 88 societies (or 55% of the sample). Other frequent causes of divorce or marital dissolution included sterility (usually that of wives [47% of societies]), cruelty or maltreatment (primarily by husbands [34%]), and "displeasingness" or personality conflicts (32%). Interestingly, polygyny—a husband electing to add another wife to the household—and subsequent co-spouse conflict was the eighth most commonly reported cause of marital dissolution, cited by 16% of societies. As we have seen, polygyny may be an optional form of mate choice in certain cultures, but it is not common and does not necessarily produce positive outcomes for the partners. Betzig noted,

> Polygyny in effect legitimizes what would be extramarital sex on the part of a husband. The result is that, to a wife, the most important "other women" are cowives rather than lovers. When a husband has added too many of them or neglected her to favor them, a woman may divorce him. (p. 661)

Other causes of divorce appear to be culture specific. Psychological and physical abuse associated with alcohol abuse by husbands has been documented as a primary reason why many women in Poland and Russia seek divorce, increasing economic opportunities for women are associated with rising divorce rates in Japan and Africa, and political unrest (which led many men and women to marry hastily and perhaps unwisely) seems to be a factor in Iranian divorce rates (see Goodwin, 1999).

In sum, just like marriage, divorce is an increasingly common experience in the lives of men and women around the world.

ALTERNATIVES TO MARRIAGE

Marriage is no longer the only option for men and women who seek to form a more or less permanent partnership with another person. Other types of long-term romantic commitment exist. One of the most common (and increasingly popular) alternatives to marriage is *cohabitation.* Cohabitation resembles a marital relationship in that it is essentially a committed pairbond or monogamous union between two individuals who live together and who coordinate their economic, social, and sexual (and sometimes reproductive) activities. Unlike marriage, however, cohabitation is not legally formalized or sanctioned by a ceremony. Perhaps due in part to more permissive social attitudes regarding premarital sex, rates of cohabitation (at least in the United States) appear to be on the rise. For example, Robert Michael and his colleagues' (1994) large national survey revealed that only about 16% of men and 6% of women born between 1933 and 1942 had cohabited prior to marriage. This number increased to 33% for men and to 24% for women born during the decade between 1943 and 1952. More than half of the men (53%) and nearly half of the women (43%) born between 1953 and 1962 reported having cohabited prior to marriage, and a whopping two thirds of men and women born between 1963 and 1974 had cohabited before marriage. Cohabitation has become so common, in fact, that the researchers concluded the following:

> The path toward marriage, once so straight and narrow, has begun to meander and to have many side paths, one of which is being trodden into a well-traveled lane. That path is the pattern of living together before marriage. Like other recent studies, ours shows a marked shift toward living together rather than marriage as the first union of couples. (p. 96)

Within the United States, cohabitation has joined marriage as an almost universal life experience.

Cohabitation may serve a variety of functions in developing relationships. For some heterosexual couples, cohabitation may serve as a replacement to marriage. For the majority, however, cohabitation seems to function as a "trial run" for marriage. Most cohabitors expect to marry their partners (Brown & Booth, 1996; Bumpass, Sweet, & Cherlin, 1991). This form of premarital union thus provides an opportunity for partners to test their relationship and examine whether or not they are compatible before making a formal (and public) commitment via a marriage ceremony.

Another alternative to marriage is the *domestic* or *same-sex partnership*, which consists of a long-term committed union between homosexual partners. Like their heterosexual counterparts, most gay men and lesbians strongly favor "couplehood" and seek long-term pair-bonds. National surveys conducted by sociologist Janet Lever (1994, 1995) revealed that most homosexuals prefer long-term monogamous relationships over other sexual or romantic arrangements. Her results also indicated that the majority of gay men (59%) and lesbians (70%) say that they would legally marry if allowed to do so. In some countries, such as Norway and Denmark, gay and lesbian couples are permitted by law to register their relationships; these socially sanctioned partnerships thus provide homosexuals with access to many of the legal rights held by heterosexual married couples (Halvorsen, 1998). A similar trend is occurring within the United States. Hawaii has legalized marriage between same-sex partners, and Vermont has approved "civil unions" involving homosexual couples (Vaid, 1995).

One of the primary differences between marital relationships and homosexual or heterosexual cohabiting unions involves division of household labor. In general, cohabitation is characterized by a more equal division of labor than is marriage. Both homosexual and heterosexual cohabitors (as well as heterosexual married couples who cohabited prior to marriage) possess more egalitarian attitudes toward division of household labor and demonstrate a more equitable allocation of household tasks than do married couples who did not cohabit (Clarkberg, Stolzenberg, & Waite, 1995; Kurdek, 1993a; Peplau & Spalding, 2000; Shelton & John, 1993). Although other differences— between cohabitors and spouses and between long-term homosexual partners and long-term heterosexual partners—undoubtedly exist, research generally indicates that levels of overall satisfaction, well-being, and happiness are comparable across these types of committed relationship.

SUMMARY

Marriage is a cross-cultural universal, with men and women the world over seeking partners for long-term committed relationships. As we have seen, many of these relationships dissolve as the result of a variety of intervening factors. The fact that the majority of people continue to search for commitment in the face of rising rates of divorce and failed partnerships attests to the enduring importance of mate selection in human lives.

KEY CONCEPTS

Polygyny (p. 179)
Polyandry (p. 179)
Monogamy (p. 179)
Monogyny (p. 179)
Monandry (p. 179)
Polygynandry (p. 179)
Cenogamy (p. 179)
Ethnographic Atlas (p. 179)

DISCUSSION QUESTIONS

1. Discuss the various mating systems that occur throughout the world. Find examples of each system, using data from modern or ancient civilizations.

2. There is an old saying that goes something like this:

   Hogamous, higamous, man is polygamous
   Higamous, hogamous, woman is monogamous

   Evaluate this saying, using evidence from cross-cultural data on mating systems and conjugal dissolution.

3. How would social exchange models of mate selection explain the prevalence of homogamy or assortment?

4. Compare traditional and egalitarian marriages. How have media depictions of married life changed over time? Is one form more prevalent on television, for example, than the other?

5. Consider the ways in which marriage has changed over time.

RECOMMENDED READINGS

Fisher, H. E. (1992). *Anatomy of love: A natural history of mating, marriage, and why we stray.* New York: Fawcett Columbine.

This well-written book is designed for a general audience. The author is a respected social scientist who presents interesting anecdotes and empirical evidence about the mating arrangements and habits of men and women living in diverse cultures around the world. The book is a fascinating read.

Daly, M., & Wilson, M. (1983). *Sex, evolution, and behavior* (2nd ed.). Belmont, CA: Wadsworth.

These authors present one of the first (and most widely cited) cross-cultural investigations of marriage and mate selection.

Peplau, L. A., & Spalding, L. (2000). The close relationships of lesbians, gay men, and bisexuals. In C. Hendrick & S. S. Hendrick (Eds.), *Close relationships: A sourcebook* (pp. 111-123). Thousand Oaks, CA: Sage.

These authors review the literature on same-sex unions.

Schwartz, P. (1994). *Peer marriage: How love between equals really works*. New York: Free Press.

This interesting book explores the topic of peer or egalitarian marriage.

PART IV

INDIVIDUAL DIFFERENCES

Both the positive and negative events that occur within mating relationships are affected by a variety of factors. Many of these factors are interpersonal in nature and involve the exchanges that happen over time between the two partners; we have seen how reciprocal self-disclosure, the formation of intimate connections, and the giving and receiving of rewards contribute to the quality and stability of romantic partnerships. Some of these factors are produced by the sociocultural context. The presence or absence of alternative romantic and sexual partners, the way in which the relationship is viewed by friends and family members, and the cultural rules that govern sexuality, mate selection, and marriage all work together to influence the outcomes experienced by relational partners. And some of these factors are individual in nature. Each man and woman possesses—and brings to his or her relationships—a host of dispositional characteristics that can have important relational consequences. For example, people with certain traits may have increased opportunities for sexual and/or romantic interaction. A highly extraverted outgoing person is perhaps more likely to seek out potential partners than is a shy withdrawn individual. Similarly, a person's disposition may influence how he or she interprets interpersonal events as well as his or her behavior toward relational partners. A secure, psychologically well-adjusted individual may be more able and willing than an emotionally unstable individual to attribute positive motives to the partner and to engage in other relationship-enhancing behavior during times of conflict.

The following three chapters explore the association between a person's enduring dispositional characteristics and his or her romantic opportunities, responses from others, and own interpersonal behavior. Chapter 14 considers the attribute of maleness or femaleness, examining the interpersonal correlates of biological sex and psychological gender. Chapter 15 explores the association between relational events and global personality characteristics. And Chapter 16 examines the ways in which a person's interpersonal belief systems may influence his or her relational experiences.

14

Maleness
and Femaleness

Chapter Outline

Perhaps the most fundamental dimension along which we classify ourselves and our mates is that of maleness-femaleness. *Biological sex* refers to whether a person possesses male or female chromosomes (XY or XX) and secondary sex characteristics (e.g., penis and testes or vagina and ovaries). *Psychological gender* or *sex role orientation* refers to whether a person possesses traits or characteristics that are believed to be associated with, and that are considered socially appropriate for, each biological sex. Maleness-femaleness is a powerful individual difference variable that influences many aspects of a person's relational world.

BIOLOGICAL SEX

We have seen in earlier chapters that men and women often exhibit similar sexual and romantic attitudes and behaviors. For example, they hold many of the same beliefs about love and report many of the same experiences in their love relationships. Both sexes also endorse many of the same sexual standards and express similar sexual preferences. And they tend to prefer the same attributes—kindness, intelligence, honesty, attractiveness, humor—in their potential mates.

These basic similarities aside, however, the interpersonal events, experiences, and outcomes of men and women are far from identical. In fact, one of the most common findings in the relationship literature is that women's experiences in dating and marital relationships are often less overtly positive than those of men. For example, women report higher amounts of discord and conflict—ranging from communication problems and inequity to sexual violence and emotional abuse—in their romantic relationships than do men (e.g., Davis, Emerson, & Williams, 1997; Eells & O'Flaherty, 1996; Foshee, 1996; Waldner-Haugrud & Magruder, 1995). Similarly, married women experience more loneliness and less overall satisfaction than do married men (e.g., Bouchard, Lussier, & Sabourin, 1999; Schumm, Webb, & Bollman, 1998; Stack, 1998; Tornstam, 1992).

Many scientists now believe that *relational standards*—the beliefs that men and women have about the qualities that a relationship should possess—are at the root of this particular sex difference. Two theoretical perspectives have been advanced during recent years, each presenting a particular view of the way in which relational standards are implicated in sex differences.

Different Cultures or Different Experiences?

According to the *Different Cultures Model*, men and women are socialized to construct and perceive relationships in very different ways. (Note the similarities between this model and other social context models that we examined in Chapter 8.) This framework suggests that men and women approach relationships from a different cultural perspective and adopt a different set of standards with respect to relationships (e.g., Maccoby, 1990; Tannen, 1990; Wood, 1994). For example, women traditionally are socialized to value interdependence, to establish intimacy through self-disclosure and affective communication, and to pursue communal goals within their close relationships. Conversely, men are socialized to value independence, to establish intimacy through shared activities, and to maintain power and autonomy in their close relationships.

Sociolinguist Deborah Tannen has written several scholarly and popular press books exploring the different expectations, goals, values, and standards that men and women bring to their interpersonal interactions and romantic relationships. Tannen (1990) suggested, as have other theorists who adopt the Different Cultures Model, that men and women inhabit separate worlds:

> *Intimacy* is key in a world of connection where individuals negotiate complex networks of friendship, minimize differences, try to reach consensus, and avoid the appearance of superiority, which would highlight differences. In a world of status, *independence* is key, because a primary means of establishing status is to tell others what to do, and taking orders is a marker of low status. Though all humans need both intimacy and independence, women tend to focus on the first and men on the second. It is as if their lifeblood ran in different directions. (p. 26, italics in original)

This fundamental difference between independence-oriented men and intimacy-oriented women is posited to have significant consequences in many relational domains, including communication. For example, Tannen (1990) suggested that in the world of women, "conversations are negotiations for closeness in which people try to seek and give confirmation and support, and to reach consensus" (p. 25). In the world of men, however, conversations serve a very different purpose; they are "negotiations in which people try to achieve and maintain the upper hand if they can, and protect themselves from others' attempts to put them down and push them around" (pp. 24-25). According to this framework, then, the different experiences that men and women have in dating and mating relationships stem from the vastly different worlds they inhabit.

Conversely, the *Different Experiences Model* portrays men and women as inhabiting essentially the same world. Specifically, this framework suggests that the sexes approach their romantic relationships with similar expectations, goals, and values but then experience differential fulfillment of those needs and expectations. According to this view, the attitudes and behaviors typically displayed by women are more likely to fulfill common relational standards and values than are those demonstrated by men. Women, for example, generally possess better communication skills than do men (see Guerrero & Reiter, 1998; Noller, 1984). Women also are more likely than men to provide support and nurturance, and to express feelings of appreciation and other positive emotions, to their partners (e.g., Cutrona, 1996; Helgeson, Shaver, & Dyer, 1987; Sprecher & Sedikides, 1993). Insofar as these kinds of supportive, expressive, and communicative behaviors are associated with (heterosexual) relationship satisfaction (Fitzpatrick & Sollie, 1999; Sprecher, Metts, Burleson, Hatfield, & Thompson, 1995), women's partners (i.e., men) may find their needs and standards met more completely than do men's partners (i.e., women).

So, which model best accounts for the differences between men's and women's interpersonal experiences? Research suggests that the second model may provide the more compelling explanation (Burleson, Kunkel, Samter, & Werking, 1996). For example, in one study, relationship scholars Anita Vangelisti and John Daly (1997) asked a sample of men and women to read a description of 30 different standards (reflecting seven general categories) involved in long-term romantic relationships. Participants reported how important they believed each standard was for a successful relationship and then rated the extent to which their current romantic relationships actually reflected the standard. The results revealed that men and women generally did not differ in the *importance* ratings they assigned to each category of standard. For example, both sexes believed that standards associated with *trust* (including fidelity, honesty and trustworthiness, commitment, and privacy) and *affective accessibility* (including openness and self-disclosure as well as demonstrations of love, liking, and affection) were strongly implicated in romantic relationship success. In addition, both sexes attached high importance to standards related to *integration* (including acceptance of each other's faults and weaknesses, respect, compatibility of values and needs, and comfort or ease in each other's presence), *flexibility* (including the ability and willingness to adapt to each other's changing needs, respect for each other's rights and need for space, and a sense of fun and enjoyment in the relationship), and *relational identity* (including having an integrated network of friends and relatives, spending time together, feeling emotionally attached, being recognized as a "couple," and jointly sharing and owning possessions).

However, men and women did report experiencing differential *fulfillment* of these standards in their actual romantic relationships. Specifically, men indicated that their standards, overall, were met more fully in the context of their current romantic relationships than did women. In fact, an examination of the fulfillment ratings that participants gave to each set of standards revealed that men's needs and expectations for six of the seven general categories (affective accessibility, integration, flexibility, relational identity, future orientation, and role fulfillment) were fulfilled more completely than were women's. The researchers also explored the discrepancies or differences between the importance and fulfillment ratings made by men and women; this enabled them to test whether the "gap" between what participants said was important and what they actually obtained from their relationships differed for men and women. It did. As compared with men, women encountered more of a discrepancy between what they wanted (or attached importance to) and what they got from their current romantic relationships in terms of trust, relational identity, integration, affective accessibility, future orientation, and role fulfillment. As noted by Vangelisti and Daly (1997), these results provide support for the Different Experiences Model:

> The findings indicate that women and men report that they have similar standards for their relationships, but that women are more likely than men to believe that their standards are not fulfilled. These results support the notion that women and men have different experiences of romantic relationships and provide a testable explanation for why women suggest they have more problems in their relationships than do men. (p. 217)

Although this study indicates that men and women enter romantic relationships with similar expectations which are then differentially fulfilled, it is also the case that the socialization pressures brought to bear on each sex are somewhat different (see Chapter 8). Thus, both factors—different cultures and different experiences—undoubtedly play a role in accounting for the oft-observed sex differences in communication, satisfaction, equity, and well-being that characterize many dating and mating relationships.

PSYCHOLOGICAL GENDER OR SEX ROLE ORIENTATION

In addition to their biological makeup, people differ in the extent to which they possess or endorse attributes that stereotypically are associated with each sex. The Bem Sex Role Inventory developed by Sandra Bem (1974) is one of the most commonly used measures of psychological gender. In this 60-item inventory, a person's gender is determined

by his or her self-ratings on various attribute dimensions. One third of
the dimensions are considered stereotypically male or socially acceptable
for men to possess, including the following:

- Self-reliant 7
- Independent 6
- Assertive 4
- Forceful 2
- Analytical 4
- Willing to take risks 4
- Self-sufficient 7
- Acts as a leader 6
- Competitive 6
- Ambitious 5

$$\frac{51}{10} = 5.1$$

androgynous = 1

One third of the items are considered stereotypically female or socially
acceptable for women to possess. Examples include the following:

- Yielding 4
- Shy 2
- Affectionate 6
- Sympathetic 5
- Sensitive to the needs of others 7
- Childlike 5
- Warm 6
- Tender 6
- Eager to soothe hurt feelings 6
- Gentle 5

$$\frac{52}{10} = 5.2$$

An additional one third of the items consist of neutral characteristics
that are considered equally desirable for men and women to possess
(e.g., adaptable, friendly, truthful).

Individuals (men or women) who describe themselves as possessing stereotypically male traits are considered *masculine*. Those who present themselves as possessing stereotypically female traits are
considered *feminine*. Men and women who endorse both male and
female attributes are classified as *androgynous,* and those who believe
they possess neither male nor female traits are considered *undifferentiated*. Individuals whose biological sex "matches" their psychological
gender (i.e., men who endorse masculine attributes and women who

endorse feminine attributes) often are identified as *sex-typed* or *traditional* in their gender or sex role orientation.

There is some evidence that the combination of instrumental masculine and expressive feminine attributes characteristic of people with an androgynous sex role orientation may contribute positively to relationship development and maintenance. For example, androgynous men and women generally are more willing to disclose information on a variety of impersonal and personal topics to other people than are sex-typed or undifferentiated individuals (e.g., Lavine & Lombardo, 1984; Sollie & Fischer, 1985). This willingness to self-disclose is likely to create and enhance feelings of intimacy between the androgynous individual and his or her romantic partner; this, in turn, will fuel the development of their relationship. ⟶ long term

Androgyny also appears to be associated with a number of positive interpersonal outcomes. For example, Michel Alain and Yvan Lussier (1988) investigated the postdivorce or separation experiences of a sample of androgynous, masculine, feminine, and undifferentiated men and women. Participants responded to a series of questions concerning their level of upset and preoccupation with the ex-partner (e.g., "I'm always thinking about my ex-partner"), their desire for the ex-partner (e.g., "I'm still attracted to my ex-partner"), and their feelings of affliction about the loss of their partner (e.g., being "depressed about one's future"). They also completed measures of psychological and social adaptation (e.g., happiness and going out to social events such as parties), self-satisfaction and adaptation potential (e.g., how much they experience self-blame and report having problems in adapting to their new life), and social skills (e.g., being "at ease with people" and being "sociable"). The results revealed that androgynous men and women reported the highest levels of psychological well-being and social adjustment, as well as self-satisfaction and adaptation potential, following divorce or separation. Undifferentiated participants reported the lowest levels. Interestingly, masculine and androgynous men and women reported significantly less desire for the ex-partner, upset and preoccupation with the ex-partner, and affliction than did feminine or undifferentiated individuals. In general, this pattern of results suggests that individuals who possess both masculine and feminine attributes, and who therefore have access to a wide array of potential responses, may be better equipped to deal with changes and disruptions in their romantic relationships. ⟶ grouped

Additional evidence that androgyny is associated with relationship adjustment and positive interpersonal outcomes was provided by a study conducted by psychologist Cynthia Peterson and her colleagues (Peterson, Baucom, Elliott, & Farr, 1989). These researchers assessed sex role orientation and marital adjustment (using a standard self-report scale of global marital satisfaction) in a large sample of married couples. Half of the couples were recruited from a psychology clinic and were seeking marital therapy; the other half were recruited from the community at large. The researchers first classified each husband and wife with respect to sex role orientation (masculine, feminine, androgynous, or undifferentiated) and then tallied the frequency of each possible husband-wife pairing (e.g., androgynous husband-androgynous wife, androgynous husband-masculine wife, androgynous husband-feminine wife, androgynous husband-undifferentiated wife). Next, the researchers compared the sex role distributions of the clinic sample and the nonclinic sample—and discovered a striking difference. Specifically, of the 16 possible husband-wife sex role pairings, androgynous husband-androgynous wife was the *most* frequent pairing among the nonclinic couples and the *least* frequent pairing among the clinic couples. The exact opposite pattern was found when the undifferentiated husband-undifferentiated wife pairing was considered. This was the *most* frequent pattern for clinic couples and the *least* frequent pattern for nonclinic couples. In addition, there was a higher frequency of nonclinic couples than of clinic couples in each of the six sex role pairings that involved only one androgynous spouse (e.g., androgynous wife-masculine husband, androgynous wife-feminine husband). Thus, androgyny—of one or both partners—seems to characterize married couples who are not seeking therapy, and undifferentiation (and lack of androgyny) seems to be common among clinically distressed married couples.

The researchers also examined the relation between sex role orientation and marital satisfaction and adjustment scores in the total sample of couples. This analysis revealed that adjustment/satisfaction scores were higher for both men and women when the two partners were androgynous than when they demonstrated any other pattern of husband-wife sex role pairing. In fact, with only one exception, men and women who had androgynous spouses achieved higher than average scores on marital well-being—regardless of their own sex role orientation. (The one exception was that undifferentiated women married to androgynous men had lower than average marital adjustment scores.) Femininity also appeared to be correlated with marital well-being. Specifically, feminine men and women married to feminine spouses (i.e., a feminine husband-feminine wife pairing) demonstrated marital adjustment scores well above average, and average or above-average adjustment was also seen in couples with one feminine partner (except, as before, when the other partner was undifferentiated). The only sex role orientation consistently associated with *lack* of marital well-being was undifferentiation. Men and women married to undifferentiated partners generally scored below average in terms of their levels of marital satisfaction, and the lowest levels of satisfaction and adjustment occurred in pairings involving two undifferentiated individuals or an undifferentiated person married to a masculine one. Taken as a whole, these results provide additional evidence that sex role orientation is an important factor in relationship outcomes.

SUMMARY

Each person possesses a host of characteristics or attributes that can influence both the quantity and quality of his or her interpersonal interactions and the relationships he or she forms with others. One of the most significant of these attributes is maleness or femaleness. Both biological sex and psychological gender are associated with a variety of relational experiences and outcomes. In Chapter 15, we consider another set of dispositional variables that appear to play a role in the dating and mating experiences of men and women.

KEY CONCEPTS

Biological sex (p. 195)
Psychological gender (p. 195)
Sex role orientation (p. 195)
Relational standards (p. 196)
Different Cultures Model (p. 196)
Different Experiences Model (p. 197)
Bem Sex Role Inventory (p. 199)
Masculine sex role (p. 200)
Feminine sex role (p. 200)
Androgynous sex role (p. 200)
Undifferentiated sex role (p. 200)
Sex-typed gender (pp. 200-201)
Traditional sex role orientation (pp. 200-201)

DISCUSSION QUESTIONS

1. Evaluate the following statement, using what you know about theories and research on sex differences in men's and women's relationship experiences: "Men and women are from completely different planets."

2. How do the Different Cultures Model and Different Experiences Model account for sex differences in relationship experience? Is it possible that both models explain men's and women's romantic experiences?

3. Find your sex role orientation using the 20 sample items from the Bem Sex Role Inventory included in the chapter. Use the following scale to indicate how well each item describes you:

1	2	3	4	5	6	7
Never or almost never true					Always or almost always true	

   Add up your total for the 10 femininity items and divide by 10. This is your femininity score. Do the same for the 10 masculinity items. This is your masculinity score. Find your androgyny score by subtracting your femininity score from your masculinity score (or vice versa) and taking the absolute value of the result (i.e., ignore the sign—positive or negative—of the result). Androgynous people show relatively equal amounts of both masculine and feminine attributes, and the difference score (the result of the subtraction) will therefore be close to zero. What is your sex role orientation, according to this measure? Do you possess many more feminine attributes than masculine ones? More masculine traits than feminine ones? Relatively equal amounts of both? What role do you think your sex role orientation has played so far in your romantic experiences?

4. Discuss the association between sex role orientation and relational outcomes. Explain why androgyny might produce positive interpersonal outcomes.

RECOMMENDED READINGS

Burleson, B. R., Kunkel, A. W., Samter, W., & Werking, K. J. (1996). Men's and women's evaluations of communication skills in personal relationships:

When sex differences make a difference—and when they don't. *Journal of Social and Personal Relationships, 13,* 201-224.

Vangelisti, A. L., & Daly, J. A. (1997). Gender differences in standards for romantic relationships: Different cultures or different experiences? *Personal Relationships, 4,* 203-219.

These two articles compare and contrast the different models that have been used to explain sex differences in romantic experience.

Tannen, D. (1990). *You just don't understand: Women and men in conversation.* New York: William Morrow.

This popular press book exemplifies the "different cultures" perspective and is more grounded in science than are others.

15

Personality

Chapter Outline

I n addition to being male or female, each person possesses a distinctive and stable pattern of behaviors, thoughts, and emotions, called
personality or *temperament,* that appears to have implications for mating
relationships. In this chapter, we consider how three personality
dimensions—traits, self-monitoring, and sociosexual orientation—are
related to people's sexual and romantic experiences.

SUPERTRAITS

Meta-analyses of existing empirical investigations of personality
generally reveal five basic traits—the "Big Five"—that are heritable,
stable across the life span, and culturally universal and that seem to
adequately capture much of the variance in human temperament (e.g.,
McCrae & Costa, 1997; for reviews, see Digman, 1990; Goldberg, 1993;

Hampson, 1999). These *supertraits* are extraversion, neuroticism, openness to experience, agreeableness, and conscientiousness. Researchers interested in dating and mating relationships have tended to focus on two particular supertraits: extraversion and neuroticism.

Extraversion

Extraversion reflects the degree to which an individual is oriented toward the social environment. People high on this personality dimension possess an active and positive orientation toward the social environment. They seek out others, take pleasure in social interaction, behave in an outgoing and sociable manner, and tend to be cheerful, energetic, and self-confident. People low on extraversion (often called *introverts*) are wary of social interaction, prefer solitary activities, and direct their attention inward to their own thoughts and feelings. Introverts are generally withdrawn, quiet, and reserved, and they report lower levels of energy, self-confidence, and positive emotional experience.

A great deal of scientific attention has been devoted to examining the association between extraversion and various marital outcomes. To date, the results are inconclusive. For instance, although some researchers find that extraversion in one or both spouses is associated with *higher* levels of marital adjustment (e.g., Nemechek & Olson, 1996), others find that extraversion is correlated with *lower* levels of adjustment and well-being (e.g., Bouchard, Lussier, & Sabourin, 1999; Lester, Haig, & Monello, 1989). The results are also mixed with respect to the association between extraversion and marital dissolution. Some researchers find that this personality trait is significantly associated with the likelihood of divorce. For example, psychologists Victor Jockin, Matt McGue, and David Lykken (1996) asked a sample of more than 3,000 men and women who had been married at least once to complete a personality inventory that measured their levels of extraversion (called "positive emotionality") and various other traits. Participants also provided information about their marital histories, including whether or not they had ever divorced. The researchers then examined whether the participants' divorce status could be predicted reliably from their extraversion scores. The results indicated that it could be; that is, the higher men and women scored on extraversion, the more likely they had experienced marital dissolution. Other researchers, however, have not found any direct relationship between this personality trait and relationship termination (e.g., Kurdek, 1993b).

It is possible that extraversion does not directly influence relationship stability but rather has an indirect effect by influencing how partners interact with each other. In one study, researchers Carolyn Cutrona, Robert Hessling, and Julie Suhr (1997) assessed the personality traits of a sample of 100 married couples prior to observing each couple in a 10-minute interaction. These interactions took place in a laboratory furnished to resemble a comfortable living room. One partner was randomly chosen by the researchers to play the role of "support recipient." The support recipient was asked to describe a recent personally stressful situation to his or her spouse. The other member of the couple was assigned the role of "support provider." The support provider was instructed to simply listen to his or her partner and then react spontaneously and naturally. The two partners then switched roles, and the process was repeated. These interactions were videotaped, and the researchers examined the support providers' verbal behavior for the presence of four types of positive communication: *emotional support* (expressing love, concern, or empathy for the partner), *esteem support* (communicating respect for the partner and confidence in his or her abilities), *informational support* (providing information about the stressful situation or advice about how to deal with it), and *tangible aid* (providing or offering to provide goods, services, or other explicit forms of assistance needed to deal with the stressful situation). The frequencies with which these four types of positive communication occurred during the interaction were summed to create an overall index of support behavior provided by each spouse.

The results revealed that this overall measure was positively correlated with extraversion levels. Specifically, husbands and wives higher in extraversion made more positive supportive statements overall to their support-seeking spouses than did less extraverted individuals—but they did not receive more support themselves from those spouses. In discussing this interesting pattern, Cutrona and her colleagues (1997) concluded,

The results that emerged for extraversion highlight the importance of considering the personal characteristics of both the individual and his or her primary source of social support. Contrary to prediction, the extraversion of support *recipients* did not directly predict the amount of support they received from the spouse.

Rather, the extraversion of support *providers* proved to be most important. Thus, a shy introvert who married a gregarious extravert might be amply supplied with a lifetime of social support, by virtue of his or her partner's interpersonally oriented nature. (p. 390, italics in original)

Further analyses also revealed that reciprocity of support was evident in the couples' behavior. That is, the more support a husband or wife *provided* during the first interaction, the more support he or she subsequently *received* during the second interaction—regardless of the level of extraversion of either spouse. This result suggests that extraverted people may indirectly affect their own relational outcomes via the support they provide for their partners. Specifically, extraverted men and women tend to give their partners a great deal of social support; these positive behaviors, in turn, seem to evoke corresponding supportive reactions from those partners.

Thus, it is possible that the personality attributes—specifically, the extraversion levels—of romantic partners may influence the nature of their interactions. Over time, these interpersonal dynamics may work to either enhance or erode the quality and stability of the relationship.

Neuroticism

Neuroticism, also called emotional instability or negative affectivity, refers to a person's sensitivity to negative stimuli, propensity to experience negative emotions, and stability of behavior over time. Individuals high on neuroticism hold negativistic views of themselves and the world around them, tend to feel inadequate and dissatisfied, and are prone to frequent and intense negative emotions. They are generally moody, highly strung, sensitive, and touchy. People low on this personality dimension are emotionally stable and much less prone to negative emotional experiences. In general, they are calm, even-tempered, relaxed, and secure. Neuroticism is implicated strongly in several romantic relationship outcomes, including dissolution (e.g., Cramer, 1993; Eysenck, 1980; Tucker, Kressin, Spiro, & Ruscio, 1998) and satisfaction or adjustment (e.g., Bouchard et al., 1999; Karney & Bradbury, 1997).

In one classic longitudinal investigation, E. Lowell Kelly and James Conley (1987) followed a sample of 249 married couples from the time of their engagement during the 1930s to 1980. The first data collection took place during the period from 1935 to 1941. During these years, and prior to their marriage, the members of each couple were rated by five of their acquaintances on various personality traits, including neuroticism. In addition, after marriage, the spouses provided annual reports about their current levels of marital satisfaction (on a scale ranging from *extraordinarily happy* to *extremely unhappy*); these annual reports were averaged to provide a measure of marital satisfaction in early marriage. The second data collection occurred in 1954-1955, and the third and final collection took place in 1980-1981. During these two periods, husbands and wives were asked how satisfied they were with their marriage, whether they would still marry their spouse if they had their life to live over, whether they had ever regretted their marriage, and whether they had ever considered divorce or separation from their spouse. Responses to these four questions were then summed to create an overall index of marital satisfaction. At each of the various assessment times, the researchers also collected information on each couple's marital status (i.e., whether or not the spouses had gotten divorced).

The results revealed that both marital outcomes—dissolution and satisfaction—were predicted by initial levels of neuroticism. For example, the men and women who divorced early (between 1935 and 1954) or late (between 1955 and 1980) in life had higher premarriage levels of neuroticism than did their still-married counterparts. In addition, their neuroticism seemed to be strongly implicated in the dissolution of their marriages. Specifically, when asked by the researchers why they decided to divorce, more than one third (36%) cited various manifestations of their own or their partner's neuroticism, including "emotional instability," "emotional overreactions," "emotional disorder," "emotional problems," "emotional reactions," "irritability," and "emotional immaturity."

The researchers also examined whether neuroticism was related to satisfaction among stably married couples (defined as spouses who were still married at the time of any given assessment). For men, premarriage neuroticism levels (as assessed by acquaintances) were negatively correlated with satisfaction scores at the first and second data collection times. That is, men who were higher in neuroticism at the beginning of the study reported more unhappiness and less satisfaction with their marriages early and later on in their lives than did men with lower levels of this trait. Women's neuroticism levels were similarly negatively associated with their marital satisfaction at the second and third data collection times. Specifically, women high in premarriage neuroticism were less satisfied and more regretful about their marriages later on than were women who possessed lower levels of neuroticism. These results, along with those of other longitudinal investigations (e.g., Kurdek, 1993b), provide evidence that neuroticism is associated with both the quality and stability of romantic relationships.

During recent years, social scientists have sought to discover why this particular personality trait seems to negatively affect an individual's ability to find relational happiness and stability. One possibility they have explored is that neuroticism may contribute to dysfunctional exchanges between romantic partners. Using a procedure very similar to the one used by Cutrona and colleagues (1997) and described earlier in this chapter, Lauri Pasch, Thomas Bradbury, and Joanne Davila (1997) examined the relationship between neuroticism and supportive behavior in newlywed couples. Couples completed measures of marital satisfaction and neuroticism and then were audiotaped during two interactions. In the first interaction, one spouse was randomly selected to serve as the "helpee." The helpee was instructed to talk about an important personal characteristic, problem, or issue that he or she would like to change about himself or herself (and that was not a source of tension in the marriage). The other spouse served as the "helper." The helper was simply asked to be involved in the discussion and to respond in whatever way he or she wished. The spouses then switched roles so that both had the opportunity to function as helper and helpee.

The verbal behaviors displayed by helpers and helpees were then examined for the presence of various positive and negative features. For example, *positive helpee behaviors* included offering a specific and clear analysis of the problem, expressing feelings related to the problem, and asking for help or stating needs in a useful way. *Positive helper behaviors* included such instrumental acts as making specific suggestions and giving helpful advice as well as emotional acts ranging from providing reassurance, to giving encouragement, to conveying love and esteem to the helpee. *Negative helpee behaviors* ranged from making demands for help, to criticizing the helper, to whining or complaining about the situation. *Negative helper behaviors* included criticizing or blaming the spouse and offering inconsiderate advice.

The analyses revealed that, for husbands, neuroticism was negatively correlated with providing positive instrumental communications to the helpee. The higher a husband scored on neuroticism, the less often he offered specific suggestions and gave helpful advice to his wife. A similar pattern was found among wives. The higher a wife scored on neuroticism, the less often she displayed positive behavior—and the more often she displayed negative behavior—toward the helpee (her husband). Thus, men and women who were high in neuroticism seemed to provide support in a largely negative and unhelpful manner.

The researchers then examined the audiotaped conversations for evidence of "negative reciprocity" of social support behavior—that is, exchanges characterized by reciprocal displays of negative communications (e.g., the helpee complains and the helper then criticizes, the helper blames and the helpee then demands help). Analysis of these data indicated that husbands who scored high on neuroticism were more likely to reciprocate their wives' negative behavior when the husbands were in the role of helper; the husbands were also more likely to have their negative helper behavior reciprocated by their wives. The wives' level of neuroticism, however, was not related to reciprocity of negative behavior. In discussing their entire set of results, Pasch and her colleagues (1997) concluded,

> Although support provision is associated with negative affectivity [neuroticism] for husbands and wives, it is the husband's negative affectivity that may have the most detrimental effect on actual interactions between husbands and wives. When husbands were in the role of providing support to their wives and when they were high in negative affectivity, social support interactions were characterized by extended sequences involving negative reciprocity. That is, husbands and wives were engaged in a cycle of negative support solicitation and provision to the extent that husbands were high in negative affectivity. These types of behavioral sequences have been shown to be associated with poor marital outcome . . . , and it is plausible to assume that negative reciprocity occurring in the context of soliciting and providing social support may have negative consequences for the marriage and the individual. (p. 376)

The evidence with respect to neuroticism, then, is clear. High levels of this personality trait are associated with marital disruption and dissatisfaction. In addition, neuroticism appears to manifest itself in maladaptive behaviors—including a failure to provide positive support and the reciprocation of negative displays—that are not at all conducive to relational well-being.

SELF-MONITORING

In addition to underlying personality traits, individuals differ in the domain of self-presentation and expressive behavior. *Self-monitoring* refers to the dispositional tendency to monitor or regulate the images that one presents to others (Snyder, 1987). High self-monitors essentially treat their social interactions as dramatic performances that can be used to gain attention, entertain, and make impressions. These "social chameleons" are strongly motivated to modify their self-presentations, are able to present themselves in a variety of ways to different audiences, and are attentive to social cues and the impressions they make on others. Low self-monitors, in contrast, are motivated to convey their authentic feelings, attitudes, and dispositions to others; are more attentive to their own internal states than to the social climate; and behave consistently across situations and audiences.

The difference between high and low self-monitors becomes clearer when we consider some of the items on the original Self-Monitoring Scale developed by social psychologist Mark Snyder (1974). Examples include the following:

- When I am uncertain how to act in a social situation, I look to the behavior of others for cues.
- I sometimes appear to others to be experiencing deeper emotions than I actually am.
- In different situations and with different people, I often act like very different persons.
- I'm not always the person I appear to be.
- I may deceive people by being friendly when I really dislike them.
- My behavior is usually an expression of my true inner feelings, attitudes, and beliefs.
- I have trouble changing my behavior to suit different people and different situations.
- I find it hard to imitate the behavior of other people.
- I can only argue for ideas in which I already believe.
- I would not change my opinions (or the way I do things) in order to please other people or win their favor.

High self-monitors tend to agree with the first five statements and believe that they are very self-descriptive; they tend to disagree with the last five statements. Low self-monitors typically demonstrate the opposite pattern; that is, they do not believe that the first five statements apply to them, but they find the last five to be very self-descriptive.

Self-monitoring is implicated in a number of romantic relationship phenomena. For example, high self-monitors pay considerably more attention to the external physical attributes of their romantic partners than to their internal dispositional characteristics; low self-monitors do the opposite (e.g., Jones, 1993; Snyder, 1987). In fact, experiments reveal that when forced to choose between two prospective dates—one with a great personality and an unattractive appearance, the other with an undesirable personality and an attractive appearance—high self-monitors willingly sacrifice personality for looks, whereas low self-monitors eschew looks in favor of personality (Snyder, Berscheid, & Glick, 1985).

High and low self-monitoring individuals also have very different experiences in their romantic relationships. Some research suggests, in fact, that high self-monitors are less commitment oriented, and tend to have less stable and satisfying relationships, compared with low self-monitors (e.g., Goodwin & Soon, 1994). For example, in one study, Mark Snyder and Jeffry Simpson (1984) surveyed undergraduates (who were previously classified as high or low self-monitors) about aspects of their dating lives. Their results revealed that high self-monitors had dated nearly twice as many different partners during the previous 12 months as had low self-monitors. In addition, among those participants who were currently involved in exclusive dating relationships, high self-monitors reported having been involved in those relationships only half as long as did low self-monitors. The researchers concluded,

> Together these analyses reveal substantial differences in the structural features of the dating lives of individuals high and low in self-monitoring. For those involved in multiple relationships, it is high self-monitoring individuals who have dated a greater number of different partners, a finding that seems to be another reflection of an uncommitted orientation to dating relationships. For those involved in single relationships, it is low self-monitoring individuals who are involved in relationships of relatively long duration, an occurrence that may be another manifestation of a committed orientation to dating relationships. (p. 1286)

Similar results were reported more recently by Stacy Norris and Richard Zweigenhaft (1999). These researchers asked a sample of heterosexual dating couples to complete both the Self-Monitoring Scale

(Snyder, 1974) and a measure of interpersonal trust that assessed participants' perceptions of their partners' predictability (the extent to which their behavior is consistent and stable), dependability (the extent to which they are honest and reliable), and faith (the extent to which they are believed to have a continuing commitment to the relationship). Participants also estimated the likelihood (in percentages) that they would eventually marry their partners. The researchers found a tendency for people with similar self-monitoring scores to pair romantically; within each couple, the self-monitoring scores for the partners were correlated significantly, and in the majority of couples (63%), both partners were either high or low in terms of self-monitoring. (The remaining couples demonstrated a mixed self-monitoring pattern, with one partner relatively high and the other relatively low on this personality dimension.) The results revealed that the partners in low self-monitoring unions scored higher than individuals in high self-monitoring relationships on all three aspects of interpersonal trust. For example, they believed in each other's honesty, reliability, and commitment to the relationship more than did couples consisting of two high self-monitors. In addition, low self-monitoring was associated with a higher estimated likelihood of marriage. Men and women in low self-monitoring relationships believed it was more likely that they would marry their current partners (75%) than did men and women in high self-monitoring relationships (51%). As noted by the researchers, these perceptions may be quite accurate. High self-monitors do not consider it highly likely that they will make formal long-term commitments (via marriage) to their current partners, and when asked to evaluate the commitment of their partners (who are typically also high self-monitors and presumably just as commitment shy as they are themselves), they provide equally low estimates.

Although other researchers have not found a significant association between self-monitoring and aspects of romantic relationship commitment and adjustment (see Richmond, Craig, & Ruzicka, 1991), the empirical evidence in general seems to indicate that this personality dimension does play at least some role in love and mating.

SOCIOSEXUAL ORIENTATION

Sociosexual orientation is another dispositional variable that may have relational consequences. Sociosexuality reflects the extent to which people require emotional intimacy and commitment before becoming sexually involved with a romantic partner (Gangestad & Simpson, 1990). Men and women who possess a *restricted* sociosexual orientation generally are unwilling to engage in sex outside of a committed relationship, and they require greater emotional closeness and commitment before engaging in sexual activity with a romantic partner. Men and women with an *unrestricted* or permissive orientation require substantially less affection or commitment before having sex with a romantic partner. The seven-item Sociosexual Orientation Inventory (SOI) used to measure this personality construct was developed by Jeffry Simpson and Steven Gangestad (1991). Respondents provide information about various aspects of their *sexual behavior* (e.g., the number of one-time sex partners they have had, the number of different sex partners they have had during the previous year), *sexual cognitions* (e.g., how often they fantasize about having sex with someone other than their current dating partner), and *sexual attitudes* (e.g., the extent to which they agree with the statement "Sex without love is okay").

Sociosexuality is correlated with a number of romantic and sexual experiences. For example, restricted and unrestricted men and women prefer different types of characteristics in their dating partners. Unrestricted individuals tend to focus on external attributes that are related to sexuality, physical appearance, and social status, whereas restricted individuals tend to pay more attention to internal dispositional features and attitudinal similarity (see Jones, 1998; Sprecher, Regan, McKinney, Maxwell, & Wazienski, 1997). For example, in a study conducted by Simpson and Gangestad (1992), a group of men and women completed the SOI and rated the importance of 15 characteristics according to how much the characteristics influenced their "selection of a romantic partner." Correlational analyses revealed a strong association between SOI scores and attribute ratings for both men and women. In general, the more unrestricted a woman was in her sociosexual orientation, the more importance she attached to a romantic partner's physical attractiveness and sex appeal and the less importance she placed on dispositional attributes (e.g., kindness and understanding, faithfulness and loyalty, similar values and beliefs) and parenting qualities (e.g., desire for children, qualities of a good parent). Similarly, the more unrestricted a man was in terms of sociosexuality, the more importance he placed on a romantic partner's physical attractiveness, sex appeal, social status, and financial resources and the less importance he attached to various dispositional and parenting qualities (e.g., kindness and understanding, responsibility, similar values and beliefs, qualities of a good parent).

In a second investigation, the researchers examined the attributes actually possessed by the romantic partners of people with differing sociosexual orientations. Heterosexual dating couples completed Zick Rubin's (1970) Companionate Love Scale (a scale, you may recall from Chapter 2, that assesses feelings of affection, caring, trust, and other elements of this type of love), a three-item index that assessed the likelihood that their current relationship would endure over time (e.g., "What is the likelihood that you will be dating your current partner one year from now?"), the SOI, and various other measures. In addition, each participant was evaluated by three observers, who rated his or her physical and sexual attractiveness. The researchers then correlated each participant's SOI score with the love, attractiveness, and other scores of the participant's dating partner. These analyses indicated that SOI scores for both men and women were significantly associated with the companionate love and relationship endurance scores of their partners. Specifically, the more unrestricted men and women were, the less affectionate love their partners felt for them and the less likely their partners were to believe that their relationships would endure over time. For men, SOI scores were also correlated with their partners' physical and sexual attractiveness; the more unrestricted men were, the more attractive their partners were, according to ratings made by observers (this association nearly reached statistical significance for women). These investigations provide evidence that restricted and unrestricted individuals desire and actually acquire romantic partners who possess different sets of attributes. Men and women with an unrestricted sociosexual orientation seek out partners who are more socially visible and physically appealing, whereas those with a restricted sociosexual orientation prefer and select partners who demonstrate more kindness, affection, loyalty, commitment, and other positive dispositional attributes.

Sociosexuality, like self-monitoring, does have implications for the formation and maintenance of romantic relationships.

SUMMARY

This chapter has explored the ways in which a person's global personality traits and dispositional tendencies are related to his or her sexual and romantic experiences. Some traits and attributes seem to promote positive interpersonal outcomes. For example, highly extraverted men and women are likely to provide—and to receive—emotional support during times of stress. Low self-monitors and individuals with a restricted sociosexual orientation tend to offer their partners commitment and stability. Other attributes appear detrimental to relational well-being. Emotionally unstable neurotic individuals often experience unstable and unsatisfying partnerships. High self-monitors may leave a date or mate if a more attractive alternative presents himself or herself. People with an unrestricted sociosexual orientation tend to become involved in relationships characterized by relatively low levels of affection and love. In sum, who we are to some extent determines the quality of our relationships.

KEY CONCEPTS

Personality (p. 206)
Temperament (p. 206)
The Big Five (p. 206)
Supertraits (p. 207)
Extraversion (p. 207)
Introverts (p. 207)
Neuroticism (p. 209)
Self-monitoring (p. 213)
High self-monitors (p. 213)
Low self-monitors (p. 213
Sociosexual orientation (pp. 215-216)
Restricted sociosexual orientation (p. 216)
Unrestricted sociosexual orientation (p. 216)

DISCUSSION QUESTIONS

1. What is extraversion? How is this personality dimension related to relationship experiences and outcomes?

2. In Chapter 9, we reviewed evidence suggesting that men and women around the world prefer mates who are emotionally stable. Does this universal preference make sense? In other words, is emotional stability related to relationship outcomes? Should men and women be concerned about a partner's emotional stability? Why or why not?

3. Using the sample items from the Self-Monitoring Scale included in the chapter, decide whether you are a high or a low self-monitor (or somewhere in the middle). How is this disposition related to romantic relationship events?

RECOMMENDED READINGS

Digman, J. M. (1990). Personality structure: Emergence of the five-factor model. *Annual Review of Psychology, 41*, 417-440.

McCrae, R. R., & Costa, P. T., Jr. (1997). Personality trait structure as a human universal. *American Psychologist, 52*, 509-516.

These articles are good introductory reviews of basic personality theory and research. In fact, any recent issue of the journal Annual Review of Psychology will provide up-to-date information on work in the field of personality psychology.

Cutrona, C. E., Hessling, R. M., & Suhr, J. A. (1997). The influence of husband and wife personality on marital social support interactions. *Personal Relationships, 4,* 379-393.

Pasch, L. A., Bradbury, T. N., & Davila, J. (1997). Gender, negative affectivity, and observed social support behavior in marital interaction. *Personal Relationships, 4,* 361-378.

These articles explore the ways in which personality may be implicated in ongoing social and interpersonal interaction. Of particular interest are the methodologies used to examine interaction.

16

Interpersonal Belief Systems

Chapter Outline

Attachment Styles
Rejection Sensitivity
Romanticism
Summary

People bring to relationships not only their own enduring personality traits and dispositional tendencies but also a variety of stable relationship-relevant beliefs and expectations. These mental representations—also called *relational schemata* or *implicit relationship theories*—consist of a rich web of beliefs, attitudes, values, and expectations and are presumed to develop over time and to influence interpersonal behavior (Baldwin, 1992, 1995; Fletcher & Thomas, 1996). This chapter explores three of these important belief systems.

ATTACHMENT STYLES

John Bowlby (e.g., 1969) originally proposed the evolutionary concept of *attachment* or the innate and adaptive "propensity of human beings to make strong affectional bonds to particular others" (Bowlby, 1977,

p. 201). Bowlby hypothesized that human infants come into the world essentially predisposed to form relationships and that this innate predisposition manifests itself in behavioral responses (e.g., crying, clinging, smiling) that promote physical proximity between vulnerable infants and their caregivers and thereby enhance the infants' chances of survival. Over time, and as a result of the caregivers' responses to these proximity-seeking behaviors and the nature of the early interactions between the caregivers and infants, children are presumed to develop an *internal working model* about relationships—a set of internalized "expectations of the accessibility and responsiveness of attachment figures" (Bowlby, 1973, p. 235)—that serves as a prototype for later relationships and influences subsequent interpersonal outcomes.

Building on the theoretical foundation laid by Bowlby, social and personality theorists have proposed the concept of adult *attachment style* (Bartholomew & Horowitz, 1991; Collins, 1996; Hazan & Shaver, 1987), which refers to a person's characteristic beliefs, attitudes, and expectations about the self (worthy of love and support vs. not worthy of love and support), other people (available and supportive vs. unavailable and rejecting), and relationships (rewarding vs. punishing). Men and women who possess a *secure* attachment style believe that they are worthy of love and support and expect to receive these responses from others; they are comfortable with closeness and believe that relationships can be—and often are—highly rewarding. Men and women with an *avoidant* style expect close relationships to be sources of pain rather than pleasure. These self-reliant people protect themselves from potential disappointment or rejection by maintaining distance from others and avoiding intimacy. Finally, men and women with an *anxious/ambivalent* style are preoccupied with relationship and intimacy issues. Feeling unworthy of love, these individuals are highly dependent on others for approval, seek rapid intimate involvement, and are anxious about being abandoned.

There are a number of self-report measures of adult attachment style. One of the first was developed by psychologists Cindy Hazan and Phillip Shaver (1987). This forced-choice measure presents people with three possible scenarios and asks them to select the one that best reflects their basic orientation toward romantic relationships:

Scenario 1: I find it relatively easy to get close to others and am comfortable depending on them and having them depend on me. I don't often worry about being abandoned or about someone getting too close to me.

Scenario 2: I am somewhat uncomfortable being close to others; I find it difficult to trust them completely, difficult to allow myself to depend on them. I am nervous when anyone gets too close, and often, love partners want me to be more intimate than I feel comfortable being.

Scenario 3: I find that others are reluctant to get as close as I would like. I often worry that my partner doesn't really love me or won't want to stay with me. I want to merge completely with another person, and this desire sometimes scares people away.

Based on their self-reports, individuals are categorized as secure (Scenario 1), avoidant (Scenario 2), or anxious/ambivalent (Scenario 3). Some theorists have proposed additional attachment styles and multi-item measurement instruments (e.g., Bartholomew & Horowitz, 1991; Collins & Read, 1990).

Research reveals that individual differences in attachment style are associated with qualitative differences in romantic relationship experiences. For example, individuals who possess a secure attachment style are preferred as potential romantic partners by both men and women (Chappell & Davis, 1998; Latty-Mann & Davis, 1996). In addition, the experiences that securely attached persons have within their ongoing romantic relationships are very different from those reported by insecure (i.e., anxious or avoidant) individuals. Compared with their insecure counterparts, secure men and women hold more positive views of their partners' personalities; experience more happiness, satisfaction, and love within their relationships; are more committed to their partners; and exhibit fewer negative emotions (Feeney, 1999; Jones & Cunningham, 1996; Young & Acitelli, 1998).

In addition to these qualitative differences in relationship experience, a study conducted by psychologist Nancy Collins (1996) provides evidence that people's attachment orientation biases the way in which they interpret and explain interpersonal events in their ongoing romantic relationships. Participants who were currently involved in a romantic relationship were asked to imagine that their partner had engaged in four potentially negative behaviors: not responding when the participant wanted to cuddle, not providing comfort when the participant was "feeling down," wanting to spend an evening by himself or herself, and leaving the participant standing alone at a party. After reading about each of these events, participants were asked to write a free-response explanation for the partner's behavior and to rate the extent to which the event would make them feel distressed (e.g., angry, hurt, disappointed, sad, unloved), nervous (e.g., nervous, confused, helpless), and unemotional or indifferent.

Analyses of the free-response essays revealed that participants who possessed an anxious/ambivalent attachment style explained the event in highly negative and pessimistic ways. Specifically, they were more likely than securely attached (and, in some cases, avoidant) participants to indicate that the partner was unresponsive, unloving, and untrustworthy and that the partner was purposely rejecting them. For example, when asked to explain why the partner would not want to cuddle, some gave responses such as the following: "He feels detached, doesn't want to be close to me," "She doesn't like me anymore," and "He's mad at me and this is his way of punishing me." Securely attached participants were more likely to give explanations that minimized the negative impact of the event. An example was "She just had a bad day and wasn't in the mood to cuddle." This suggests that people with different attachment styles explain and interpret interpersonal events—in this case, potentially negative behavior by a romantic partner—in ways consistent with their internal working models. As Collins (1996) noted,

> Preoccupied individuals were likely to construct explanations that offered much more negative views of their partner and more negative interpretations of events. Consistent with participants' expectations, their explanations were more likely to suggest that their relationship was in jeopardy, and that their partner was unresponsive to their needs, not trustworthy, and purposely rejecting closeness. Their explanations also reflected lower self-worth and self-reliance. In contrast, secure adults provided much more positive explanations. Consistent with their optimistic models of self and others, their explanations were more likely to communicate confidence in their relationship and in their partner's love, they were less likely to view their partner's behavior as purposely rejecting closeness, and overall they tended to construe events in ways that minimized their negative impact and limited their importance for broader issues of relationship stability. (p. 826)

Analysis of the emotional response data provided evidence that men and women with different attachment styles also differ in their affective reactions to potentially negative relationship events. As expected, anxious/ambivalent participants reported exaggerated levels of negative emotion. They indicated that they would feel much more emotional distress, helplessness, and nervous confusion in the face of the various partner behaviors as compared with securely attached participants. Avoidant participants, on the other hand, reported that they would feel *less* distress as compared with securely attached participants; in fact, the former's primary emotional response was indifference.

Taken altogether, these results suggest that when men and women with insecure (i.e., anxious/ambivalent or avoidant) attachment orientations are faced with an interpersonal event that lends itself to a potentially negative interpretation, they are likely to respond cognitively and emotionally in ways that are unpleasant for the partner and harmful to the relationship. Craving closeness and validation from the partner—yet feeling unworthy of such things—anxious/ambivalent individuals are only too ready to believe the worst. They assume that the event is caused by the partner's lack of love, concern, and trustworthiness, and they consequently experience overwhelming and excessive distress. Avoidant men and women also readily attribute negative motives to the partner, but their intense need for self-protection produces a very different emotional response—a noncommunicative display of unconcern and stoic indifference. These cognitive and emotional responses are unlikely to produce beneficial outcomes for the partner or the relationship.

In sum, men and women with a secure attachment orientation enter their relationships expecting positive outcomes and then engage in behaviors that seem to promote intimacy and increase the likelihood that they actually will obtain those positive outcomes.

REJECTION SENSITIVITY

Another class of beliefs and expectations—having to do specifically with rejection—also has clear implications for romantic relationships. Drawing on Bowlby's attachment theory, psychologist Geraldine Downey and her colleagues (e.g., Downey, Bonica, & Rincon, 1999) proposed that *rejection sensitivity*—defined as the tendency to anxiously anticipate, readily perceive, and emotionally and behaviorally overreact to rejection from significant others—develops as a self-protective response to parental rejection. Specifically, these theorists suggested the following:

Our model proposes that when parents tend to meet children's expressed needs with rejection, children become sensitive to rejection. That is, they develop the expectation that when they seek acceptance and support from significant others they will probably be rejected, and they learn to place a particularly high value on avoiding such rejection. They thus experience anticipatory anxiety when expressing needs or vulnerabilities to significant others. These anxious expectations of rejection make them hypervigilant for signs of rejection. When they encounter rejection cues, however minimal or ambiguous, they readily perceive intentional rejection and experience feelings of rejection. The perceived rejection is then likely to prompt both affective and behavioral overreactions, which may include anger and hostility, despondency, withdrawal of support, jealousy, and inappropriate attempts to control the significant other's behavior. (Downey & Feldman, 1996, p. 1328)

Rejection sensitivity is typically assessed by asking individuals to imagine being in various situations that involve making requests or asking for assistance from acquaintances, romantic partners, or family members (e.g., asking a classmate to borrow his or her notes, asking a boyfriend/girlfriend to cohabit, asking parents for help in deciding what college programs to apply for). For each situation, participants are asked whether they would be concerned or anxious about the response to their request from the person or persons involved and whether they would expect the other(s) to honor or reject the request. People who are high in rejection sensitivity usually express anxiety and concern about the outcome of their request, coupled with an expectation of rejection; those who are low in rejection sensitivity report less anxiety and concern and express a calm expectation of assistance.

There is growing evidence that rejection-sensitive men and women essentially are primed to perceive rejection in the behavior of others—even when no rejection is intended. For example, in one study, Geraldine Downey and Scott Feldman (1996) asked a group of college students, each of whom had recently begun a new romantic relationship, to imagine that their partner had committed three insensitive but ambiguous actions that conceivably could have occurred for a number of reasons: had acted cool and distant, had begun to spend less time with them, and had been intolerant of something the participant did. Participants then indicated the extent to which they believed each action reflected the partner's intentional desire to hurt them. The results revealed a positive correlation between rejection sensitivity (as assessed with the multi-item scale) and perceived hurtful intent; the more sensitive participants were to rejection, the greater the amount of hurtful intent they perceived in the partner's actions. Thus, it seems that men and women who anxiously anticipate rejection do actually "see" rejection in the actions of their intimate partners.

In addition, rejection sensitivity is associated with a number of negative romantic outcomes. For example, compared with people who are low in rejection sensitivity, rejection-sensitive people—and their partners—are less satisfied with their romantic relationships (Downey & Feldman, 1996). They are also more likely to be involved in unstable relationships. In one longitudinal study (Downey, Freitas, Michaelis, & Khouri, 1998), dating couples completed a measure of rejection sensitivity and then were recontacted 1 year later and asked to indicate their relationship status (i.e., whether the partners were still together). The results revealed that 44% of the couples who included a rejection-sensitive female partner had broken up, compared with 15% of the couples who included a non-rejection-sensitive female partner. Similarly, 42% of the couples who included a rejection-sensitive male partner had broken up over the 12-month period, compared with 15% of the couples who included a non-rejection-sensitive male partner. Dissolution is a common event in relationships involving at least one rejection-sensitive partner.

Rejection-sensitive men and women also tend to magnify the extent of their partners' dissatisfaction and lack of commitment; in other words, rejection-sensitive people believe that their dating partners are less satisfied and committed than is actually the case. In addition, they often exhibit hostile, jealous, emotionally unsupportive, and otherwise negative interpersonal behavior (according to their own and their partners' self-reports and laboratory observations of dyadic interaction). Interestingly, there appears to be a sex difference in how rejection-sensitive people manifest their insecurities within close romantic relationships. Specifically, men high in rejection sensitivity are more likely to display jealousy and suspicion and to seek to control their partners' contact with other people, whereas women high in rejection sensitivity are more likely to blame their partners unjustly and to display hostile and unsupportive behavior toward them (Downey & Feldman, 1996). There is also some evidence that rejection-sensitive men are more likely to engage in aggressive or coercive behaviors toward dating partners than are non-rejection-sensitive men (Downey, Feldman, & Ayduk, 2000).

In sum, rejection-sensitive people think about and behave toward their partners in ways that appear to undermine the quality of their interactions and limit their chances of developing and maintaining satisfying and stable romantic relationships.

ROMANTICISM

In addition to their implicit theories about relationships in general (i.e., that they are rewarding or punishing), men and women possess a subset of beliefs, values, and expectations that are specific to romantic relationships. The *romantic ideal* encompasses five central notions: the importance of love as a basis for marriage, the idea that love strikes without warning and often at first sight, the belief that there exists only one true love for each person, the idea that true love endures forever, and the notion that love can conquer all obstacles (e.g., Knee, 1998; Sprecher & Metts, 1989).

The most recent and thorough measure of romanticism was created by Susan Sprecher and Sandra Metts (1989), who drew on previous measurement instruments and theoretical statements about romantic ideology. The Romantic Beliefs Scale contains items that reflect the essential tenets of romanticism: Love Finds a Way ("If a relationship I have was meant to be, any obstacle can be overcome"), Love at First Sight ("I am likely to fall in love almost immediately if I meet the right person"), One and Only ("There will be only one real love for me"), and Idealization ("The relationship I will have with my true love will be nearly perfect").

Romanticism is associated with several relationship experiences, including (not surprisingly) feelings of love for the partner. For example, men and women who strongly endorse the romantic ideal generally report higher levels of passionate love and liking for their partners than do their less romantic counterparts, and the former tend to fall in love with their partners at an earlier stage in their relationships (Sprecher & Metts, 1989). Romanticism also appears to be associated with several other aspects of relationship quality. Highly romantic men and women think about the relationship more during a partner's absence (Cate, Koval, Lloyd, & Wilson, 1995), and they feel higher amounts of satisfaction with and commitment to the partner and the relationship

(Sprecher & Metts, 1999). Men and women who subscribe to a generalized romantic ideal may be more likely to feel passion, more eager to commit, and more inclined to view their partners and their relationships in a positive light than are their less overtly romantic counterparts. As noted by Sprecher and Metts (1999), "General positive beliefs about relationships tend to be associated with positive feelings and experiences (love, satisfaction, commitment) within a specific relationship" (p. 846).

SUMMARY

Over time and as a result of the interpersonal events we experience, each of us develops a host of relationship-relevant beliefs, attitudes, values, and expectations. Like our biological sex, psychological gender, and temperament, these mental representations can influence our interpersonal behavior and the nature of the romantic associations we form with others. Of course, it is important to keep in mind that no single disposition or set of beliefs inevitably determines what happens between partners or the fate of their relationship. Rather, it may be the particular constellation of beliefs, traits, and dispositional features that one person possesses, and how well those attributes mesh with the enduring characteristics of his or her partner, that ultimately proves to have the greatest impact on any given relationship. Thus, an extraverted, securely attached person may experience unhappiness, conflict, and romantic instability, and an emotionally unstable, insecure, rejection-sensitive person may find lasting love and satisfaction. In the realm of dating and mating, anything is possible.

KEY CONCEPTS

Relational schemata (p. 220)
Implicit relationship theories (p. 220)
Attachment (pp. 220-221)
Internal working model (p. 221)
Attachment style (p. 221)
Secure attachment style (p. 221)
Avoidant attachment style (p. 221)
Anxious/ambivalent attachment style (p. 221)

Rejection sensitivity (p. 224)
Romantic ideal (p. 227)

DISCUSSION QUESTIONS

1. Define the concept of relational schemata or implicit relationship theories. In what ways is a prototype similar to these concepts?

2. Identify the three primary styles of adult attachment. Do you think a person's attachment style can change over time?

3. What is rejection sensitivity? Compare this belief system with that of attachment style. How are they similar?

4. Find social scientific research on a phenomenon called "behavioral confirmation" or the "self-fulfilling prophecy." Drawing on this literature, explain how rejection-sensitive people might actually create their own unpleasant interpersonal realities.

5. Define the romantic ideal. In what ways is romanticism related to relationship outcomes?

RECOMMENDED READINGS

Ainsworth, M. D. S., Blehar, M. C., Waters, E., & Wall, S. (1978). *Patterns of attachment: A psychological study of the strange situation.* Hillsdale, NJ: Lawrence Erlbaum.

These researchers designed a classification system, based on behavioral observation of infant-caregiver interactions, that could be used to describe the quality of the infant-caregiver attachment. This book describes their work.

Baldwin, M. W. (1992). Relational schemas and the processing of social information. *Psychological Bulletin, 112,* 461-484.

Baldwin, M. W. (1995). Relational schemas and cognition in close relationships. *Journal of Social and Personal Relationships, 12,* 547-552.

These two articles serve as a nice introduction to the topic of relationship cognition.

Belsky, J., & Cassidy, J. (1995). Attachment: Theory and evidence. In M. L. Rutter, D. F. Hays, & S. Baron-Cohen (Eds.), *Developmental principles and clinical issues in psychology and psychiatry* (pp. 373-402). Oxford, UK: Blackwell.

Bowlby argued that infants and children develop "working models" of relationships as a result of the interactions they have with their caregivers. These working models presumably influence later relationship events and experiences. This review article examines whether attachment behavior during early childhood does, in fact, predict subsequent interpersonal outcomes.

Karen, R. (1990, February). Becoming attached. *The Atlantic Monthly,* pp. 35-70.

This article presents an excellent overview of the concept of attachment and should be required reading for anyone interested in that area.

Concluding Remarks

What does it mean to be in love with someone? How long does love last? What characteristics make someone desirable as a mate? What role does sex play in love and love relationships? What variables influence whether marriages and other romantic relationships endure or dissolve? My purpose in writing this text was to address these questions (and, I hope, to provide some answers to them) by considering theories of love, mate selection, relationship development, and relational sexuality and by reviewing empirical research on these interlinked life experiences.

We have seen that romantic relationships provide people with the opportunity to experience a panoply of positive and affirming events—passion and joy, affection and trust, desire and sexual expression. We have also seen how they can be a source of unhappiness and torment, ranging from incompatibility and dissatisfaction to obsession, coercion, and sometimes even violence. Whatever their outcomes, and regardless of the form they take, the love relationships that we form with others clearly have profound implications for the quality of our lives. I hope that this text has shed some small light on these important and fascinating human experiences.

References

Abbey, A. (1982). Sex differences in attributions for friendly behavior: Do males misperceive females' friendliness? *Journal of Personality and Social Psychology, 42*, 830-838.

Abbey, A. (1987). Misperceptions of friendly behavior as sexual interest: A survey of naturally occurring incidents. *Psychology of Women Quarterly, 11*, 173-194.

Abbey, A., & Melby, C. (1986). The effects of nonverbal cues on gender differences in perceptions of sexual intent. *Sex Roles, 15*, 283-298.

Abrahams, M. F. (1994). Perceiving flirtatious communication: An exploration of the perceptual dimensions underlying judgments of flirtatiousness. *Journal of Sex Research, 31*, 283-292.

Adams, J. S. (1965). Inequity in social exchange. In L. Berkowitz (Ed.), *Advances in experimental social psychology* (Vol. 2, pp. 267-299). New York: Academic Press.

Ainsworth, M. D. S., Blehar, M. C., Waters, E., & Wall, S. (1978). *Patterns of attachment: A psychological study of the strange situation.* Hillsdale, NJ: Lawrence Erlbaum.

Alain, M., & Lussier, Y. (1988). Sex-role attitudes and divorce experience. *Journal of Social Psychology, 128*, 143-152.

Altman, I., & Taylor, D. A. (1973). *Social penetration: The development of interpersonal relationships.* New York: Holt, Rinehart & Winston.

Amato, P. R., & Rogers, S. J. (1997). A longitudinal study of marital problems and subsequent divorce. *Journal of Marriage and the Family, 59*, 612-624.

Aron, A., & Henkemeyer, L. (1995). Marital satisfaction and passionate love. *Journal of Social and Personal Relationships, 12*, 139-146.

Aron, A., & Westbay, L. (1996). Dimensions of the prototype of love. *Journal of Personality and Social Psychology, 70*, 535-551.

Atkins, D. C., Baucom, D. H., & Jacobson, N. S. (2001). Understanding infidelity: Correlates in a national random sample. *Journal of Family Psychology, 15*, 735-749.

Attridge, M., & Berscheid, E. (1994). Entitlement in romantic relationships in the United States: A social exchange perspective. In M. J. Lerner & G. Mikula (Eds.), *Entitlement and the affectional bond: Justice in close relationships* (pp. 117-148). New York: Plenum.

Ault, L. K., & Philhower, C. (2001, July). *Allergen avoidance: Qualities in romantic partners that are shunned by lovers and their parents.* Paper presented at the joint conference of the International Network on Personal Relationships and the International Society for the Study of Personal Relationships, Prescott, AZ.

Baldwin, M. W. (1992). Relational schemas and the processing of social information. *Psychological Bulletin, 112,* 461-484.

Baldwin, M. W. (1995). Relational schemas and cognition in close relationships. *Journal of Social and Personal Relationships, 12,* 547-552.

Bartholomew, K., & Horowitz, L. M. (1991). Attachment styles among young adults: A test of a four-category model. *Journal of Personality and Social Psychology, 61,* 226-244.

Baumeister, R. F., & Wotman, S. R. (1992). *Breaking hearts: The two sides of unrequited love.* New York: Guilford.

Baumeister, R. F., Wotman, S. R., & Stillwell, A. M. (1993). Unrequited love: On heartbreak, anger, guilt, scriptlessness, and humiliation. *Journal of Personality and Social Psychology, 64,* 377-394.

Baxter, L. A. (1985). Accomplishing relationship disengagement. In S. Duck & D. Perlman (Eds.), *Understanding personal relationships: An interdisciplinary approach* (pp. 243-265). London: Sage.

Baxter, L. A., & Bullis, C. (1986). Turning points in developing romantic relationships. *Human Communication Research, 12,* 469-493.

Beaver, E. D., Gold, S. R., & Prisco, A. G. (1992). Priming macho attitudes and emotions. *Journal of Interpersonal Violence, 7,* 321-333.

Belsky, J., & Cassidy, J. (1995). Attachment: Theory and evidence. In M. L. Rutter, D. F. Hays, & S. Baron-Cohen (Eds.), *Developmental principles and clinical issues in psychology and psychiatry* (pp. 373-402). Oxford, UK: Blackwell.

Bem, S. L. (1974). The measurement of psychological androgyny. *Journal of Consulting and Clinical Psychology, 42,* 155-162.

Berscheid, E. (1983). Emotion. In H. H. Kelley, E. Berscheid, A. Christensen, J. H. Harvey, G. Levinger, E. McClintock, L. A. Peplau, & D. R. Peterson (Eds.), *Close relationships* (pp. 110-168). New York: Freeman.

Berscheid, E. (1985). Interpersonal attraction. In G. Lindzey & E. Aronson (Eds.), *The handbook of social psychology* (3rd ed., Vol. 2, pp. 413-484). New York: Random House.

Berscheid, E. (1988). Some comments on love's anatomy: Or, whatever happened to old-fashioned lust? In R. J. Sternberg & M. L. Barnes (Eds.), *The psychology of love* (pp. 359-374). New Haven, CT: Yale University Press.

Berscheid, E., & Reis, H. T. (1998). Attraction and close relationships. In D. T. Gilbert, S. T. Fiske, & G. Lindzey (Eds.), *The handbook of social psychology* (4th ed., pp. 193-281). New York: McGraw-Hill.

Berscheid, E., & Walster, E. (1974). A little bit about love. In T. L. Huston (Ed.), *Foundations of interpersonal attraction* (pp. 355-381). New York: Academic Press.

Bertrand, J. T., Makani, B., Edwards, M. P., & Baughman, N. C. (1996). The male versus the female perspective on family planning: Kinshasa, Zaire. *Journal of Biosocial Science, 28,* 37-55.

Bettor, L., Hendrick, S. S., & Hendrick, C. (1995). Gender and sexual standards in dating relationships. *Personal Relationships, 2,* 359-369.

Betzig, L. (1989). Causes of conjugal dissolution: A cross-cultural study. *Current Anthropology, 30,* 654-676.

Biernat, M., & Wortman, C. B. (1991). Sharing of home responsibilities between professionally employed women and their husbands. *Journal of Personality and Social Psychology, 60,* 844-860.

Blair, S. L., & Johnson, M. P. (1992). Wives' perceptions of the fairness of the division of household labor: The intersection of housework and ideology. *Journal of Marriage and the Family, 54,* 570-581.

Blair, S. L., & Lichter, D. T. (1991). Measuring the division of household labor: Gender segregation of housework among American couples. *Journal of Family Issues, 12,* 91-113.

Blau, P. M. (1964). *Exchange and power in social life.* New York: John Wiley.

Blood, R. O., Jr., & Wolfe, D. M. (1960). *Husbands and wives: The dynamics of married living.* Glencoe, IL: Free Press.

Blumstein, P., & Schwartz, P. (1983). *American couples.* New York: William Morrow.

Bouchard, G., Lussier, Y., & Sabourin, S. (1999). Personality and marital adjustment: Utility of the five-factor model of personality. *Journal of Marriage and the Family, 61,* 651-660.

Bowlby, J. (1969). *Attachment and loss. Vol. 1. Attachment.* New York: Basic Books.

Bowlby, J. (1973). *Attachment and loss. Vol. 2. Separation: Anxiety and anger.* New York: Basic Books.

Bowlby, J. (1977). The making and breaking of affectional bonds. *British Journal of Psychiatry, 130,* 201-210.

Bradbury, T. N., & Fincham, F. D. (1990). Attributions in marriage: Review and critique. *Psychological Bulletin, 107,* 3-33.

Braiker, H. B., & Kelley, H. H. (1979). Conflict in the development of close relationships. In R. L. Burgess & T. L. Huston (Eds.), *Social exchange in developing relationships* (pp. 135-168). New York: Academic Press.

Brehm, S. S. (1985). *Intimate relationships.* New York: Random House.

Brines, J. (1994). Economic dependency, gender, and division of labor at home. *American Journal of Sociology, 100,* 652-660.

Bringle, R. G., & Buunk, B. P. (1991). Extradyadic relationships and sexual jealousy. In K. McKinney & S. Sprecher (Eds.), *Sexuality in close relationships* (pp. 135-153). Hillsdale, NJ: Lawrence Erlbaum.

Brook, J. S., Balka, E. B., Abernathy, T., & Hamburg, B. A. (1994). Sequence of sexual behavior and its relationship to other problem behaviors in African American and Puerto Rican adolescents. *Journal of Genetic Psychology, 155,* 107-114.

Brown, M., & Auerback, A. (1981). Communication patterns in initiation of marital sex. *Medical Aspects of Human Sexuality, 15,* 105-117.

Brown, S. L., & Booth, A. (1996). Cohabitation versus marriage: A comparison of relationship quality. *Journal of Marriage and the Family, 58,* 668-678.

Bumpass, L. L., Sweet, J. A., & Cherlin, A. (1991). The role of cohabitation in declining rates of marriage. *Journal of Marriage and the Family, 53,* 913-927.

Burgoon, J. K., Buller, D. B., Hale, J. L., & deTurck, M. A. (1984). Relational messages associated with nonverbal behaviors. *Human Communication Research, 10,* 351-378.

Burleson, B. R., Kunkel, A. W., Samter, W., & Werking, K. J. (1996). Men's and women's evaluations of communication skills in personal relationships: When sex differences make a difference—and when they don't. *Journal of Social and Personal Relationships, 13,* 201-224.

Burt, M. R. (1980). Cultural myths and supports for rape. *Journal of Personality and Social Psychology, 38,* 217-230.

Buss, D. M. (1985). Human mate selection. *American Scientist, 73,* 47-51.

Buss, D. M. (1988). Love acts: The evolutionary biology of love. In R. J. Sternberg & M. L. Barnes (Eds.), *The psychology of love* (pp. 100-118). New Haven, CT: Yale University Press.

Buss, D. M. (1989). Sex differences in human mate preferences: Evolutionary hypotheses tested in 37 cultures. *Behavioral and Brain Sciences, 12,* 1-49.

Buss, D. M., Abbott, M., et al. (1990). International preferences in selecting mates: A study of 37 cultures. *Journal of Cross-Cultural Psychology, 21,* 5-47.

Buss, D. M., & Kenrick, D. T. (1998). Evolutionary social psychology. In D. T. Gilbert, S. T. Fiske, & G. Lindzey (Eds.), *The handbook of social psychology* (4th ed., Vol. 2, pp. 982-1026). New York: McGraw-Hill.

Buss, D. M., & Schmitt, D. P. (1993). Sexual strategies theory: An evolutionary perspective on human mating. *Psychological Review, 100,* 204-232.

Buunk, B. P. (1995). Sex, self-esteem, dependency and extradyadic sexual experience as related to jealousy responses. *Journal of Social and Personal Relationships, 12,* 147-153.

Buunk, B. P., & Bakker, A. B. (1995). Extradyadic sex: The role of descriptive and injunctive norms. *Journal of Sex Research, 32,* 313-318.

Byers, E. S., Demmons, S., & Lawrance, K. (1998). Sexual satisfaction within dating relationships: A test of the interpersonal exchange model of sexual satisfaction. *Journal of Social and Personal Relationships, 15,* 257-267.

Byers, E. S., & Heinlein, L. (1989). Predicting initiations and refusals of sexual activities in married and cohabiting heterosexual couples. *Journal of Sex Research, 26,* 210-231.

Call, V., Sprecher, S., & Schwartz, P. (1995). The incidence and frequency of marital sex in a national sample. *Journal of Marriage and the Family, 57,* 639-650.

Canary, D. J., & Stafford, L. (1992). Relational maintenance strategies and equity in marriage. *Communication Monographs, 59,* 243-267.

Carroll, J. L., Volk, K. D., & Hyde, J. S. (1985). Differences between males and females in motives for engaging in sexual intercourse. *Archives of Sexual Behavior, 14,* 131-139.

Castañeda, D. M. (1993). The meaning of romantic love among Mexican-Americans. *Journal of Social Behavior and Personality, 8,* 257-272.

Castro-Martin, T., & Bumpass, L. (1989). Recent trends in marital disruption. *Demography, 26,* 37-51.

Cate, R. M., Huston, T. L., & Nesselroade, J. R. (1986). Premarital relationships: Toward the identification of alternative pathways to marriage. *Journal of Social and Clinical Psychology, 4,* 3-22.

Cate, R. M., Koval, J., Lloyd, S. A., & Wilson, G. (1995). Assessment of relationship thinking in dating relationships. *Personal Relationships, 2,* 77-95.

Cate, R. M., & Lloyd, S. A. (1992). *Courtship*. Newbury Park, CA: Sage.

Cate, R. M., Long, E., Angera, J. J., & Draper, K. K. (1993). Sexual intercourse and relationship development. *Family Relations, 42*, 158-164.

Chappell, K. D., & Davis, K. E. (1998). Attachment, partner choice, and perception of romantic partners: An experimental test of the attachment-security hypothesis. *Personal Relationships, 5*, 327-342.

Charny, I. W., & Parnass, S. (1995). The impact of extramarital relationships on the continuation of marriages. *Journal of Sex & Marital Therapy, 21*, 100-115.

Christensen, A., & Heavey, C. L. (1990). Gender and social structure in the demand/withdraw pattern of marital conflict. *Journal of Personality and Social Psychology, 59*, 73-81.

Christensen, H. T. (1947). Student views on mate selection. *Marriage and Family Living, 9*, 85-88.

Christopher, F. S. (2001). *To dance the dance: A symbolic interactional exploration of premarital sexuality*. Mahwah, NJ: Lawrence Erlbaum.

Christopher, F. S., & Cate, R. M. (1984). Factors involved in premarital sexual decision-making. *Journal of Sex Research, 20*, 363-376.

Christopher, F. S., & Cate, R. M. (1985). Premarital sexual pathways and relationship development. *Journal of Social and Personal Relationships, 2*, 271-288.

Christopher, F. S., & Frandsen, M. M. (1990). Strategies of influence in sex and dating. *Journal of Social and Personal Relationships, 7*, 89-105.

Christopher, F. S., & Lloyd, S. A. (2000). Physical and sexual aggression in relationships. In C. Hendrick & S. S. Hendrick (Eds.), *Close relationships: A sourcebook* (pp. 331-343). Thousand Oaks, CA: Sage.

Christopher, F. S., Owens, L. A., & Stecker, H. L. (1993). An examination of single men's and women's sexual aggressiveness in dating relationships. *Journal of Social and Personal Relationships, 10*, 511-527.

Christopher, F. S., & Sprecher, S. (2000). Sexuality in marriage, family, and other relationships: A decade review. *Journal of Marriage and the Family, 62*, 999-1017.

Clark, C. L., Shaver, P. R., & Abrahams, M. F. (1999). Strategic behaviors in romantic relationship initiation. *Personality and Social Psychology Bulletin, 25*, 707-720.

Clarkberg, M., Stolzenberg, R. M., & Waite, L. J. (1995). Attitudes, values, and entrance into cohabitational versus marital unions. *Social Forces, 74*, 609-632.

Cleek, M. G., & Pearson, T. A. (1985). Perceived causes of divorce: An analysis of interrelationships. *Journal of Marriage and the Family, 47*, 179-183.

Coleman, F. L. (1997). Stalking behavior and the cycle of domestic violence. *Journal of Interpersonal Violence, 12*, 420-432.

Collins, N. L. (1996). Working models of attachment: Implications for explanation, emotion, and behavior. *Journal of Personality and Social Psychology, 71*, 810-832.

Collins, N. L., & Read, S. J. (1990). Adult attachment, working models, and relationship quality in dating couples. *Journal of Personality and Social Psychology, 58*, 644-663.

Contreras, R., Hendrick, S. S., & Hendrick, C. (1996). Perspectives on marital love and satisfaction in Mexican American and Anglo couples. *Journal of Counseling and Development, 74*, 408-415.

Coombs, R. H. (1991). Marital status and personal well-being: A literature review. *Family Relations, 40,* 97-102.

Cosmides, L., & Tooby, J. (1997). *Evolutionary psychology: A primer.* [Online]. Available: www.psych.ucsb.edu/research/cep/primer.htm

Cramer, D. (1993). Personality and marital dissolution. *Personality and Individual Differences, 14,* 605-607.

Cunningham, M. R., Barbee, A. P., & Druen, P. B. (1996). Social allergens and the reactions that they produce: Escalation of annoyance and disgust in love and work. In R. M. Kowalski (Ed.), *Aversive interpersonal behaviors* (pp. 189-214). New York: Plenum.

Cunningham, M. R., Druen, P. B., & Barbee, A. P. (1997). Angels, mentors, and friends: Trade-offs among evolutionary, social, and individual variables in physical appearance. In J. A. Simpson & D. T. Kenrick (Eds.), *Evolutionary social psychology* (pp. 109-140). Mahwah, NJ: Lawrence Erlbaum.

Cupach, W. R., & Comstock, J. (1990). Satisfaction with sexual communication in marriage: Links to sexual satisfaction and dyadic adjustment. *Journal of Social and Personal Relationships, 7,* 179-186.

Cupach, W. R., & Metts, S. (1991). Sexuality and communication in close relationships. In K. McKinney & S. Sprecher (Eds.), *Sexuality in close relationships* (pp. 93-110). Hillsdale, NJ: Lawrence Erlbaum.

Cupach, W. R., & Spitzberg, B. H. (1997, February). *The incidence and perceived severity of obsessive relational intrusion behaviors.* Paper presented at the meeting of the Western States Communication Association, Monterey, CA.

Cupach, W. R., & Spitzberg, B. H. (1998). Obsessive relational intrusion and stalking. In B. H. Spitzberg & W. R. Cupach (Eds.), *The dark side of close relationships* (pp. 233-263). Mahwah, NJ: Lawrence Erlbaum.

Cutrona, C. E. (1996). *Social support in couples: Marriage as a resource in times of stress.* Thousand Oaks, CA: Sage.

Cutrona, C. E., Hessling, R. M., & Suhr, J. A. (1997). The influence of husband and wife personality on marital social support interactions. *Personal Relationships, 4,* 379-393.

Dainton, M. (2000). Maintenance behaviors, expectations for maintenance, and satisfaction: Linking comparison levels to relational maintenance strategies. *Journal of Social and Personal Relationships, 17,* 827-842.

Dainton, M., & Stafford, L. (1993). Routine maintenance behaviors: A comparison of relationship type, partner similarity, and sex differences. *Journal of Social and Personal Relationships, 10,* 255-272.

Daly, M., & Wilson, M. (1983). *Sex, evolution, and behavior* (2nd ed.). Belmont, CA: Wadsworth.

Darling, C. A., Davidson, J. K., & Cox, R. P. (1991). Female sexual response and the timing of partner orgasm. *Journal of Sex & Marital Therapy, 17,* 3-21.

Darwin, C. (1859). *On the origin of the species by means of natural selection: Or, preservation of favoured races in the struggle for life.* London: J. Murray.

Darwin, C. (1871). *The descent of man, and selection in relation to sex.* London: J. Murray.

D'Augelli, A., & D'Augelli, J. F. (1985). The enhancement of sexual skills and competence: Promoting lifelong sexual unfolding. In L. L'Abate &

M. A. Milan (Eds.), *Handbook of social skills training and research* (pp. 170-191). New York: John Wiley.

Davis, J. A., & Smith, T. (1991). *General social surveys, 1972-1991*. Storrs, CT: University of Connecticut, Roper Center for Public Opinion Research.

Davis, K. E., & Latty-Mann, H. (1987). Love styles and relationship quality: A contribution to validation. *Journal of Social and Personal Relationships, 4*, 409-428.

Davis, K. E., & Todd, M. J. (1982). Friendship and love relationships. In K. E. Davis & T. Mitchell (Eds.), *Advances in descriptive psychology* (Vol. 2, pp. 79-122). Greenwich, CT: JAI.

Davis, L. E., Emerson, S., & Williams, J. H. (1997). Black dating professionals' perceptions of equity, satisfaction, power, and romantic alternatives and ideals. *Journal of Black Psychology, 23*, 148-164.

Davis, S. (1990). Men as success objects and women as sex objects: A study of personal advertisements. *Sex Roles, 23*, 43-50.

Deaux, K., & Hanna, R. (1984). Courtship in the personals column: The influence of gender and sexual orientation. *Sex Roles, 11*, 363-375.

De Becker, G. (1998). *The gift of fear: Survival signals that protect us from violence.* New York: Dell.

Demo, D. H., & Acock, A. C. (1996). Singlehood, marriage, and remarriage: The effects of family structure and family relationships on mothers' well-being. *Journal of Family Issues, 17*, 388-407.

Dickson, L. (1993). The future of marriage and family in black America. *Journal of Black Studies, 23*, 472-491.

Digman, J. M. (1990). Personality structure: Emergence of the five-factor model. *Annual Review of Psychology, 41*, 417-440.

Dindia, K. (2000). Relational maintenance. In C. Hendrick & S. S. Hendrick (Eds.), *Close relationships: A sourcebook* (pp. 287-299). Thousand Oaks, CA: Sage.

Dion, K. L., & Dion, K. K. (1993). Gender and ethnocultural comparisons in styles of love. *Psychology of Women Quarterly, 17*, 463-473.

Donnelly, D. A. (1993). Sexually inactive marriages. *Journal of Sex Research, 30*, 171-179.

Downey, G., Bonica, C., & Rincon, C. (1999). Rejection sensitivity and adolescent romantic relationships. In W. Furman, B. B. Brown, & C. Feiring (Eds.), *The development of romantic relationships in adolescence* (pp. 148-174). New York: Cambridge University Press.

Downey, G., & Feldman, S. I. (1996). Implications of rejection sensitivity for intimate relationships. *Journal of Personality and Social Psychology, 70*, 1327-1343.

Downey, G., Feldman, S., & Ayduk, O. (2000). Rejection sensitivity and male violence in romantic relationships. *Personal Relationships, 7*, 45-61.

Downey, G., Freitas, A. L., Michaelis, B., & Khouri, H. (1998). The self-fulfilling prophecy in close relationships: Rejection sensitivity and rejection by romantic partners. *Journal of Personality and Social Psychology, 75*, 545-560.

Downey, J. L., & Damhave, K. W. (1991). The effects of place, type of comment, and effort expended on the perception of flirtation. *Journal of Social Behavior and Personality, 6*, 35-43.

Drigotas, S. M., Rusbult, C. E., & Verette, J. (1999). Level of commitment, mutuality of commitment, and couple well-being. *Personal Relationships, 6,* 389-409.

Duck, S. (1982). A topography of relationship disengagement and dissolution. In S. Duck (Ed.), *Personal relationships. Vol. 4. Dissolving personal relationships* (pp. 1-30). London: Academic Press.

Dunn, J. L. (1999). What love has to do with it: The cultural construction of emotion and sorority women's responses to forcible interaction. *Social Problems, 46,* 440-459.

Dutton, D. G., & Aron, A. P. (1974). Some evidence for heightened sexual attraction under conditions of high anxiety. *Journal of Personality and Social Psychology, 30,* 510-517.

Eagly, A. H. (1987). *Sex differences in social behavior: A social-role interpretation.* Hillsdale, NJ: Lawrence Erlbaum.

Eagly, A. H., & Karau, S. J. (1991). Gender and the emergence of leaders: A meta-analysis. *Journal of Personality and Social Psychology, 60,* 685-710.

Eells, L. W., & O'Flaherty, K. (1996). Gender perceptual differences in relation to marital problems. *Journal of Divorce and Remarriage, 25,* 95-116.

Ellis, A. (1954). *The American sexual tragedy.* New York: Twayne.

Emerson, R. M., Ferris, K. O., & Gardner, C. B. (1998). On being stalked. *Social Problems, 45,* 289-314.

Eysenck, H. J. (1980). Personality, marital satisfaction, and divorce. *Psychological Reports, 47,* 1235-1238.

Feeney, J. A. (1999). Adult attachment, emotional control, and marital satisfaction. *Personal Relationships, 6,* 169-185.

Feeney, J., Peterson, C., & Noller, P. (1994). Equity and marital satisfaction over the family life cycle. *Personal Relationships, 1,* 83-99.

Fehr, B. (1988). Prototype analysis of the concepts of love and commitment. *Journal of Personality and Social Psychology, 55,* 557-579.

Fehr, B., & Russell, J. A. (1991). The concept of love viewed from a prototype perspective. *Journal of Personality and Social Psychology, 60,* 425-438.

Feingold, A. (1990). Gender differences in effects of physical attractiveness on romantic attraction: A comparison across five research paradigms. *Journal of Personality and Social Psychology, 59,* 981-993.

Feingold, A. (1992). Gender differences in mate selection preferences: A test of the parental investment model. *Psychological Bulletin, 112,* 125-139.

Felmlee, D. H. (1995). Fatal attractions: Affection and disaffection in intimate relationships. *Journal of Social and Personal Relationships, 12,* 295-311.

Feltey, K. M., Ainslie, J. J., & Geib, A. (1991). Sexual coercion attitudes among high school students: The influence of gender and rape education. *Youth & Society, 23,* 229-250.

Finkelhor, D., & Yllö, K. (1985). *License to rape: Sexual abuse of wives.* New York: Holt, Rinehart & Winston.

Fischer, K. W., Shaver, P. R., & Carnochan, P. (1990). How emotions develop and how they organize development. *Cognition and Emotion, 4,* 81-127.

Fisher, H. E. (1989). Evolution of human serial pairbonding. *American Journal of Physical Anthropology, 78,* 331-354.

Fisher, H. E. (1992). *Anatomy of love: A natural history of mating, marriage, and why we stray.* New York: Fawcett Columbine.

Fisher, R. A. (1958). *The genetical theory of natural selection* (2nd ed.). Oxford, UK: Clarendon.

Fitzpatrick, J., & Sollie, D. L. (1999). Influence of individual and interpersonal factors on satisfaction and stability in romantic relationships. *Personal Relationships, 6,* 337-350.

Fletcher, G. J. O., & Thomas, G. (1996). Close relationship lay theories: Their structure and function. In G. J. O. Fletcher & J. Fitness (Eds.), *Knowledge structures in close relationships: A social psychological approach* (pp. 3-24). Mahwah, NJ: Lawrence Erlbaum.

Foshee, V. A. (1996). Gender differences in adolescent dating abuse prevalence, types, and injuries. *Health Education Research, 11,* 275-286.

Frayser, S. G. (1989). Sexual and reproductive relationships: Cross-cultural evidence and biosocial implications. *Medical Anthropology, 11,* 385-407.

Frazier, P., Arikian, N., Benson, S., Losoff, A., & Maurer, S. (1996). Desire for marriage and life satisfaction among unmarried heterosexual adults. *Journal of Social and Personal Relationships, 13,* 225-239.

Frazier, P. A., & Cook, S. W. (1993). Correlates of distress following heterosexual relationship dissolution. *Journal of Social and Personal Relationships, 10,* 55-67.

Fromm, E. (1956). *The art of loving.* New York: Harper & Row.

Gagnon, J. H., & Simon, W. (1973). *Sexual conduct: The social sources of human sexuality.* Chicago: Aldine.

Gangestad, S. W. (1993). Sexual selection and physical attractiveness: Implications for mating dynamics. *Human Nature, 4,* 205-235.

Gangestad, S. W., & Simpson, J. A. (1990). Toward an evolutionary history of female sociosexual variation. *Journal of Personality, 58,* 69-96.

Gilbert, L. (1993). *Two careers/one family.* Newbury Park, CA: Sage.

Givens, D. B. (1978). The nonverbal basis of attraction: Flirtation, courtship, and seduction. *Psychiatry, 41,* 346-359.

Glenn, N. D., & Weaver, N. (1979). Attitudes toward premarital, extramarital, and homosexual relations in the U.S. in the 1970s. *Journal of Sex Research, 15,* 108-119.

Goldberg, L. R. (1993). The structure of phenotypic personality traits. *American Psychologist, 48,* 26-34.

Goodwin, R. (1999). *Personal relationships across cultures.* London: Routledge.

Goodwin, R., & Soon, A. P. Y. (1994). Self-monitoring and relationship adjustment: A cross-cultural analysis. *Journal of Social Psychology, 134,* 35-39.

Goodwin, R., & Tang, D. (1991). Preferences for friends and close relationship partners: A cross-cultural comparison. *Journal of Social Psychology, 131,* 579-581.

Gottman, J. M., & Levenson, R. W. (1988). The social psychophysiology of marriage. In P. Noller & M. A. Fitzpatrick (Eds.), *Perspectives on marital interaction* (pp. 182-200). Philadelphia: Multilingual Matters.

Gottman, J. M., & Levenson, R. W. (1992). Marital processes predictive of later dissolution: Behavior, physiology, and health. *Journal of Personality and Social Psychology, 63,* 221-233.

Graziano, W. G., Jensen-Campbell, L. A., Todd, M., & Finch, J. F. (1997). Interpersonal attraction from an evolutionary psychology perspective: Women's reactions to dominant and prosocial men. In J. A. Simpson & D. T. Kenrick (Eds.), *Evolutionary social psychology* (pp. 141-167). Mahwah, NJ: Lawrence Erlbaum.

Greeley, A. M. (1991). *Faithful attraction: Discovering intimacy, love, and fidelity in American marriage.* New York: St. Martin's.

Green, S. K., & Sandos, P. (1983). Perceptions of male and female initiators of relationships. *Sex Roles, 9,* 849-852.

Greenblat, C. S. (1983). The salience of sexuality in the early years of marriage. *Journal of Marriage and the Family, 45,* 289-299.

Guerrero, L. K., & Reiter, R. L. (1998). Expressing emotion: Sex differences in social skills and communicative responses to anger, sadness, and jealousy. In D. J. Canary & K. Dindia (Eds.), *Sex differences and similarities in communication: Critical essays and empirical investigations of sex and gender in interaction* (pp. 321-350). Mahwah, NJ: Lawrence Erlbaum.

Haas, S. M., & Stafford, L. (1998). An initial examination of maintenance behaviors in gay and lesbian relationships. *Journal of Social and Personal Relationships, 15,* 846-855.

Hall, H. F. (1901). *Napoleon's letters to Josephine, 1796-1812.* London: J. M. Dent.

Halvorsen, R. (1998). The ambiguity of lesbian and gay marriages: Continuity and change in the symbolic order. *Journal of Homosexuality, 35,* 207-231.

Hampson, S. (1999). State of the art: Personality. *The Psychologist, 12,* 284-288.

Harvey, J. H., Flanary, R., & Morgan, M. (1986). Vivid memories of vivid loves gone by. *Journal of Social and Personal Relationships, 3,* 359-373.

Harvey, J. H., Weber, A. L., Galvin, K. S., Huszti, H. C., & Garnick, N. N. (1986). Attribution in the termination of close relationships: A special focus on the account. In R. Gilmour & S. Duck (Eds.), *The emerging field of close relationships* (pp. 189-201). Hillsdale, NJ: Lawrence Erlbaum.

Hatfield, E., Greenberger, D., Traupmann, J., & Lambert, P. (1982). Equity and sexual satisfaction in recently married couples. *Journal of Sex Research, 17,* 18-32.

Hatfield, E., & Rapson, R. L. (1993). *Love, sex, and intimacy: Their psychology, biology, and history.* New York: HarperCollins.

Hatfield, E., & Rapson, R. L. (1996). *Love and sex: Cross-cultural perspectives.* Needham Heights, MA: Allyn & Bacon.

Hatfield, E., & Sprecher, S. (1986). Measuring passionate love in intimate relationships. *Journal of Adolescence, 9,* 383-410.

Hatfield, E., Traupmann, J., & Sprecher, S. (1984). Older women's perceptions of their intimate relationships. *Journal of Social and Clinical Psychology, 2,* 108-124.

Hatfield, E., Utne, M. K., & Traupmann, J. (1979). Equity theory and intimate relationships. In R. L. Burgess & T. L. Huston (Eds.), *Social exchange in developing relationships* (pp. 99-133). New York: Academic Press.

Hatfield, E., & Walster, G. W. (1978). *A new look at love.* Reading, MA: Addison-Wesley.

Hazan, C., & Shaver, P. (1987). Romantic love conceptualized as an attachment process. *Journal of Personality and Social Psychology, 52,* 510-524.

Heaton, T. B. (1991). Time-related determinants of marital dissolution. *Journal of Marriage and the Family, 53*, 285-295.

Heavey, C. L., Christensen, A., & Malamuth, N. M. (1995). The longitudinal impact of demand and withdrawal during marital conflict. *Journal of Consulting and Clinical Psychology, 63*, 797-801.

Heavey, C. L., Layne, C., & Christensen, A. (1993). Gender and conflict structure in marital interaction: A replication and extension. *Journal of Consulting and Clinical Psychology, 61*, 16-27.

Helgeson, V. S., Shaver, P., & Dyer, M. (1987). Prototypes of intimacy and distance in same-sex and opposite-sex relationships. *Journal of Social and Personal Relationships, 4*, 195-233.

Henderson-King, D. H., & Veroff, J. (1994). Sexual satisfaction and marital well-being in the first years of marriage. *Journal of Social and Personal Relationships, 11*, 509-534.

Hendrick, C., & Hendrick, S. S. (1986). A theory and method of love. *Journal of Personality and Social Psychology, 50*, 392-402.

Hendrick, C., & Hendrick, S. S. (1988). Lovers wear rose colored glasses. *Journal of Social and Personal Relationships, 5*, 161-183.

Hendrick, C., & Hendrick, S. S. (1989). Research on love: Does it measure up? *Journal of Personality and Social Psychology, 56*, 784-794.

Hendrick, C., & Hendrick, S. S. (1990). A relationship-specific version of the Love Attitudes Scale. *Journal of Social Behavior and Personality, 5*, 239-254.

Hendrick, C., Hendrick, S. S., & Dicke, A. (1998). The Love Attitudes Scale: Short Form. *Journal of Social and Personal Relationships, 15*, 147-159.

Hendrick, C., Hendrick, S. S., Foote, F. H., & Slapion-Foote, M. J. (1984). Do men and women love differently? *Journal of Social and Personal Relationships, 1*, 177-195.

Hendrick, S. S., & Hendrick, C. (1987). Love and sex attitudes and religious beliefs. *Journal of Social and Clinical Psychology, 5*, 391-398.

Hendrick, S. S., & Hendrick, C. (1992). *Liking, loving, and relating* (2nd ed.). Pacific Grove, CA: Brooks/Cole.

Hendrick, S. S., & Hendrick, C. (1995). Gender differences and similarities in sex and love. *Personal Relationships, 2*, 55-65.

Hendrick, S. S., Hendrick, C., & Adler, N. L. (1988). Romantic relationships: Love, satisfaction, and staying together. *Journal of Personality and Social Psychology, 54*, 980-988.

Hendrick, S. S., Hendrick, C., Slapion-Foote, M. J., & Foote, F. H. (1985). Gender differences in sexual attitudes. *Journal of Personality and Social Psychology, 48*, 1630-1642.

Herold, E. S., Mantle, D., & Zemitis, O. (1979). A study of sexual offenses against females. *Adolescence, 14*, 65-72.

Hill, C. A., Blakemore, J. E. O., & Drumm, P. (1997). Mutual and unrequited love in adolescence and young adulthood. *Personal Relationships, 4*, 15-23.

Hill, R. (1945). Campus values in mate-selection. *Journal of Home Economics, 37*, 554-558.

Hobart, C. (1993). Interest in marriage among Canadian students at the end of the eighties. *Journal of Comparative Family Studies, 24*, 45-61.

Hogben, M., & Byrne, D. (1998). Using social learning theory to explain individual differences in human sexuality. *Journal of Sex Research, 35,* 58-71.

Holmes, J. G. (2000). Social relationships: The nature and function of relational schemas. *European Journal of Social Psychology, 30,* 447-495.

Homans, G. (1961). *Social behavior: Its elementary forms.* New York: Harcourt, Brace & World.

Hoyt, L. L., & Hudson, J. W. (1981). Personal characteristics important in mate preference among college students. *Social Behavior and Personality, 9,* 93-96.

Hudson, J. W., & Henze, L. F. (1969). Campus values in mate selection: A replication. *Journal of Marriage and the Family, 31,* 772-775.

Hunt, M. (1974). *Sexual behavior in the 1970s.* Chicago: Playboy Press.

Huston, T. L., Caughlin, J. P., Houts, R. M., Smith, S. E., & George, L. J. (2001). The connubial crucible: Newlywed years as predictors of marital delight, distress, and divorce. *Journal of Personality and Social Psychology, 80,* 237-252.

Huston, T. L., McHale, S. M., & Crouter, A. C. (1986). When the honeymoon's over: Changes in the marriage relationship over the first year. In R. Gilmour & S. Duck (Eds.), *The emerging field of personal relationships* (pp. 109-132). Hillsdale, NJ: Lawrence Erlbaum.

Huston, T. L., Surra, C. A., Fitzgerald, N. M., & Cate, R. M. (1981). From courtship to marriage: Mate selection as an interpersonal process. In S. Duck & R. Gilmour (Eds.), *Personal relationships,* Vol. 2: *Developing personal relationships* (pp. 53-88). London: Academic Press.

James, W. H. (1981). The honeymoon effect on marital coitus. *Journal of Sex Research, 17,* 114-123.

Jankowiak, W. R., & Fischer, E. F. (1992). A cross-cultural perspective on romantic love. *Ethnology, 31,* 149-155.

Jason, L. A., Reichler, A., Easton, J., Neal, A., & Wilson, M. (1984). Female harassment after ending a relationship: A preliminary study. *Alternative Lifestyles, 6,* 259-269.

Jefferis, B. G., & Nichols, J. L. (1896). *Search lights on health. Light on dark corners. A complete sexual science and a guide to purity and physical manhood. Advice to maiden, wife, and mother. Love, courtship and marriage* (18th ed.). Naperville, IL: J. L. Nichols.

Jensen-Campbell, L. A., Graziano, W. G., & West, S. (1995). Dominance, prosocial orientation, and female preferences: Do nice guys really finish last? *Journal of Personality and Social Psychology, 68,* 427-440.

Jesser, C. J. (1978). Male responses to direct verbal sexual initiatives of females. *Journal of Sex Research, 14,* 118-128.

Jessor, R., Costa, F., Jessor, L., & Donovan, J. E. (1983). Time of first intercourse: A prospective study. *Journal of Personality and Social Psychology, 44,* 608-626.

Jockin, V., McGue, M., & Lykken, D. T. (1996). Personality and divorce: A genetic analysis. *Journal of Personality and Social Psychology, 71,* 288-299.

Johnson, M. D., & Bradbury, T. N. (1999). Marital satisfaction and topographical assessment of marital interaction: A longitudinal analysis of newlywed couples. *Personal Relationships, 6,* 19-40.

Jones, J. T., & Cunningham, J. D. (1996). Attachment styles and other predictors of relationship satisfaction in dating couples. *Personal Relationships, 3,* 387-399.

Jones, M. (1993). Influence of self-monitoring on dating motivations. *Journal of Research in Personality, 27,* 197-206.

Jones, M. (1998). Sociosexuality and motivations for romantic involvement. *Journal of Research in Personality, 32,* 173-182.

Juhasz, A. M., Kaufman, B., & Meyer, H. (1986). Adolescent attitudes and beliefs about sexual behavior. *Child and Adolescent Social Work, 3,* 177-193.

Kamo, Y. (1993). Determinants of marital satisfaction: A comparison of the United States and Japan. *Journal of Social and Personal Relationships, 10,* 551-568.

Kanin, E. J. (1967). An examination of sexual aggression as a response to sexual frustration. *Journal of Marriage and the Family, 29,* 428-433.

Kanin, E. J. (1984). Date rape: Unofficial criminals and victims. *Victimology: An International Journal, 9,* 95-108.

Kanin, E. J. (1985). Date rapists: Differential sexual socialization and relative deprivation. *Archives of Sexual Behavior, 14,* 219-231.

Kaplan, H. S. (1979). *Disorders of sexual desire and other new concepts and techniques in sex therapy.* New York: Simon & Schuster.

Karen, R. (1990, February). Becoming attached. *The Atlantic Monthly,* pp. 35-70.

Karney, B. R., & Bradbury, T. N. (1997). Neuroticism, marital interaction, and the trajectory of marital satisfaction. *Journal of Personality and Social Psychology, 72,* 1075-1092.

Karra, M. V., Stark, N. N., & Wolf, J. (1997). Male involvement in family planning: A case study spanning five generations of a South Indian family. *Studies in Family Planning, 28,* 24-34.

Kelley, H. H., Berscheid, E., Christensen, A., Harvey, J. H., Levinger, G., McClintock, E., Peplau, L. A., & Peterson, D. R. (Eds.). (1983). *Close relationships.* New York: Freeman.

Kelly, E. L., & Conley, J. J. (1987). Personality and compatibility: A prospective analysis of marital stability and marital satisfaction. *Journal of Personality and Social Psychology, 52,* 27-40.

Kenrick, D. T., Groth, G. E., Trost, M. R., & Sadalla, E. K. (1993). Integrating evolutionary and social exchange perspectives on relationships: Effects of gender, self-appraisal, and involvement level on mate selection criteria. *Journal of Personality and Social Psychology, 64,* 951-969.

Kenrick, D. T., Sadalla, E. K., Groth, G., & Trost, M. R. (1990). Evolution, traits, and the stages of human courtship: Qualifying the parental investment model. *Journal of Personality, 58,* 97-116.

Kephart, W. M. (1967). Some correlates of romantic love. *Journal of Marriage and the Family, 29,* 470-474.

Kerckhoff, A. C., & Davis, K. E. (1962). Value consensus and need complementarity in mate selection. *American Sociological Review, 27,* 295-303.

Kinsey, A. C., Pomeroy, W. B., & Martin, C. E. (1948). *Sexual behavior in the human male.* Philadelphia: W. B. Saunders.

Kinsey, A. C., Pomeroy, W. B., Martin, C. E., & Gebhard, P. H. (1953). *Sexual behavior in the human female.* Philadelphia: W. B. Saunders.

Knee, C. R. (1998). Implicit theories of relationships: Assessment and prediction of romantic relationship initiation, coping, and longevity. *Journal of Personality and Social Psychology, 74,* 360-370.

Koss, M. P., Gidycz, C. A., & Wisniewski, N. (1987). The scope of rape: Incidence and prevalence of sexual aggression and victimization in a national sample of higher education students. *Journal of Consulting and Clinical Psychology, 55,* 162-170.

Kowalski, R. M. (1992). Nonverbal behaviors and perceptions of sexual intentions: Effects of sexual connotativeness, verbal response, and rape outcome. *Basic and Applied Social Psychology, 13,* 427-445.

Kowalski, R. M. (1993). Inferring sexual interest from behavioral cues: Effects of gender and sexually relevant attitudes. *Sex Roles, 29,* 13-36.

Kposowa, A. J. (1998). The impact of race on divorce in the United States. *Journal of Comparative Family Studies, 29,* 529-548.

Kumagai, F. (1995). Families in Japan: Beliefs and realities. *Journal of Comparative Family Studies, 26,* 135-163.

Kurdek, L. A. (1991a). Marital stability and changes in marital quality in newlywed couples: A test of the contextual model. *Journal of Social and Personal Relationships, 8,* 27-48.

Kurdek, L. A. (1991b). Sexuality in homosexual and heterosexual couples. In K. McKinney & S. Sprecher (Eds.), *Sexuality in close relationships* (pp. 177-191). Hillsdale, NJ: Lawrence Erlbaum.

Kurdek, L. A. (1993a). The allocation of household labor in gay, lesbian, and heterosexual married couples. *Journal of Social Issues, 49,* 127-139.

Kurdek, L. A. (1993b). Predicting marital dissolution: A 5-year prospective longitudinal study of newlywed couples. *Journal of Personality and Social Psychology, 64,* 221-242.

Kurdek, L. A. (1998). Developmental changes in marital satisfaction: A 13-year prospective longitudinal study of newlywed couples. In T. N. Bradbury (Ed.), *The developmental course of marital dysfunction* (pp. 180-204). New York: Cambridge University Press.

Kurdek, L. A. (2000). Attractions and constraints as determinants of relationship commitment: Longitudinal evidence from gay, lesbian, and heterosexual couples. *Personal Relationships, 7,* 245-262.

Lamm, H., & Wiesmann, U. (1997). Subjective attributes of attraction: How people characterize their liking, their love, and their being in love. *Personal Relationships, 4,* 271-284.

Langlois, J. H., Kalakanis, L., Rubenstein, A. J., Larson, A., Hallam, M., & Smoot, M. (2000). Maxims or myths of beauty? A meta-analytic and theoretical review. *Psychological Bulletin, 126,* 390-423.

Latty-Mann, H., & Davis, K. E. (1996). Attachment theory and partner choice: Preference and actuality. *Journal of Social and Personal Relationships, 13,* 5-23.

Lavine, L. O., & Lombardo, J. P. (1984). Self-disclosure: Intimate and nonintimate disclosures to parents and best friends as a function of Bem sex-role category. *Sex Roles, 11,* 735-744.

Lawrance, K., & Byers, E. S. (1995). Sexual satisfaction in long-term heterosexual relationships: The interpersonal exchange model of sexual satisfaction. *Personal Relationships, 2,* 267-285.

Lee, J. A. (1973). *Colours of love: An exploration of the ways of loving.* Toronto: New Press.

Lee, J. A. (1977). A typology of styles of loving. *Personality and Social Psychology Bulletin, 3,* 173-182.

Lee, J. A. (1988). Love-styles. In R. J. Sternberg & M. L. Barnes (Eds.), *The psychology of love* (pp. 38-67). New Haven, CT: Yale University Press.

Leiblum, S. R., & Rosen, R. C. (1988). Introduction: Changing perspectives on sexual desire. In S. R. Leiblum & R. C. Rosen (Eds.), *Sexual desire disorders* (pp. 1-17). New York: Guilford.

Leigh, B. C. (1989). Reasons for having and avoiding sex: Gender, sexual orientation, and relationship to sexual behavior. *Journal of Sex Research, 26,* 199-209.

Leitenberg, H., & Saltzman, H. (2000). A statewide survey of age at first intercourse for adolescent females and age of their male partners: Relation to other risk behaviors and statutory rape implications. *Archives of Sexual Behavior, 29,* 203-215.

Leites, E. (1982). The duty to desire: Love, friendship, and sexuality in some Puritan theories of marriage. *Journal of Social History, 15,* 383-408.

Lennon, M. C., & Rosenfield, S. (1994). Relative fairness and the division of housework: The importance of options. *American Journal of Sociology, 100,* 506-531.

Leonard, R., Ling, L. C., Hankins, G. A., Maidon, C. H., Potorti, P. F., & Rogers, J. M. (1993). Sexual harassment at North Carolina State University. In G. L. Kreps (Ed.), *Sexual harassment: Communication implications* (pp. 170-194). Cresskill, NJ: Hampton.

Lester, D. (1996). Trends in divorce and marriage around the world. *Journal of Divorce and Remarriage, 25,* 169-171.

Lester, D., Haig, C., & Monello, R. (1989). Spouses' personality and marital satisfaction. *Personality and Individual Differences, 10,* 253-254.

Lever, J. (1994, August 23). The 1994 *Advocate* survey of sexuality and relationships: The men. *The Advocate: The National Gay & Lesbian Newsmagazine,* pp. 17-24.

Lever, J. (1995, August 22). The 1995 *Advocate* survey of sexuality and relationships: The women. *The Advocate: The National Gay & Lesbian Newsmagazine,* pp. 22-30.

Levine, S. B. (1984). An essay on the nature of sexual desire. *Journal of Sex & Marital Therapy, 10,* 83-96.

Levinger, G. (1965). Marital cohesiveness and dissolution: An integrative view. *Journal of Marriage and the Family, 27,* 19-28.

Levinger, G. (1976). A social psychological perspective on marital dissolution. *Journal of Social Issues, 32,* 21-47.

Levinger, G. (1983). Development and change. In H. H. Kelley, E. Berscheid, A. Christensen, J. H. Harvey, T. L. Huston, G. Levinger, E. McClintock, L. A. Peplau, & D. R. Peterson (Eds.), *Close relationships* (pp. 315-359). New York: Freeman.

Levinger, G., Senn, D. J., & Jorgensen, B. W. (1970). Progress toward permanence in courtship: A test of the Kerckhoff-Davis hypothesis. *Sociometry, 33,* 427-443.

Lewis, C. S. (1988). *The four loves.* New York: Harcourt Brace. (Original work published 1960)

Logan, T. K., Leukefeld, C., & Walker, B. (2000). Stalking as a variant of intimate violence: Implications from a young adult sample. *Violence & Victims, 15,* 91-111.

Luepnitz, D. A. (1988). *The family interpreted.* New York: Basic Books.

Maccoby, E. E. (1990). Gender and relationships: A developmental account. *American Psychologist, 45,* 513-520.

Major, B. (1993). Gender, entitlement, and the distribution of family labor. *Journal of Social Issues, 49,* 141-159.

Maneker, J. S., & Rankin, R. P. (1997). A comparison of couples completing and not completing marital dissolution in California. *Journal of Divorce and Remarriage, 27,* 51-60.

Marston, P. J., Hecht, M. L., Manke, M. L., McDaniel, S., & Reeder, H. (1998). The subjective experience of intimacy, passion, and commitment in heterosexual love relationships. *Personal Relationships, 5,* 15-30.

Martin, P. V., & Hummer, R. A. (1989). Fraternities and rape on campus. *Gender & Society, 3,* 457-473.

Masters, W. H., & Johnson, V. E. (1979). *Homosexuality in perspective.* Boston: Little, Brown.

McCabe, M. P., & Collins, J. K. (1984). Measurement of depth of desired and experienced sexual involvement at different stages of dating. *Journal of Sex Research, 20,* 377-390.

McCormick, N. B. (1979). Come-ons and put-offs: Unmarried students' strategies for having and avoiding sexual intercourse. *Psychology of Women Quarterly, 4,* 194-211.

McCormick, N. B., & Jones, A. J. (1989). Gender differences in nonverbal flirtation. *Journal of Sex Education and Therapy, 15,* 271-282.

McCrae, R. R., & Costa, P. T., Jr. (1997). Personality trait structure as a human universal. *American Psychologist, 52,* 509-516.

McGinnis, R. (1958). Campus values in mate selection: A repeat study. *Social Forces, 36,* 368-373.

McGonagle, K. A., Kessler, R. C., & Schilling, E. A. (1992). The frequency and determinants of marital disagreements in a community sample. *Journal of Social and Personal Relationships, 9,* 507-524.

McKinney, K., & Sprecher, S. (Eds.). (1991). *Sexuality in close relationships.* Hillsdale, NJ: Lawrence Erlbaum.

McNamara, J. R., & Grossman, K. (1991). Initiation of dates and anxiety among college men and women. *Psychological Reports, 69,* 252-254.

Meeks, B. S., Hendrick, S. S., & Hendrick, C. (1998). Communication, love and relationship satisfaction. *Journal of Social and Personal Relationships, 15,* 755-773.

Meloy, J. R. (1989). Unrequited love and the wish to kill: Diagnosis and treatment of borderline erotomania. *Bulletin of the Menninger Clinic, 53,* 477-492.

Metts, S., Sprecher, S., & Regan, P. C. (1998). Communication and sexual desire. In P. A. Andersen & L. K. Guerrero (Eds.), *Handbook of communication and emotion: Research, theory, applications, and contexts* (pp. 353-377). Orlando, FL: Academic Press.

Meyers, S., & Berscheid, E. (1996). The language of love: The difference a preposition makes. *Personality and Social Psychology Bulletin, 23,* 347-362.

Michael, R. T., Gagnon, J. H., Laumann, E. O., & Kolata, G. (1994). *Sex in America: A definitive survey.* Boston: Little, Brown.

Mintz, E. E. (1980). Obsession with the rejecting beloved. *Psychoanalytic Review, 67,* 479-492.

Mischel, W. (1966). A social-learning view of sex differences in behavior. In E. E. Maccoby (Ed.), *The development of sex differences* (pp. 513-581). Stanford, CA: Stanford University Press.

Mongeau, P. A., & Johnson, K. L. (1995). Predicting cross-sex first-date sexual expectations and involvement: Contextual and individual difference factors. *Personal Relationships, 2,* 301-312.

Moore, M. M. (1985). Nonverbal courtship patterns in women: Context and consequences. *Ethology and Sociobiology, 6,* 237-247.

Morrow, G. D., Clark, E. M., & Brock, K. F. (1995). Individual and partner love styles: Implications for the quality of romantic involvements. *Journal of Social and Personal Relationships, 12,* 363-387.

Morrow, G. D., & O'Sullivan, C. (1998). Romantic ideals as comparison levels. Implications for satisfaction and commitment in romantic involvements. In V. C. de Munck (Ed.), *Romantic love and sexual behavior: Perspectives from the social sciences* (pp. 171-199). Westport, CT: Praeger.

Mosher, D. L., & Anderson, R. D. (1986). Macho personality, sexual aggression, and reactions to guided imagery of realistic rape. *Journal of Research in Personality, 18,* 150-163.

Muehlenhard, C. L. (1988). "Nice women" don't say yes and "real men" don't say no: How miscommunication and the double standard can cause sexual problems. *Women and Therapy, 7,* 95-108.

Muehlenhard, C. L., Goggins, M. F., Jones, J. M., & Satterfield, A. T. (1991). Sexual violence and coercion in close relationships. In K. McKinney & S. Sprecher (Eds.), *Sexuality in close relationships* (pp. 155-175). Hillsdale, NJ: Lawrence Erlbaum.

Muehlenhard, C. L., & Miller, E. N. (1988). Traditional and nontraditional men's responses to women's dating initiation. *Behavior Modification, 12,* 385-403.

Mullen, P. E., & Pathé, M. (1994). Stalking and the pathologies of love. *Australian and New Zealand Journal of Psychiatry, 28,* 469-477.

Muram, D., Rosenthal, T. L., Tolley, E. A., Peeler, M. M., & Dorko, B. (1991). Race and personality traits affect high school senior girls' sexual reports. *Journal of Sex Education and Therapy, 17,* 231-243.

Murdock, G. P. (1967). Ethnographic atlas: A summary. *Ethnology, 6,* 109-236.

Murstein, B. I. (1970). Stimulus-value-role: A theory of marital choice. *Journal of Marriage and the Family, 32,* 465-481.

Murstein, B. I. (1976). *Who will marry whom? Theories and research in marital choice.* New York: Springer.

Murstein, B. I. (1980). Mate selection in the 1970s. *Journal of Marriage and the Family, 42,* 777-792.

Murstein, B. I. (1987). A clarification and extension of the SVR theory of dyadic pairing. *Journal of Marriage and the Family, 49,* 929-947.

Murstein, B. I. (1988). A taxonomy of love. In R. J. Sternberg & M. L. Barnes (Eds.), *The psychology of love* (pp. 13-37). New Haven, CT: Yale University Press.

Murstein, B. I., Merighi, J. R., & Vyse, S. A. (1991). Love styles in the United States and France: A cross-cultural comparison. *Journal of Social and Clinical Psychology, 10,* 37-46.

Nemechek, S., & Olson, K. R. (1996). Personality and marital adjustment. *Psychological Reports, 78,* 26.

Noller, P. (1984). *Nonverbal communication and marital interaction.* Oxford, UK: Pergamon.

Noller, P., Feeney, J. A., Bonnell, D., & Callan, V. J. (1994). A longitudinal study of conflict in early marriage. *Journal of Social and Personal Relationships, 11,* 233-252.

Norris, S. L., & Zweigenhaft, R. L. (1999). Self-monitoring, trust, and commitment in romantic relationships. *Journal of Social Psychology, 139,* 215-220.

Oliver, M. B., & Hyde, J. S. (1993). Gender differences in sexuality: A meta-analysis. *Psychological Bulletin, 114,* 29-51.

Orvis, B. R., Kelley, H. H., & Butler, D. (1976). Attributional conflict in young couples. In J. H. Harvey, W. J. Ickes, & R. F. Kidd (Eds.), *New directions in attribution research* (Vol. 1, pp. 353-386). Hillsdale, NJ: Lawrence Erlbaum.

O'Sullivan, L. F. (1995). Less is more: The effects of sexual experience on judgments of men's and women's personality characteristics and relationship desirability. *Sex Roles, 33,* 159-181.

O'Sullivan, L. F., & Byers, E. S. (1993). Eroding stereotypes: College women's attempts to influence reluctant male sexual partners. *Journal of Sex Research, 30,* 270-282.

O'Sullivan, L. F., & Gaines, M. E. (1998). Decision-making in college students' heterosexual dating relationships: Ambivalence about engaging in sexual activity. *Journal of Social and Personal Relationships, 15,* 347-363.

Painter, K., & Farrington, D. P. (1998). Marital violence in Great Britain and its relationship to marital and non-marital rape. *International Review of Victimology, 5,* 257-276.

Pasch, L. A., Bradbury, T. N., & Davila, J. (1997). Gender, negative affectivity, and observed social support behavior in marital interaction. *Personal Relationships, 4,* 361-378.

Pennebaker, J. W., Dyer, M. A., Caulkins, R. S., Litowitz, D. L., Ackreman, P. L., Anderson, D. B., & McGraw, K. M. (1979). Don't the girls get prettier at closing time: A country and western application to psychology. *Personality and Social Psychology Bulletin, 5,* 122-125.

Peplau, L. A. (1983). Roles and gender. In H. H. Kelley, E. Berscheid, A. Christensen, J. H. Harvey, T. L. Huston, G. Levinger, E. McClintock, L. A. Peplau, & D. R. Peterson (Eds.), *Close relationships* (pp. 220-264). New York: Freeman.

Peplau, L. A., Rubin, Z., & Hill, C. T. (1977). Sexual intimacy in dating relationships. *Journal of Social Issues, 33,* 86-109.

Peplau, L. A., & Spalding, L. (2000). The close relationships of lesbians, gay men, and bisexuals. In C. Hendrick & S. S. Hendrick (Eds.), *Close relationships: A sourcebook* (pp. 111-123). Thousand Oaks, CA: Sage.

Perlman, S. D., & Abramson, P. R. (1982). Sexual satisfaction among married and cohabiting individuals. *Journal of Consulting and Clinical Psychology, 50,* 458-460.

Perper, T., & Weis, D. L. (1987). Proceptive and rejective strategies of U.S. and Canadian college women. *Journal of Sex Research, 23,* 455-480.

Peterson, C. D., Baucom, D. H., Elliott, M. J., & Farr, P. A. (1989). The relationship between sex role identity and marital adjustment. *Sex Roles, 21,* 775-787.

Pinney, E. M., Gerrard, M., & Denney, N. W. (1987). The Pinney Sexual Satisfaction Inventory. *Journal of Sex Research, 23,* 233-251.

Prager, K. J., & Buhrmester, D. (1998). Intimacy and need fulfillment in couple relationships. *Journal of Social and Personal Relationships, 15,* 435-469.

Press, J. E., & Townsley, E. (1998). Wives' and husbands' housework reporting: Gender, class, and social desirability. *Gender & Society, 12,* 188-218.

Proite, R., Dannells, M., & Benton, S. L. (1993). Gender, sex-role stereotypes, and the attribution of responsibility for date and acquaintance rape. *Journal of College Student Development, 34,* 411-417.

Pryor, J. B., & Merluzzi, T. V. (1985). The role of expertise in processing social interaction scripts. *Journal of Experimental Social Psychology, 21,* 362-379.

Rao, K. V., & DeMaris, A. (1995). Coital frequency among married and cohabiting couples in the United States. *Journal of Biosocial Science, 27,* 135-150.

Regan, P. C. (1998a). Minimum mate selection standards as a function of perceived mate value, relationship context, and gender. *Journal of Psychology and Human Sexuality, 10,* 53-73.

Regan, P. C. (1998b). Of lust and love: Beliefs about the role of sexual desire in romantic relationships. *Personal Relationships, 5,* 139-157.

Regan, P. (1998c). Romantic love and sexual desire. In V. C. de Munck (Ed.), *Romantic love and sexual behavior: Perspectives from the social sciences* (pp. 91-112). Westport, CT: Praeger.

Regan, P. C. (1998d). What if you can't get what you want? Willingness to compromise ideal mate selection standards as a function of sex, mate value, and relationship context. *Personality and Social Psychology Bulletin, 24,* 1288-1297.

Regan, P. C. (2000a). Love relationships. In L. T. Szuchman & F. Muscarella (Eds.), *Psychological perspectives on human sexuality* (pp. 232-282). New York: John Wiley.

Regan, P. C. (2000b). The role of sexual desire and sexual activity in dating relationships. *Social Behavior and Personality, 28,* 51-60.

Regan, P. C. (2002). Functional features: An evolutionary perspective on inappropriate relationships. In R. Goodwin & D. Cramer (Eds.), *Inappropriate relationships: The unconventional, the disapproved, and the forbidden* (pp. 25-42). Mahwah, NJ: Lawrence Erlbaum.

Regan, P. C., & Berscheid, E. (1995). Gender differences in beliefs about the causes of male and female sexual desire. *Personal Relationships, 2,* 345-358.

Regan, P. C., & Berscheid, E. (1997). Gender differences in characteristics desired in a potential sexual and marriage partner. *Journal of Psychology and Human Sexuality, 9,* 25-37.

Regan, P. C., & Berscheid, E. (1999). *Lust: What we know about human sexual desire.* Thousand Oaks, CA: Sage.

Regan, P. C., Kocan, E. R., & Whitlock, T. (1998). Ain't love grand! A prototype analysis of romantic love. *Journal of Social and Personal Relationships, 15,* 411-420.

Reik, T. (1941). *Of love and lust.* New York: Bantam Books.

Reis, H. T., & Patrick, B. C. (1996). Attachment and intimacy: Component processes. In E. T. Higgins & A. Kruglanski (Eds.), *Social psychology: Handbook of basic principles* (pp. 523-563). New York: Guilford.

Reis, H. T., & Shaver, P. (1988). Intimacy as an interpersonal process. In S. Duck (Ed.), *Handbook of personal relationships: Theory, research, and interventions* (pp. 367-389). Chichester, UK: Wiley.

Reiss, I. L. (1960). Toward a sociology of the heterosexual love relationship. *Marriage and Family Living, 22,* 139-145.

Reiss, I. L. (1964). The scaling of premarital sexual permissiveness. *Journal of Marriage and the Family, 26,* 188-198.

Reiss, I. L. (1967). *The social context of premarital sexual permissiveness.* New York: Holt, Rinehart & Winston.

Reiss, I. L. (1973). *Heterosexual relationships inside and outside of marriage* (University Programs Modular Series). Morristown, NJ: General Learning Press.

Reiss, I. L. (1980). *Family systems in America* (3rd ed.). New York: Holt, Rinehart & Winston.

Reiss, I. L. (1981). Some observations on ideology and sexuality in America. *Journal of Marriage and the Family, 43,* 271-283.

Reiss, I. L. (1986). *Journey into sexuality: An exploratory voyage.* Englewood Cliffs, NJ: Prentice Hall.

Reiss, I. L., & Lee, G. R. (1988). *Family systems in America* (4th ed.). New York: Holt, Rinehart & Winston.

Renne, E. P. (1997). The meaning of contraceptive choice and constraint for Hausa women in a northern Nigerian town. *Anthropology & Medicine, 4,* 159-175.

Richmond, L. D., Craig, S. S., & Ruzicka, M. F. (1991). Self-monitoring and marital adjustment. *Journal of Research in Personality, 25,* 177-188.

Ridge, R. D., & Berscheid, E. (1989, May). *On loving and being in love: A necessary distinction.* Paper presented at the meeting of the Midwestern Psychological Association, Chicago.

Robinson, I. E., Balkwell, J. W., & Ward, D. M. (1980). Meaning and behavior: An empirical study in sociolinguistics. *Social Psychology Quarterly, 43,* 253-258.

Robinson, J. P. (1977). *How Americans use time: A social-psychological analysis.* New York: Praeger.

Robinson, J. P., Yerby, J., Fieweger, M., & Somerick, N. (1977). Sex-role differences in time use. *Sex Roles, 3,* 443-458.

Roche, J. P., & Ramsbey, T. W. (1993). Premarital sexuality: A five-year follow-up study of attitudes and behavior by dating stage. *Adolescence, 28,* 67-80.

Rosch, E. H. (1973). On the internal structure of perceptual and semantic categories. In T. E. Moore (Ed.), *Cognitive development and the acquisition of language* (pp. 111-144). New York: Academic Press.

Rosch, E. (1975). Cognitive representations of semantic categories. *Journal of Experimental Psychology, 104,* 192-233.

Rosch, E. (1978). Principles of categorization. In E. Rosch & B. B. Lloyd (Eds.), *Cognition and categorization* (pp. 27-48). Hillsdale, NJ: Lawrence Erlbaum.

Roscoe, B., Strouse, J. S., & Goodwin, M. P. (1994). Sexual harassment: Early adolescent self-reports of experiences and acceptance. *Adolescence, 29,* 515-523.

Rose, S., & Frieze, I. H. (1989). Young singles' scripts for a first date. *Gender & Society, 3,* 258-268.

Rose, S., & Frieze, I. H. (1993). Young singles' contemporary dating scripts. *Sex Roles, 28,* 499-509.

Rosenfeld, L. B., & Bowen, G. L. (1991). Marital disclosure and marital satisfaction: Direct-effect versus interaction-effect models. *Western Journal of Speech Communication, 55,* 69-84.

Rotenberg, K. J., & Korol, S. (1995). The role of loneliness and gender in individuals' love styles. *Journal of Social Behavior and Personality, 10,* 537-546.

Rowatt, T. J., Cunningham, M. R., Rowatt, W. C., Miles, S. S., Ault-Gauthier, L. K., Georgianna, J., & Shamblin, S. (1997, July). *Men and women are from Earth: Life-span strategy dynamics in mate choices.* Paper presented at the meeting of the International Network on Personal Relationships, Oxford, OH.

Rubin, L. (1976). *Worlds of pain: Life in the working class family.* New York: Basic Books.

Rubin, Z. (1970). Measurement of romantic love. *Journal of Personality and Social Psychology, 16,* 265-273.

Rubin, Z. (1973). *Liking and loving: An invitation to social psychology.* New York: Holt, Rinehart & Winston.

Rubin, Z., Hill, C. T., Peplau, L. A., & Dunkel-Schetter, C. (1980). Self-disclosure in dating couples: Sex roles and the ethic of openness. *Journal of Marriage and the Family, 42,* 305-317.

Rusbult, C. E. (1983). A longitudinal test of the investment model: The development (and deterioration) of satisfaction and commitment in heterosexual involvements. *Journal of Personality and Social Psychology, 45,* 101-117.

Rusbult, C. E., & Buunk, B. P. (1993). Commitment processes in close relationships: An interdependence analysis. *Journal of Social and Personal Relationships, 10,* 175-204.

Rusbult, C. E., Johnson, D. J., & Morrow, G. D. (1986). Predicting satisfaction and commitment in adult romantic involvements: An assessment of the generalizability of the investment model. *Social Psychology Quarterly, 49,* 81-89.

Rusbult, C. E., Martz, J. M., & Agnew, C. R. (1998). The Investment Model Scale: Measuring commitment level, satisfaction level, quality of alternatives, and investment size. *Personal Relationships, 5,* 357-391.

Rusbult, C. E., Zembrodt, I. M., & Gunn, L. K. (1982). Exit, voice, loyalty, and neglect: Responses to dissatisfaction in romantic relationships. *Journal of Personality and Social Psychology, 43,* 1230-1242.

Sagrestano, L. M., Christensen, A., & Heavey, C. L. (1998). Social influence techniques during marital conflict. *Personal Relationships, 5,* 75-89.

Samson, J. M., Levy, J. J., Dupras, A., & Tessier, D. (1991). Coitus frequency among married or cohabiting heterosexual adults: A survey in French-Canada. *Australian Journal of Marriage & Family, 12,* 103-109.

Scanzoni, J., Polonko, K., Teachman, J., & Thompson, L. (1989). *The sexual bond: Rethinking families and close relationships.* Newbury Park, CA: Sage.

Scheib, J. E. (2001). Context-specific mate choice criteria: Women's trade-offs in the contexts of long-term and extra-pair mateships. *Personal Relationships, 8,* 371-389.

Schumm, W. R., Webb, F. J., & Bollman, S. R. (1998). Gender and marital satisfaction: Data from the National Survey of Families and Households. *Psychological Reports, 83,* 319-327.

Schwartz, P. (1994). *Peer marriage: How love between equals really works.* New York: Free Press.

Schwartz, P., & Rutter, V. (1998). *The gender of sexuality.* Thousand Oaks, CA: Pine Forge.

Seal, D. W., Agostinelli, G., & Hannett, C. A. (1994). Extradyadic romantic involvement: Moderating effects of sociosexuality and gender. *Sex Roles, 31,* 1-22.

Secord, P. F. (1983). Imbalanced sex ratios: The social consequences. *Personality and Social Psychology Bulletin, 9,* 525-543.

Sedikides, C., Oliver, M. B., & Campbell, W. K. (1994). Perceived benefits and costs of romantic relationships for women and men: Implications for exchange theory. *Personal Relationships, 1,* 5-21.

Shaver, P., Hazan, C., & Bradshaw, D. (1988). Love as attachment: The integration of three behavioral systems. In R. J. Sternberg & M. L. Barnes (Eds.), *The psychology of love* (pp. 68-99). New Haven, CT: Yale University Press.

Shaver, P., Schwartz, J., Kirson, D., & O'Connor, C. (1987). Emotion knowledge: Further exploration of a prototype approach. *Journal of Personality and Social Psychology, 52,* 1061-1086.

Shaver, P. R., & Hazan, C. (1988). A biased overview of the study of love. *Journal of Social and Personal Relationships, 5,* 473-501.

Shelton, B. A., & John, D. (1993). Does marital status make a difference? Housework among married and cohabiting men and women. *Journal of Family Issues, 14,* 401-420.

Sherwin, R., & Corbett, S. (1985). Campus sexual norms and dating relationships: A trend analysis. *Journal of Sex Research, 21,* 258-274.

Sillars, A., Roberts, L. J., Leonard, K. E., & Dun, T. (2000). Cognition during marital conflict: The relationship of thought and talk. *Journal of Social and Personal Relationships, 17,* 479-502.

Simon, W., & Gagnon, J. H. (1986). Sexual scripts: Permanence and change. *Archives of Sexual Behavior, 15,* 97-120.

Simpson, J. A., Campbell, B., & Berscheid, E. (1986). The association between romantic love and marriage: Kephart (1967) twice revisited. *Personality and Social Psychology Bulletin, 12,* 363-372.

Simpson, J. A., & Gangestad, S. W. (1991). Individual differences in sociosexuality: Evidence for convergent and discriminant validity. *Journal of Personality and Social Psychology, 60,* 870-883.

Simpson, J. A., & Gangestad, S. W. (1992). Sociosexuality and romantic partner choice. *Journal of Personality, 60,* 31-51.

Small, M. F. (1992). The evolution of female sexuality and mate selection in humans. *Human Nature, 3,* 133-156.

Snyder, M. (1974). The self-monitoring of expressive behavior. *Journal of Personality and Social Psychology, 30,* 526-537.

Snyder, M. (1987). *Public appearances/private realities: The psychology of self-monitoring.* New York: Freeman.

Snyder, M., Berscheid, E., & Glick, P. (1985). Focusing on the exterior and the interior: Two investigations of the initiation of personal relationships. *Journal of Personality and Social Psychology, 48,* 1427-1439.

Snyder, M., & Simpson, J. A. (1984). Self-monitoring and dating relationships. *Journal of Personality and Social Psychology, 47,* 1281-1291.

Soames, M. (1979). *Clementine Churchill.* London: Cassell.

Sollie, D. L., & Fischer, J. L. (1985). Sex-role orientation, intimacy of topic, and target person differences in self-disclosure among women. *Sex Roles, 12,* 917-929.

South, S. J. (1995). Do you need to shop around? Age at marriage, spousal alternatives, and marital dissolution. *Journal of Family Issues, 16,* 432-449.

South, S. J., & Lloyd, K. M. (1995). Spousal alternatives and marital dissolution. *American Sociological Review, 60,* 21-35

South, S. J., & Spitze, G. (1994). Housework in marital and nonmarital households. *American Sociological Review, 59,* 327-347.

Spanier, G. B., & Margolies, R. L. (1983). Marital separation and extramarital sexual behavior. *Journal of Sex Research, 19,* 23-48.

Spitzberg, B. H., & Cupach, W. R. (1996, July). *Obsessive relational intrusion: Victimization and coping.* Paper presented at the meeting of the International Society for the Study of Personal Relationships, Banff, Alberta.

Spitzberg, B. H., & Cupach, W. R. (Eds.). (1998). *The dark side of close relationships.* Mahwah, NJ: Lawrence Erlbaum.

Spitzberg, B. H., & Cupach, W. R. (2001). Paradoxes of pursuit: Toward a relational model of stalking-related phenomena. In J. A. Davis (Ed.), *Stalking crimes and victim protection: Prevention, intervention, and threat assessment* (pp. 97-136). Boca Raton, FL: CRC Press.

Spitzberg, B. H., & Cupach, W. R. (2002). The inappropriateness of relational intrusion. In R. Goodwin & D. Cramer (Eds.), *Inappropriate relationships: The unconventional, the disapproved, and the forbidden* (pp. 191-219). Mahwah, NJ: Lawrence Erlbaum.

Spitzberg, B. H., Nicastro, A. M., & Cousins, A. V. (1998). Exploring the interactional phenomenon of stalking and obsessive relational intrusion. *Communication Reports, 11,* 33-47.

Spreadbury, C. L. (1982). First date. *Journal of Early Adolescence, 2,* 83-89.

Sprecher, S. (1989). Importance to males and females of physical attractiveness, earning potential, and expressiveness in initial attraction. *Sex Roles, 21,* 591-607.

Sprecher, S. (1992). How men and women expect to feel and behave in response to inequity in close relationships. *Social Psychology Quarterly, 55,* 57-69.

Sprecher, S. (1998). Social exchange theories and sexuality. *Journal of Sex Research, 35,* 32-43.

Sprecher, S., Aron, A., Hatfield, E., Cortese, A., Potapova, E., & Levitskaya, A. (1994). Love: American style, Russian style, and Japanese style. *Personal Relationships, 1,* 349-369.

Sprecher, S., & Chandak, R. (1992). Attitudes about arranged marriages and dating among men and women from India. *Free Inquiry in Creative Sociology, 20*, 59-69.

Sprecher, S., & Hatfield, E. (1995). Premarital sexual standards among U.S. college students: Comparison with Russian and Japanese students. *Archives of Sexual Behavior, 25*, 261-288.

Sprecher, S., & McKinney, K. (1993). *Sexuality*. Thousand Oaks, CA: Sage.

Sprecher, S., McKinney, K., Walsh, R., & Anderson, C. (1988). A revision of the Reiss premarital sexual permissiveness scale. *Journal of Marriage and the Family, 50*, 821-828.

Sprecher, S., & Metts, S. (1989). Development of the "Romantic Beliefs Scale" and examination of the effects of gender and gender-role orientation. *Journal of Social and Personal Relationships, 6*, 387-411.

Sprecher, S., & Metts, S. (1999). Romantic beliefs: Their influence on relationships and patterns of change over time. *Journal of Social and Personal Relationships, 16*, 834-851.

Sprecher, S., Metts, S., Burleson, B., Hatfield, E., & Thompson, A. (1995). Domains of expressive interaction in intimate relationships: Associations with satisfaction and commitment. *Family Relations: Journal of Applied Family & Child Studies, 44*, 203-210.

Sprecher, S., & Regan, P. C. (1998). Passionate and companionate love in courting and young married couples. *Sociological Inquiry, 68*, 163-185.

Sprecher, S., & Regan, P. C. (2000). Sexuality in a relational context. In C. Hendrick & S. S. Hendrick (Eds.), *Close relationships: A sourcebook* (pp. 217-227). Thousand Oaks, CA: Sage.

Sprecher, S., Regan, P. C., & McKinney, K. (1998). Beliefs about the outcomes of extramarital sexual relationships as a function of the gender of the "cheating spouse." *Sex Roles, 38*, 301-311.

Sprecher, S., Regan, P. C., McKinney, K., Maxwell, K., & Wazienski, R. (1997). Preferred level of sexual experience in a date or mate: The merger of two methodologies. *Journal of Sex Research, 34*, 327-337.

Sprecher, S., & Schwartz, P. (1994). Equity and balance in the exchange of contributions in close relationships. In M. J. Lerner & G. Mikula (Eds.), *Entitlement and the affectional bond: Justice in close relationships* (pp. 11-42). New York: Plenum.

Sprecher, S., & Sedikides, C. (1993). Gender differences in perceptions of emotionality: The case of close heterosexual relationships. *Sex Roles, 28*, 510-530.

Sprecher, S., Sullivan, Q., & Hatfield, E. (1994). Mate selection preferences: Gender differences examined in a national sample. *Journal of Personality and Social Psychology, 66*, 1074-1080.

Stack, S. (1998). Marriage, family, and loneliness: A cross-national study. *Sociological Perspectives, 41*, 415-432.

Sternberg, R. J. (1986). A triangular theory of love. *Psychological Review, 93*, 119-135.

Sternberg, R. J. (1988). Triangulating love. In R. J. Sternberg & M. L. Barnes (Eds.), *The psychology of love* (pp. 119-138). New Haven, CT: Yale University Press.

Sternberg, R. J. (1998). *Cupid's arrow: The course of love through time*. Cambridge, UK: Cambridge University Press.

Sternberg, R. J., & Barnes, M. L. (Eds.). (1988). *The psychology of love*. New Haven, CT: Yale University Press.

Surra, C. A. (1985). Courtship types: Variations in interdependence between partners and social networks. *Journal of Personality and Social Psychology, 49*, 357-375.

Talmadge, L. D., & Talmadge, W. C. (1986). Relational sexuality: An understanding of low sexual desire. *Journal of Sex & Marital Therapy, 12*, 3-21.

Tamplin, R. (1995). *Famous love letters: Messages of intimacy and passion*. New York: Andromeda Oxford.

Tannen, D. (1990). *You just don't understand: Women and men in conversation*. New York: William Morrow.

Tennov, D. (1979). *Love and limerence*. New York: Stein & Day.

Thibaut, J. W., & Kelley, H. H. (1959). *The social psychology of groups*. New York: John Wiley.

Thompson, A. P. (1984). Emotional and sexual components of extramarital relations. *Journal of Marriage and the Family, 46*, 35-42.

Tjaden, P., & Thoennes, N. (2000). Prevalence and consequences of male-to-female and female-to-male intimate partner violence as measured by the National Violence Against Women Survey. *Violence Against Women, 6*, 142-161.

Tolhuizen, J. H. (1989). Communication strategies for intensifying dating relationships: Identification, use, and structure. *Journal of Social and Personal Relationships, 6*, 413-434.

Tooby, J., & Cosmides, L. (1992). The psychological foundations of culture. In J. H. Barrow, L. Cosmides, & J. Tooby (Eds.), *The adapted mind: Evolutionary psychology and the generation of culture* (pp. 19-136). Oxford, UK: Oxford University Press.

Tornstam, L. (1992). Loneliness in marriage. *Journal of Social and Personal Relationships, 9*, 197-217.

Townsend, J. M., & Levy, G. D. (1990). Effects of potential partners' costume and physical attractiveness on sexuality and partner selection. *Journal of Psychology, 124*, 371-389.

Tucker, J. S., Kressin, N. R., Spiro, A., III, & Ruscio, J. (1998). Intrapersonal characteristics and the timing of divorce: A prospective investigation. *Journal of Social and Personal Relationships, 15*, 210-225.

Tucker, M. B., & Mitchell-Kernan, C. (1995). *The decline in marriage among African Americans: Causes, consequences, and policy implications*. New York: Russell Sage.

Tucker, P., & Aron, A. (1993). Passionate love and marital satisfaction at key transition points in the family life cycle. *Journal of Social and Clinical Psychology, 12*, 135-147.

Turner, R. H. (1970). *Family interaction*. New York: John Wiley.

U.S. Bureau of the Census. (1994). *Statistical abstracts of the United States*. Washington, DC: Government Printing Office.

U.S. Bureau of the Census. (1998). *Marital status and living arrangements: March 1998* (Current Population Reports, Series P20-514). Washington, DC: Government Printing Office.

Useche, B., Villegas, M., & Alzate, H. (1990). Sexual behavior of Colombian high school students. *Adolescence, 25,* 291-304.

Vaid, U. (1995). *Virtual equality: The mainstreaming of gay and lesbian liberation.* Garden City, NY: Anchor.

Vaillant, C. O., & Vaillant, G. E. (1993). Is the U-curve of marital satisfaction an illusion? A 40-year study of marriage. *Journal of Marriage and the Family, 55,* 230-239.

van den Berghe, P. L. (1979). *Human family systems: An evolutionary view.* New York: Elsevier.

Vangelisti, A. L., & Daly, J. A. (1997). Gender differences in standards for romantic relationships: Different cultures or different experiences? *Personal Relationships, 4,* 203-219.

Villasmil Prieto, M. C. (1997). Social representation of feminine sexuality: An interpretation from a gender perspective. *Sociologica, 12,* 159-182.

von Krafft-Ebing, R. (1945). *Psychopathia sexualis* (12th ed.). New York: Pioneer Publishing. (Original work published 1886)

Vorauer, J. D., & Ratner, R. K. (1996). Who's going to make the first move? Pluralistic ignorance as an impediment to relationship formation. *Journal of Social and Personal Relationships, 13,* 483-506.

Waldner-Haugrud, L. K., & Magruder, B. (1995). Male and female victimization in dating relationships: Gender differences in coercion techniques and outcomes. *Violence & Victims, 10,* 203-215.

Wallace, H., & Silverman, J. (1996). Stalking and posttraumatic stress syndrome. *Police Journal, 69,* 203-206.

Walster, E., Walster, G. W., & Berscheid, E. (1978). *Equity: Theory and research.* Boston: Allyn & Bacon.

Weber, A. L. (1998). Losing, leaving, and letting go: Coping with nonmarital breakups. In B. H. Spitzberg & W. R. Cupach (Eds.), *The dark side of close relationships* (pp. 267-306). Mahwah, NJ: Lawrence Erlbaum.

Weinberg, M. S., Swensson, R. G., & Hammersmith, S. K. (1983). Sexual autonomy and the status of women: Models of female sexuality in U.S. sex manuals from 1950 to 1980. *Social Problems, 30,* 312-324.

Wiederman, M. W., & Allgeier, E. R. (1992). Gender differences in mate selection criteria: Sociobiological or socioeconomic explanation? *Ethology and Sociobiology, 13,* 115-124.

Wiederman, M. W., & Allgeier, E. R. (1996). Expectations and attributions regarding extramarital sex among young married individuals. *Journal of Psychology and Human Sexuality, 8,* 21-35.

Wilkie, J. R., Ferree, M. M., & Ratcliff, K. S. (1998). Gender and fairness: Marital satisfaction in two-earner couples. *Journal of Marriage and the Family, 60,* 577-594.

Wood, J. T. (1994). *Gendered lives: Communication, gender, and culture.* Belmont, CA: Wadsworth.

Xu, X., & Whyte, M. K. (1990). Love matches and arranged marriages: A Chinese replication. *Journal of Marriage and the Family, 52,* 709-722.

Young, A. M., & Acitelli, L. K. (1998). The role of attachment style and relationship status of the perceiver in the perceptions of romantic partner. *Journal of Social and Personal Relationships, 15,* 161-173.

Young, M., Denny, G., Luquis, R., & Young, T. (1998). Correlates of sexual satisfaction in marriage. *Canadian Journal of Human Sexuality, 7,* 115-127.

Zellman, G. L., & Goodchilds, J. D. (1983). Becoming sexual in adolescence. In E. A. Allgeier & N. B. McCormick (Eds.), *Changing boundaries: Gender roles and sexual behavior* (pp. 49-63). Palo Alto, CA: Mayfield.

Zelnik, M., & Kantner, J. F. (1980). Sexual activity, contraceptive use, and pregnancy among metropolitan-area teenagers: 1971-1979. *Family Planning Perspectives, 12,* 230-237.

Author Index

Subject Index

About the Author

Pamela Regan is Associate Professor of Psychology and Director of the Social Relations Lab at California State University, Los Angeles. She received her Ph.D. in Psychology from the University of Minnesota and her undergraduate degree in English from Williams College. Her research interests are in the areas of close relationships and human sexuality, with an emphasis on passionate love, sexual desire, and mate preference. She has published more than 40 journal articles, book chapters, and reviews (and has given close to 60 professional presentations) on the dynamics of sex, love, and human mating, and she is the coauthor (with Ellen Berscheid) of *Lust: What We Know About Human Sexual Desire* (Sage, 1999).